To Lynette and [...]
with love

Andy

Sept '94

Feminist Readings in Middle English Literature

This volume, designed with the student reader in mind, provides an indispensable blend of key essays in the field with specially commissioned new material by feminist scholars from the UK and the US. The essays address a diversity of texts and feminist approaches and are framed by a substantial and illuminating introduction by the editors, and an annotated list of further reading which offers preliminary guidance to the reader approaching the topic of gender and medieval literature for the first time.

Works and writers covered include:

- Chaucer
- Margery Kempe
- Christine de Pisan
- The Katherine Group of Saints' lives
- Langland's *Piers Plowman*
- Medieval cycle drama

Students of both medieval and feminist literature will find this an essential work for study and reference.

Contributors: Mary Carruthers; Sheila Delany; Ruth Evans; Lesley Johnson; Julia Long; Colette Murphy; Felicity Riddy; Susan Schibanoff; Jocelyn Wogan-Browne.

Ruth Evans is a lecturer in the School of English Studies, Communication and Philosophy at the University of Wales College of Cardiff. **Lesley Johnson** is a lecturer in the School of English at the University of Leeds.

Feminist Readings in Middle English Literature

The Wife of Bath and all her sect

Edited by Ruth Evans and
Lesley Johnson

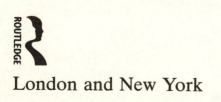

London and New York

First published 1994
by Routledge
11 New Fetter Lane, London EC4P 4EE

Simultaneously published in the USA and Canada
by Routledge
29 West 35th Street, New York, NY 10001

Phototypeset in Times by Intype, London
Printed and bound in Great Britain by
TJ Press (Padstow) Ltd, Padstow, Cornwall

British Library Cataloguing in Publication Data
A catalogue record for this book is available from the British
Library

Library of Congress Cataloging in Publication Data
Feminist readings in Middle English literature: the Wife of Bath
    and all her sect/edited by Ruth Evans and Lesley Johnson.
        p.   cm.
    Includes bibliographical references and index.
    1. English literature – Middle English, 1100–1500 – History and
    criticism.   2. Women and literature – England – History.
    3. Feminism and literature – England – History.   4. Sex
    role in literature.   5. Chaucer, Geoffrey, d. 1400.
    Canterbury tales.
    I. Evans, Ruth.   II. Johnson, Lesley.
    PR275.W6F46   1994
    820.9′352042′0902 – dc20   93–46923

ISBN 0–415–05818–X (hbk)
        0–415–05819–8 (pbk)

For

Jean and John Evans
Hilda and Colby Johnson

Contents

Contributors

Mary Carruthers is a professor in the Department of English, New York University.

Sheila Delany is a professor in the Department of English, Simon Fraser University, Burnaby, British Columbia.

Ruth Evans is a lecturer in the School of English Studies, Communication and Philosophy at the University of Wales College of Cardiff.

Lesley Johnson is a lecturer in the School of English at the University of Leeds.

Julia Long teaches English at a sixth-form college in Cambridge.

Colette Murphy is Head of English and Drama at the Royal Bridewell Hospital School, Witley.

Felicity Riddy is a professor in the Centre for Medieval Studies, University of York.

Susan Schibanoff is a professor in the Department of English, University of New Hampshire.

Jocelyn Wogan-Browne is a lecturer in the Department of English Language and Literature at the University of Liverpool.

Acknowledgements

We are very grateful to the following authors and presses for their permission to reprint previously published material. Mary Carruthers' essay, 'The Wife of Bath and the painting of lions', was previously published in *PMLA*, 1979, vol. 94, pp. 209–22 and is reprinted here, as Chapter 2 of this collection, by permission of the Modern Language Association of America. Sheila Delany's 'Sexual economics, Chaucer's Wife of Bath and *The Book of Margery Kempe*' is taken from Sheila Delany, *Writing Women*, New York, Schocken Books, 1983, pp. 76–92 and is reprinted here, as Chapter 4 of this collection, by permission of Sheila Delany. Susan Schibanoff's essay, ' "Taking the gold out of Egypt"; the art of reading as a woman', was originally published in Elizabeth Flynn and Patrocinio Schweickart (eds) *Gender and Reading*, Baltimore, Johns Hopkins University Press, 1986, pp. 83–106 and is reprinted here, as Chapter 10, with the permission of the Johns Hopkins University Press. We have reformatted the notes of these three essays in order to maintain the same documentary conventions throughout this collection.

We would like to thank all our co-contributors, our colleagues and students past and present: we hope this collection will prove to be a useful contribution to the continuing study of Middle English texts.

1 Introduction

Ruth Evans and Lesley Johnson

THE WIFE OF BATH AND 'AL HIRE SECTE': MEDIEVAL FEMINISTS?

It is perhaps no coincidence that one of the earliest anthologies of feminist criticism which included essays on medieval texts was titled *The Authority of Experience* (edited by Arlyn Diamond and Lee R. Edwards, published in 1977 and republished in 1988).[1] This deliberate yoking together of the terms 'authority' and 'experience' which, according to the logic of 'patriarchal binary thought',[2] are usually maintained as oppositional mimes an apparently similar gesture of feminist defiance by Chaucer's Wife of Bath, whose Prologue opens:

> Experience, though noon auctoritee
> Were in this world, is right ynogh for me
> To speke of wo that is in mariage[.]
> *(Wife of Bath's Prologue,* 1–3)

The Wife of Bath has sometimes been read as the epitome of a modern feminist, insofar as she claims that experience is the ground of her authority (thus reversing the hierarchy which devalues 'feminine' experience and privileges 'masculine' authority), takes on the men at their own game of name-dropping (for she does, in fact, flesh out her argument with references to some of the most important medieval authorities), and refuses to be silenced by the patriarchal powers-that-be. Yet to commemorate the Wife as a 'feminist' simplifies both history and textuality. On the one hand, 'feminism' is not an historically portable term: during the passage of some six hundred years women's social, legal, cultural and ideological status has shifted considerably, and with it the corresponding modes of resistance. And on the other, the Wife is a textual signifier, an effect of language, whose 'meaning', like that of the historically real women with whom she is sometimes compared in this volume, is therefore subject to the play of difference in language itself. The 'Wife of Bath' does not have a single 'meaning'; the diversity of feminist and critical readings of her represented in some of the essays here suggest something of what Mary Carruthers refers to as her 'power',[3] but which could alternatively be read as her signifying surplus. One purpose of this collection is to explore that surplus in various fictions and representations of the Middle Ages.

The Wife is the focal point for this volume even though she is emphatically not the whole story. Around her cluster a number of issues central to the rereading in feminist terms of the Middle Ages. One issue is how to negotiate the alterity of the medieval past and attend to the meaning of its specific historical systems of difference. Another is how to interpret the various acts of medieval ventriloquism: the female voices which proceed, for the most part, from male authors. Such voices, like the Wife's, are equivocal. They do not wholly speak from the place of their male authors, since the meanings they embody are cultural rather than the sole property of individual authors, yet neither can they be romanticised as the repressed and marginalised voices of women from the past. Recognition of the cultural meanings that are spoken through female voices can be a starting place for the exploration of forms of power and power relations in the Middle Ages.

To think about how a voice like the Wife of Bath's might constitute a point of resistance is to move away from naïve readings of her as either a militant feminist or as trapped in the prison-house of masculinist ideology, towards a strategic exploration of how medieval subjects, female and male, are caught up in systems of power relations. Our own practice, as editors and critics, is very much shaped by a broadly post-structuralist view of the relationship between power and knowledge, language and textuality. Such a view is still often regarded by recalcitrant medievalists as incommensurate with the traditional business of medieval scholarship, yet it *necessarily* involves close exploration of cultural and historical meanings. Our understanding of what it means to 'historicise' a text thus relies absolutely on the empirical evidence provided by scholarship, but does not treat such empirical material in an empiricist fashion, as a form of 'hard data' about which no further questions can be asked. To historicise is both to seek for historical meanings and to recognise the limits of those meanings. A post-structuralist understanding of language acknowledges that meanings are plural, and are thus constantly open to revision.

One way of historicising the Wife's performance is to ask, for example, if there was a phenomenon identifiable as 'feminism' in the Middle Ages. Chaucer's Clerk appears to give support to the idea that the Wife is part of a sisterhood when he cites her as the dedicatee of his final song, offered

> for the Wyves love of Bathe –
> Whos lyf and al hire secte God mayntene
> In heigh maistrye . . .

(Clerk's Tale, 1170–2)

But who or what is the 'secte' referred to here? The word 'secte' occurs only four times in Chaucer's work (or possibly five if the English translation of the *Romaunt de la Rose* is his work),[4] but the resonances of the word in this context are difficult to pin down with any certainty. The editors of the *Riverside Chaucer* give their readers the following range of meanings, none of which they foreground as an interpretation in this instance: 'category of persons [as applied to followers of different methodologies or schools]; sex; oath-helper; lawsuit'.[5] Yet from the other collectivities ('archwyves' (1195); 'sklendre wyves' (1198)) singled out for address by the Clerk in the song dedicated to the Wife of Bath and company of pilgrims it seems possible that some kind of company of *wives* is being invoked here, but what status does this 'secte' have?

The Wife herself does not claim allegiance to any female 'secte' in her Prologue. She mentions her 'gossib', but does not conjure up the image of any kind of female countersphere in her mode of address. Feminism as a political practice in the twentieth century grounded itself, initially at least, in an essentialist notion of 'sexual identity': an identity which would allow women to organise themselves politically as a unified group to combat male oppression. The possibility of constructing a unified group on the grounds of 'womanhood' has been very much challenged on theoretical grounds since the late 1970s,[6] yet it remains the case that a feminist politics must ground itself in some sort of idea of collective identity. Yet the Wife's performance does not openly allude to any late four-teenth-century concept of a political programme committed to a struggle against all forms of female subordination, nor is there any historical evidence to suggest that any such programme existed. The rise of groups such as the beguines (lay women in Northern Europe in the thirteenth century who organised themselves in what might loosely be called religious collectives, outside the authority of the medieval Church) or the women committed to preaching and teaching in the English Lollard conventicles of the fourteenth and fifteenth centuries[7] *could* be understood in this way, but the explicit alignment of such groups with religious causes complicates the political issues involved, and raises questions about the very different historical conceptualisation of the opposition between the individual and the group in the Middle Ages.[8]

Similarly, the efforts of Christine de Pisan in the early fifteenth century to protest, via her writings, about the virulent misogyny of the European secular literary tradition could be hailed as a feminist gesture, but again only at the risk of oversimplifying issues which make her texts very much open to plural readings: her aristocratic subject-position, the political effects of her interventions, and the act of inserting herself into a prestigious masculine textual tradition of 'trafficking in women', an act which is simultaneously an exceptional *entrée* to an élite male club and a subversion of its very credentials. The scene of women versus clerks is a powerful antagonistic dynamic in the late Middle Ages: Christine de Pisan's opposition to the clerical monopoly of culture thus makes her outwardly one of the Wife's party, but it is a similarity which may obscure the differences between their tactics and voices.

The Wife, after all, appears in a specific discourse: a secular narrative poem written by a man, namely Chaucer. The textual dynamics suggest that when the Clerk aligns her with a 'secte' the Wife is 'named' rather than 'naming' herself. A male cleric is given the last word on the Wife, however much this is ironised by the writer who takes immediate responsibility for her creation. It might be argued that both Chaucer and the Clerk are 'trafficking in women' here: both are making their textual mark by dealing in textual representations of women and reworking commonplaces about collectivities of womanhood: good women; bad women; wives. 'Sectes' make good literary currency for male authors.

Yet to hear the Wife's voice only as the product of a chorus of male narrators is to arrive at an impasse that belongs to the early phase of feminist theory of the 1970s: that of seeing women as victims of patriarchy. More recent phases of feminist literary criticism are interested in how textual representations are the site where women can fight back. One way of doing this is to point out that phallocentric discourses and knowledges, like medieval anti-feminism, depend on images and metaphors of women to support and legitimate their speculations, something explicitly signalled in the Wife's performance. The binary oppositions of sexual difference which such discourses try to nail in place can be shown to undo themselves continually: the 'secte' of dominant wives conjured up at the end of the *Clerk's Tale* is itself composed of differences ('archwyves' and 'sklendre wyves'), an observation which might be used to question the unity of this collective alignment, and the clerical voice itself is not anyway a single voice on the subject of women. Actually it is not altogether clear who is speaking here.[9] To explore this area is to move from a feminist critique of man-made images, a critique which is nevertheless still indispensable to gender-conscious medievalists, to an analysis of the slipperiness of the terms involved in making such images, and thus to go some way towards undoing the fictions which have kept, and which still keep, the hierarchic oppositions of the Western (male) philosophical tradition in place.

THE WIFE OF BATH AND 'AL HIRE SECTE': FEMINIST MEDIEVALISTS?

Feminist medievalists make use of many of the tools of contemporary feminist literary theory, and engage with similar debates: how and why women have gained access to learning and culture (and which women have done so); how they have been excluded; how male authors have represented women; the question of the difference of women's writing; the kinds of meanings, recuperable for a feminist politics today, that can be released from medieval texts. However, these questions have to be asked rather differently by medievalists, because of the particular historical features of the period: few and imperfect documentary resources with which to construct an archaeology of the text; a preponderance of male readers and authors, albeit a fraction of the male population (though a number of volumes on medieval women writers offer a corrective to the notion that only men wielded the pen in this period); a memory culture, in which there is residual orality and restricted access to literacy; and the mysterious and omnipresent 'anon.', who makes the sex of the authorial 'presence' so much more equivocal than in later periods. On the other hand feminist medievalists are well-placed to treat literary texts as cultural phenomena and not as products of a privileged discourse, because of the well-established practice in medieval studies of analysing texts from both high and popular culture, such as conduct literature, penitential manuals, and scriptural commentaries, that fall out of the literary frame in other periods. The interdisciplinarity which is a feature of the institution of medieval 'literature' has facilitated certain kinds of culturally based feminist inquiry.

It is difficult to characterise the history of feminist criticism of the Middle Ages, or to give a comprehensive overview of work currently being done. Its texts are dispersed across a range of disciplines: some of the most visible, high-profile work has been in the field of history: in the work of scholars such as Susan Mosher Stuard, Martha Howell and Judith Bennett, in which feminist theory has informed vital empirical research, or in the work of the prominent social historian Caroline Walker Bynum on gendered readings of bodies, food and spirituality in the Middle Ages. It is as well to be aware that Bynum's critical and methodological assumptions have recently received some well-aimed criticism, notably in the 1993 issue of *Speculum*. Such criticism is inevitable, given Bynum's status as an almost-establishment figure and the continued need of a feminist critical practice to review its politics, yet this does not in itself invalidate the importance of her material for literary scholars, particularly those interested in medieval bodies and sexuality. The important collection *Women and Power in the Middle Ages* (edited by Mary Erhler and Maryanne Kowaleski in 1988) addressed readers of both history and literature. The picture is anyway one of uneven development, to borrow Mary Poovey's formulation for another historical period.[10] There has been a great deal of very sophisticated feminist work on Chaucer (Carolyn Dinshaw, Elaine Tuttle Hansen, Louise Fradenburg); much less, for various institutional reasons, on other areas such as the medieval drama.[11]

This volume deliberately does not set out to offer either a coherent narrative of that critical history from the 1970s to the present or a series of new essays on the cutting edge of high theory. In this collection we are reprinting three essays (by Mary Carruthers, Sheila Delany, and Susan Schibanoff), and printing six others for the first time. The intention is to offer a small corpus of more, and less, recent essays which illustrate some of the methods of analysis of immediate usefulness for feminist readers who might be encouraged to try them out on medieval texts other than those specifically discussed here, and to suggest something of the scenes of debate within the field of medieval literary studies which provide a context for these strategies of discussion and analysis. This introduction maps out some of these scenes, but is not itself outside them. We recognise here elements of the 'Caxton problematic', noticed by Susan Schibanoff:[12] that in interposing/imposing ourselves between essays and readers, we are seeking to fix our map of the field as we want it to be fixed. But our voices are not the last word: they are part of a debate.

There is, however, one thing which all the contributors here are agreed upon, more or less explicitly: that phenomena such as anti-feminism, 'courtly love' and mysticism (to name only some of the more problematic areas) are not just inscribed in medieval texts but are linked, though not in obvious or reflective ways, to historical practices which had (and continue to have) very real political conse-quences. A feminist reading is nothing if not a practice, with signifi-cant political and institutional effects.

These effects are now being felt within the context of the insti-tution of medieval studies, which has its own history and its own paradigms of reading and interpretation. In the late 1960s and 1970s, when feminism as a political movement was beginning to have an impact on the academy, there were two dominant paradigms in the study of medieval literary texts: a Robertsonian exegetical her-meneutic, whereby *all* fictional narratives, no matter how secular, were read as moral allegories, ultimately revelatory of Christian *caritas*; and the paradigm of empirical scholarship, in which an almost-fetishism for uncovering the 'facts' about a text rendered questions about the *political* significance of those facts irrelevant or simply not of concern to medievalists.[13] Both the Robertsonian and the scholarship approaches are inherently conservative; together their hold on the institution of medieval literary criticism, on its learned journals, its matrix of critical studies, its textbooks and its conferences, has made it deeply resistant to new critical methods and to the intellectual challenges posed by the newer disciplines, including feminism.

In a fairly unassuming way, Mary Carruthers broke new ground when her essay, 'The Wife of Bath and the painting of lions', first appeared in 1979. In order to understand something of the ground-breaking nature of her essay, we can read her 'Afterword' (newly written for this volume), which charts the North American medieval academic establishment's hostile response to her refusal to read the Wife of Bath according to the dominant canons of Robertsonian criticism. That academic response, incidentally, does not neatly con-firm an entrenched binarism, in which the traditional establishment pits itself against feminism, for, as Carruthers makes clear, her original essay was *not* written as a *feminist* interpretation, and the attacks on her reading came not only from conservative Chaucerians but also from critics espousing the newer disciplines of critical theory, such as 'Marxist historiography', and from 'men taking a feminist position'. What emerges forcefully in Carruthers's 'After-word' is a sense of the battle over the meaning of one of Chaucer's most hallowed creations, a battle which for Carruthers centred on the vexed question of the 'reality' of textual figures, and her concern that the Wife be read as a figure of resistance to the dominant late fourteenth-century discourses of anti-feminism and anti-matrimonialism rather than being trapped within their confines. Despite Carruthers's lack of a theoretical framework within which to articulate her response, her awareness that textual representations offer *resistance* is invaluable in the production of feminist readings.

Yet Carruthers's essay *was* shaped by the concerns of late twenti-eth-century feminism. One of its most significant insights was that the Wife of Bath puts her finger on an important sexual/textual dynamic when she refers to Aesop's fable of painting the lion: 'the "truth" of any picture often has more to do with the prejudices and predilections of the painter than with the "reality" of the subject'.[14] Without explicitly invoking feminist theory, Carruthers opened up the representation of the Wife of Bath to interrogation by a set of powerful questions which are able to structure a feminist critique of many medieval (and modern) textual representations: who made this image? What is its truth-value? Whose vested interests are at work in its production? How has this image been re-produced criti-cally? If *women* had had access to the means of production, might they have produced a different kind of truth altogether? Carruthers thus implicitly prepared the ground for *political* readings of Chaucer's text(s), readings which could demystify either the vested interests of Chaucer himself, not as an individual but as the rep-resentative of a masculine, literary culture, or those of his modern clerkly commentators who interpret the Wife as the embodiment of some eternal (female) 'truth'. It was Carruthers's decision to read the Wife as *mulier economica*, as occupying a specific historical and socio-economic space, rather than as an emblem of the dangerously carnal woman who ignores masculine 'auctoritee', which enabled her to produce a political reading of both the Prologue and Tale, as shrewd and witty exposés of the limits of that same 'auctoritee'. Something of the 'auctoritee' of academic medievalists was chal-lenged in the process.

That same resistance to allegorical, universalising interpretations, and the making of that resistance the basis for careful textual read-ings, informs Felicity Riddy's subtle analysis of the *Franklin's Tale*, 'Engendering pity in the *Franklin's Tale*'. Working in a much more openly declared feminist and materialist mode, she explores the co-articulation of gender and class in the Tale. Riddy's way into this is not so much through 'lion-painting' as 'lion-reading', by setting up a slightly different set of questions about the relationship between gender and genre: what difference it might make to consider who was reading Chaucer's texts, and how a late medieval reading culture of *women*, with reading tastes in down-market romance, might interpret the Tale's up-market textual operations. Riddy shows how in Chaucerian texts dependent and passive roles *signify* differently depending on whether the sufferer is a man or a woman. She distinguishes between the pitiable and sexually humiliated Dorigen, omitted from the line-up of (male) contestants who are the focus of the Tale's final question about 'true' nobility, and the figures of Arveragus, Aurelius and the philosopher-clerk, *ennobled* by their attitudes of 'pitee' and extravagant sensibility: 'both pitying and being pitied are, for men, positions of power'.[15] Riddy thus develops, in relation to another Chaucerian Tale, Carruthers's reading of the class and gender-specific nature of 'gentilesse' in the *Wife of Bath's Tale*.

Riddy's analysis of the *Franklin's Tale* also, and importantly, opens up the question of 'courtly love' to a specific feminist critique, revealing what is at stake for both men and women in the courtly fiction of the woman on top, and disabling the Tale's view of courtly marriage as blissful reciprocity. Moreover, her observations about the relationship between the masculine, upwardly mobile anxieties and desires of the *Franklin's Tale* and shifting social structures in the late fourteenth century raise crucial questions about the asymptotic relations between history and literary texts. These questions are of course also raised by Carruthers in her 'Afterword'; they are fundamental to the kind of historically aware feminist readings that we wish to argue for.

Such questions are also the focus of Delany's essay, 'Sexual economics, Chaucer's Wife of Bath and *The Book of Margery Kempe*' (1975), in which she develops her concept of 'sexual economics': 'the psychological effects of economic necessity, specifically upon sexual mores'.[16] According to Delany, the Wife recognises that in a mercantile society everything, including even the most private area of human sexual relations, comes under the sway of the profit motive. She thus sets out shamelessly to take advantage of this pervasive commodification, bartering her body for a measure of economic control in marriage. Where traditional critics offer hostile readings of Alice's behaviour as cynical exploitation, Delany powerfully argues that such behaviour is adaptive and strategic, the result of internalising the values of a profit-orientated bourgeoisie and a way of defending herself against female oppression.

Delany's argument is useful on two counts: it shows how Chaucer, through Alice, exposes medieval bourgeois marriage as thoroughly shot through with mercantile values, and it offers an ideological reading of the Wife's behaviour: not as voluntaristic, the result of 'free choice', but as deeply imbricated in the value systems of her society. Delany's reading does not see Alice resisting those values or asserting a different value system, but through her strategies for negotiating the oppressive norms of the society she lives in we are made aware of the extent to which those norms are internalised by women and consequently deform their sexuality.

Delany's analysis of medieval power relations invokes a single cause explanation for oppression: in this case, the classical Marxist economic model, in which the economic base of society determines the forms of consciousness displayed in the superstructure. Yet it has now become clear that this model, which provides the explanation for the classic and powerful Marxist notion of 'ideology', cannot, in fact, properly accommodate sexual difference, or indeed other kinds of difference. Delany's explanation that the Wife's situation is due to the 'special oppression of women' ducks the issue of how to integrate sexual difference into the economic model, of how sexual difference can challenge and perhaps fundamentally alter the economic model. Difference, whether of class, gender, sexuality, race or ethnicity, can no longer be 'explained' in terms of one single, overarching, privileged 'difference': one of the unresolved tensions in Delany's marxian reading is that it privileges class difference even as it takes sexual difference as its primary focus. Delany has openly denied that she is a feminist; yet this essay is very centrally concerned with female oppression, and with explaining it in terms which represent Chaucer's texts as offering a critique of that oppression.

Delany's other focus is Margery Kempe, an actual fourteenth-century woman from Lynn, in Norfolk, but no less a textual representation, available to us only in her extraordinary autobiography-cum-spiritual pilgrimage, *The Book of Margery Kempe*. For Delany, Margery's 'real' historical status shows how far Chaucer falls short of 'reality' in his representation of the Wife of Bath. Implicit in Delany's argument is the assumption that historical figures are to be privileged over and above textual ones, although there is no especial reason offered as to why this should be the case. Privileged in what way? For whom? It is anyway difficult wholly to maintain the distinction between 'historical' and 'textual', given that our access to the historical women of the Middle Ages is thoroughly textualised. This is a different matter, though, from rightly arguing for the value of paying attention to real historical women. The juxtaposition of the Wife and Kempe, however, makes the useful point that the Wife of Bath is not the whole story as far as the medieval analysis of the commodification of sexuality goes. Delany's important critique shows how far from 'natural' were the dictates of the medieval Church, and to what extent they constructed norms of femininity in the late medieval period. The twin focus of her essay also has the effect of destabilising the centrality of 'Chaucer', whose towering presence on the medieval literary scene and richly self-reflexive, ironic and *scriptible* texts have made him the most obvious focus for new theoretical readings and the construction of a 'new' Middle Ages.

Delany's explicitly theoretical approach to Margery Kempe was disturbing to a medieval academic establishment which was trying, though not succeeding very well, to read her text as a document in the tradition of Catholic mysticism, along with texts such as the writings of Richard Rolle, or the anonymous *The Cloud of Unknowing*, or the *Revelations* of Julian of Norwich. Delany offered one direction in which feminists might use Marxism as a way into Kempe's text: such a reading went deliberately against the grain in its stress on the materiality of Margery Kempe's mystical experience, a materiality which is incidentally already thoroughly inscribed in her text but which could not easily be accommodated by some Catholic and academic readers. Irked by the overtly subjective elements in her *Book*, and dismayed by its apparent lack of literary decorum, they thus pronounced its author to be 'hysterical'.

The challenge of engaging with this judgement of Kempe – and in appropriating psychoanalysis as a tool of feminist theory in relation to medieval texts – is taken up by Julia Long in her essay 'Mysticism and hysteria: the histories of Margery Kempe and Anna O.'. Delany's Marxist reading presupposed economic determinism: Margery cannot break out of her false consciousness because, as Delany rightly observes, the social conditions did not exist in the late fourteenth century which would have enabled the theorising of her position for a feminist politics. But with psychoanalytic readings do we move into a world of psychic determinism in which the careful historicising of traditional medieval scholarship is swept aside for a series of universal and historically transcendent structures? Long's subtly argued essay shows that this need not be the case.

Psychoanalysis, as it is understood in Freud and Lacan, is first of all a clinical, therapeutic practice, but that practice is underpinned by a theory of subjectivity with a powerful ability to 'explain' the crises, anxieties and desires of the 'modern' subject, that is, the post-Enlightenment subject, who makes the doctrinaire assumption that consciousness is coterminous with a subjective sense of unified self-hood: 'I think, therefore I am.' Freud's 'discovery' of the unconscious enabled a critique of this sovereign subject, revealing its wholeness to be illusory; Lacan developed Freud's 'discovery' in directions suggested by the more recent disciplines of structuralism and linguistics, and gave back to Freud's work its radical edge by representing the subject as an *effect* of language, as 'spoken by' language, and not itself as the originator and producer of that language. It is not sexuality but the hypothesis of the unconscious as a site of meaning, in both Freud's work and in Lacan's important return to Freud, which has had the most scandalous impact on the rereading of our culture and of its literary contents. That the unconscious has meaning dethrones the sovereign ego and its various incarnations, from analysts to authors to critics, thus rendering the 'meaning' of (literary) texts unstable.

Feminist medievalists are doubly challenged by psychoanalysis: on the one hand by its apparent blindness to sexual difference, insofar as it takes male sexuality to be the norm, and on the other hand by its intellectual and theoretical bases in post-Enlightenment thought, which provokes the idea that the *medieval* subject might need a rather different model of subjectivity to 'explain' it. These are very real methodological problems, which are not confronted in Long's essay and which in fact lie beyond its scope. Instead she goes straight into her reading, showing the value of comparing the very different histories and cultural contexts of Margery Kempe and 'Anna O.', the patient of Breuer's who is now credited with enabling psychoanalysis: in treating her, Breuer and Freud discovered the operations of the unconscious and the therapeutic value of speaking. Hence psychoanalysis as the 'talking cure', with its uncanny similarities to the practices of the medieval confessional, which Long touches on briefly.

By comparing the two women Long reveals not what is similar about them, but what is so different – and in doing so does not so much prise the label 'hysteric' away from Kempe, as explain why it should have been applied to her in the first place by a patriarchal academic establishment. Long's is less a psychoanalytic reading, in the sense of unravelling the 'unconscious' of the cultural texts that are the 'lives' of Bertha Pappenheim and Margery Kempe, than one which confronts subjects that have been (mis)read in psychoanalytical terms. Yet her reading is psychoanalytic insofar as it identifies some of the effects of unconscious processes at work in the texts of their lives, and in the texts associated with their names. By situating Kempe in relation to the clerical, masculine culture and society with which she engaged, and which judged her according to its canons, a culture which 'produced' her as much as early psychoanalysis, in the persons of Freud and Breuer, 'produced' Bertha Pappenheim ('Anna O.'), Long lays bare those strategies of 'lion-painting' which have a cultural persistence, whilst not traducing the very historically different situations of the two women. For Delany, it is the economic aspects of late medieval society which are primordial in determining Kempe's behaviour. For Long, it is a nexus of factors to do with class, family, sexuality and gender which are *understood* in psychoanalytic terms, that is, as processed by the mechanisms of the unconscious: repression, identification, sublimation and displacement.

Long finally addresses the question of women speaking under patriarchy. Kempe can speak only insofar as she allows God to speak through her: what, then, is she articulating? Both Kempe and Pappenheim exhibit modes of self-expression which disrupt the patriarchal Symbolic, but Long offers necessary caveats about the *political* and personal meaning of that disruption for the individuals concerned. And Long shows how in both Kempe and Pappenheim's case, subjectivity – understood in terms of a sexual identity which is inevitably already gendered – is achieved in the case of women only with extreme difficulty and risk: the risk of psychosis. The figure which emerges from Long's reading is no 'patient': Long restores to Kempe her quality of active disruptiveness, while at the same time recognising the very real ways in which she was repressed and oppressed. Delany and Long have very different kinds of feminist political and intellectual investments in the readings they produce; both, however, refuse to accept hysteria as the final diagnosis of Margery Kempe. In Delany's words, it is the very thing to be explained, the beginning of a questioning and not the answer to the question.

The issue of exactly what critical and theoretical paradigms are available for feminist scholars to use in relation to *medieval* texts, and what their possibilities and their limits might be, surfaces again in Ruth Evans's; essay, 'Body politics: engendering medieval cycle drama'. She shows how Mervyn James's highly influential anthropological reading of the Feast of Corpus Christi does not provide an adequate feminist paradigm for the interpretation of bodies in the dramatic texts and their associated practices. After offering a critique of James's thesis, she then goes on to read various textual bodies, notably that of Christ in the York *Crucifixion* pageant. Evans's decision to outline a feminist reading of this pageant – an extremely recalcitrant text from a feminist point of view because it is one of those texts which, in the words of Belsey and Moore, 'do not depict any women at all, and say nothing about gender relations'[17] – aims to open up medieval drama, and indeed the field of medieval literature as a whole, to gendered readings which do not necessarily consider only the role of women.

In so doing Evans focuses on one of the problematic aspects of medieval drama for feminist critics: its relative absence of women as central figures. This is emphatically not the case with Chaucer's texts, which is perhaps one reason why his writings have been more amenable to feminist or 'woman-centred' readings. 'Woman-centred' readings, both of medieval literature and of the culture as a whole, have been part of the critical scene since the mid-1970s, but such studies have been by no means either avowedly feminist or explicitly theoretical (Angela Lucas, Derek Baker, Peter Dronke). Yet the various anthologies of writings by medieval women or studies of medieval women writers (Dronke, Katharina Wilson, Alexandra Barratt) have had a political impact because they have highlighted previously ignored areas of medieval literature, decentred the medieval canon in which 'anon.' is assumed to be a man, opened up underexplored territories, and suggested a different reading focus. The focus has been altered in yet more complex ways by editions such as that of Bella Millett and Jocelyn Wogan-Browne, which offers a collection of texts FOR women. This not only gets away from the essentialist focus on the author in other anthologies, but suggests a wholly different set of questions about the relationship of women to literary production in the Middle Ages.

Yet, paradoxically, where Chaucer's canonical security has resulted in a number of feminist articles and book-length studies, the canonical security of other major medieval works, and the dominant grids through which they are read, have, as Colette Murphy points out in relation to *Piers Plowman*, made them appear to be more resistant to political readings, including feminist ones. Like the drama, *Piers Plowman* has been chiefly read within the context of the medieval Church: as an apocalyptic, dramatic, meditative text which is the product of religious orthodoxy, closed off to social meanings.

In her essay, 'Lady Holy Church and Meed the Maid: re-envisioning female personifications in *Piers Plowman*', Murphy turns her attention to the gendering of allegorical personifications, and in so doing opens up another route into gendered readings of allegory, a dominant and problematic medieval form, just as Riddy in her essay explores the gender and class ramifications of personifying Daunger, an attribute of the Lady, as a club-wielding peasant in the *Romance of the Rose*. It may appear that for medieval clerical readers, just as for their modern heirs within the Robertsonian school, women in the Middle Ages are situated at either end of a good/bad axis, as types of Eve or Mary, 'impure flesh' or 'pure soul'.[18] We might therefore expect to find allegorical personifications, which by their very nature remain static and unchanging, reinforcing such symbolism, and confirming a dominant medieval view of women's essential 'nature'. Murphy shows that in *Piers Plowman*, at least, this is not the case, by tracking the gender/class dynamics in the dramatisation of the complex figures of Lady Holy Church and Meed the Maid, whose relationship cannot be adequately represented as one of polarised oppositions between a 'good' and a 'bad' woman, which is how the Dreamer initially, and some modern critics more insistently, may try to see it. Murphy reveals here the possibilities of reading allegory as a dynamic form, in terms of gender and class, as a form precisely where various abstract qualities *fail* to become embodied and fixed, even as they are realised in personified bodies. This is of course of crucial interest to feminists, since it shows that historically 'Woman' (the signifier with which patriarchy puts women in their place) has not 'always been like that', but has, even in the allegorical mode, been a site of contradiction and not just a place colonised by the desires of others.

Readers today must always reckon with the vast output of 'official' Church writing which the Wife of Bath so wittily debunks. However, while the Wife can gleefully reject the Church's teachings on virginity, it is not so easy for feminist medievalists to reject the large corpus of virginity literature produced under the aegis of the Church. This is 'woman-centred' literature *par excellence*, about women and for women, but it is largely the product of a male clerical élite ostensibly anxious to promote the Church ideal of celibacy but also deeply troubled by their own feelings about sexuality, which are thence projected onto women. As Jocelyn Wogan-Browne notes in her witty and clearly argued essay 'The Virgin's Tale', this material is extremely problematic for the feminist reader: in virgin martyr hagiographies, for example, there are accounts of horrific torture of women – breasts pierced with nails and ripped off, immersion in boiling cauldrons. Their cautionary message, like that of the narrative of the latter-day saint Maria Goretti, is that it is better for women to die than to have their physical intactness and purity violated. Yet Wogan-Browne argues that such texts should not simply be received as products of medieval anti-feminism, even though they represent official Church teachings which are clearly aimed at keeping women in their place. The virgin martyrs are not passive and suffering: their narratives provide a site where women do speak with authority and autonomy, and their narratives should be accorded this recognition, even as it should be recognised at the same time that these martyrs are made to mouth the words of their loving Father. Virginity texts also offer at least a partial critique of medieval secular romance, especially its ideology of the glorious destiny of marriage or romantic love. Wogan-Browne's analysis of literary form is crucial here. The choice of form, as Riddy pointed out, is highly determining: there is not a previously existing 'knowledge' about medieval women which is then 'encoded' in a variety of genres and modes: rather, the discourse itself, be it hagiography, romance or courtly *plainte*, produces a particular kind of knowledge. This analysis goes well beyond the Wife of Bath's speculations about lion-painting, which assumed a prior 'truth' about women that depended only on women expressing it for there to be proper representation.

Lesley Johnson looks at the cultural persistence of Griselda as a signifier of femininity, and as a talking-point for both medieval and modern readers, most notably in Chaucer's *Clerk's Tale*, in 'Reincarnations of Griselda: contexts for the *Clerk's Tale*?'. In so doing she extends the question of reading raised by the Wife of Bath, the question about the production of images by men and their vested interests in producing those images. Johnson asks whether clerks have control of (hi)stories: she shows how this question is posed already in Chaucer's text, and discusses the impossibility of recovering a 'medieval' reading for this troubling and powerful icon of femininity. Johnson thus raises important questions about returning the text to its historical moment of production: we can produce ever-more detailed contexts for medieval representations, but it is vital to note that it is the power of the grids by which we read those representations which can shift a reader's expectations. Griselda will continue to be a subject for debate, and for changed 'meaning', with each new discourse in which she appears.

Johnson's essay also deals with the question of a plurality of historical readings: this is not always the case with medieval texts, not all of which have been read continually from the Middle Ages to the present (Kempe's *Book* is one example) and whose reception history is uneven. Not only are individual medieval texts read differently today, though the point about *Piers Plowman* and the drama is that they are usually *not*, but they have also been read differently in the past. This can be instructive: there is no single, true, transhistorical reading. If lion-painting is about the supremely masculine, God-like function of making the world in your own image, then lion-reading is about reproducing texts in your own image too, and about the feminist reader's ability to wrest meaning away from the patriarchal powers-that-be.

What might the (medieval) world look like if women made it too? Several of the contributors raise our awareness of the possible effects of medieval women *reading*: that this might productively reorientate our present view of the meanings of individual texts by positing a different set of expectations about the kind of historical meanings medieval women might have derived from those texts. Of course women *did* also write in the Middle Ages (as evidenced in recent anthologies of women writers, but also in the less obvious case of Margery Kempe, who gets her book written even though she is functionally illiterate), although their output was a fraction of the male one. The fifteenth-century writer Christine de Pisan is probably one of the best-known (because named) female writers. Schibanoff, in common with many of our contributors, collapses the distinction between reading and writing by showing how Christine de Pisan's *Book of the City of Ladies* thematises the difficulties of *writing* as a matter of the difficulties of *reading*, in her essay ' "Taking the gold out of Egypt": the art of reading as a woman' (1986). As Schibanoff reminds us, the genesis of de Pisan's *Book* is due to its narrator's being temporarily incapacitated by her reading of some of the central anti-marriage texts of the Middle Ages, the very texts which the Wife of Bath symbolically defaces in her act of ripping out the pages from her husband's book. If the Wife of Bath's action dramatises the *failure* of reading, since in this episode at least she shows herself unable to negotiate the text except by violent denial, then, Schibanoff argues, Christine de Pisan learns strategies of survival in her reading practices. Schibanoff raises important issues here about access to literacy: about who is reading and writing in the Middle Ages; about female and male subject-positions for reading and writing; about historical ways of resisting normative positions; about the cultural possibilities opened up by humanism and print culture. She argues, however, that increased literacy paradoxically brought not greater control for women but a greater chance that they would be subject to masculine ideology.

She advises that, at the least, we should exercise caution before we celebrate women's greater access to literacy and culture in the fifteenth century. This is not necessarily a pessimistic conclusion.

The point is that we cannot construct unified histories tracing either the advance of women's historical position or its decline. Our histories, like our readings of them, are made up of uneven developments and paradoxes: the 'relations between ideological and social change for women' is problematic, and even more so is 'women's relation to hegemonic (male) culture', as Elizabeth Fox-Genovese has pointed out in her review of women's history and culture since 1975.[19]

This collection represents the liveliness of feminist readings of medieval texts. Its political impact is less easy to calculate. Christine de Pisan, writing at a moment of social crisis and upheaval in the early fifteenth century, recognised that reading is instrumental in changing social structures. Although the feminist reader cannot determine how a work can or will be read, s/he can suggest different grids and different models of both the period and its literary texts. Above all s/he can ask different questions. The 'new' Middle Ages is taking shape, although the older ways of reading still maintain their force in certain parts of the academy, represented, for example, by neo-Robertsonian criticism (Judson Allen, Olson),[20] and by the newly visible texts of medieval literary theory, which are often presented in such a way as to reinforce a 'proper' mode of reading the culture.[21]

There are still areas in which relatively little feminist work has been done, and which we can point to as areas which are currently opening up in stimulating ways. There is the question of gender and racial, ethnic or national identity, which might make use of feminist appropriations of post-colonial literary theory: useful cultural texts here are medieval historiography, travel-writing and maps.[22] There is the important area of gay and lesbian concerns in medieval studies, and the issue of 'men in feminism'; preliminary cartography here has begun in recent issues of *Medieval Feminist Newsletter*.[23] There is the question of specifically feminist editing practices: this is not simply or only a matter of offering a 'feminist' introduction, but of introducing difference into one of the chief bastions of medieval scholarship, in ways that perhaps might seek to disrupt the traditional procedures of textual editing, wittily characterised by E. Talbot Donaldson in a revealingly gendered metaphor as 'not unlike a bachelor choosing a bride'. And there is a place for contesting periodisation and the sexual politics of that periodisation: there are continuities between the 'medieval' and 'modern' periods, just as there are discontinuities, and there is room here to challenge the ideological investment of critics in maintaining a firm division between the two. The contributors to this volume are not in the business of arbitrating between 'proper' and 'improper' readings (for that would only confirm the very binarism which feminists seek to avoid), but rather of exploding the distinction between them, revealing that it is an effect of the sexual politics of reading and writing, both in the medieval and the modern period. They aim to map out questions of sufficient power to keep generating responses and rereadings, to ensure that medieval texts are read and continue to be read in the most intellectually challenging and politically accountable ways.

NOTES

1 Arlyn Diamond and Lee R. Edwards (eds) *The Authority of Experience: Essays in Feminist Criticism*, Amherst, University of Massachusetts Press, 1977; republished in paperback in 1988.

2 The phrase is coined by Toril Moi, *Sexual/Textual Politics*, London, Methuen, 1985, pp. 104–7, to describe Hélène Cixous's analysis of binary oppositions. See Hélène Cixous, 'Sorties: out and out: attacks/ways out/ forays', in Catherine Belsey and Jane Moore (eds) *The Feminist Reader*, Basingstoke and London, Macmillan, 1989, pp. 101–16.

3 Carruthers, 'Afterword', pp. 39, 42–3.

4 J. S. P. Tatlock and A. G. Kennedy in *A Concordance to the Complete Works of Geoffrey Chaucer and to the Romaunt of the Rose*, Washington, The Carnegie Institute of Washington, 1927 note other uses of 'secte' in the *Squire's Tale* 17; *House of Fame* 342; *Romaunt of the Rose* 5745; but see also the *Legend of Good Women* 1382, which suggests the construction of a group of false male lovers as the 'sekte' to which Jason belongs.

5 Larry D. Benson (ed.) *The Riverside Chaucer*, Oxford, Oxford University Press, 1988. See also Joseph L. Baird, 'The "secte" of the Wyf of Bathe', *The Chaucer Review*, 1968, vol. 2, pp. 188–90; Lilian Hornstein, 'The Wyf of Bathe and the Merchant: from sex to "secte" ', *The Chaucer Review*, 1968, vol. 3, pp. 65–7; Joseph L. Baird, ' "Secte" and "suit" again: Chaucer and Langland', *The Chaucer Review*, 1971, vol. 6, pp. 117–19. See, too, the *Middle English Dictionary*, *sect(e)* n. 1 (d), which offers the following definition of the use of the term in the *Wife of Bath's Prologue* and in the *Legend of Good Women*: 'those of a certain way of thinking and acting, especially as parties in a controversy or lawsuit: ?also with punning reference to n. 1 (e)' [that is, 'sex', 'gender'].

6 bell hooks, *Ain't I A Woman: Black Women and Feminism*, London, Pluto, 1982. See also the debates on feminism and essentialism in the editorials of the journal *m/f* from 1978 to 1986, reprinted in Parveen

Adams and Elizabeth Cowie (eds) *The Woman in Question*, London and New York, Verso, 1990, pp. 21–39.

7 On the beguines, see Ernest W. McDonnell, *The Beguines and Beghards in Medieval Culture*, New Brunswick, New Jersey, Rutgers University Press, 1954; Elizabeth Alvilda Petroff, *Medieval Women's Visionary Literature*, New York, Oxford University Press, 1986, pp. 171–8; R. W. Southern, *Western Society and the Church in the Later Middle Ages*, Harmondsworth, Penguin, 1970, pp. 319–31. On women and Lollardy, see Margaret Aston, 'Devotional literacy', in *Lollards and Reformers: Images and Literacy in Late Medieval Religion*, London, Hambledon Press, 1984, pp. 101–33; Claire Cross, ' "Great Reasoners in Scripture": the activities of women lollards, 1380–1530', in Derek Baker (ed.) *Medieval Women*, Oxford, Basil Blackwell, 1978, pp. 359–80.

8 For a preliminary mapping-out of the problem of individual vs group identity in the Middle Ages, see Lee Patterson, 'On the margin: post-modernism, ironic history, and medieval studies', *Speculum*, 1990, vol. 65, pp. 87–108. See also David Aers, *Community, Gender and Individual Identity*, London, Routledge, 1988. For further discussion of the audiences addressed by the Wife of Bath, see Barrie Ruth Straus, 'The subversive discourse of the Wife of Bath: phallocentric discourse and the imprisonment of criticism', *English Literary History*, 1988, vol. 55, pp. 527–54.

9 For further discussion of this 'envoy', the varieties of voice in it, and confusion in manuscripts of the *Canterbury Tales* about where the Clerk's voice actually ends, see 'Reincarnations of Griselda', Chapter 9, p. 209 and especially n. 40.

10 Mary Poovey, *Uneven Developments: The Ideological Work of Gender in Mid-Victorian England*, Chicago, University of Chicago Press, 1988; republished London, Virago, 1989.

11 Carolyn Dinshaw, *Chaucer's Sexual Poetics*, Madison, Wisconsin and London, University of Wisconsin Press, 1989; Elaine Tuttle Hansen, *Chaucer and the Fictions of Gender*, Berkeley, University of California Press, 1992; and Louise O. Fradenburg, 'The Wife of Bath's passing fancy', *Studies in the Age of Chaucer*, 1986, vol. 8, pp. 31–58.

12 Schibanoff, p. 223.

13 D. W. Robertson's exegetical method is perhaps best illustrated in his essay 'The doctrine of charity in medieval literary gardens: a topical approach through symbolism and allegory', *Speculum*, 1951, vol. 26, pp. 24–49; reprinted in D. W. Robertson, Jr, *Essays in Medieval Culture*, Princeton, New Jersey, Princeton University Press, 1980, pp. 21–50; see also D. W. Robertson, Jr, *A Preface to Chaucer: Studies in Medieval Perspectives*, Princeton, New Jersey, Princeton University Press, 1963. For a summary of Robertson's criticism and the debate about its institutional effects, see Dinshaw, op. cit., pp. 31–9, and Lee Patterson, 'The historical development of Chaucer studies', in *Negotiating The Past: The Historical Understanding of Medieval Literature*, Madison, Wisconsin and London, University of Wisconsin Press, 1987, pp. 3–39. For a critique of 'scholarship' in relation to the medieval drama see, Theresa Coletti, 'Reading REED: history and the Records of Early English Drama', in Lee Patterson (ed.) *Literary Practice and Social Change in Britain, 1380–1530*,

Berkeley, Los Angeles and Oxford, University of California Press, 1990, pp. 248–84.

14 Carruthers, p. 22.

15 Riddy, p. 57.

16 Delany, p. 72.

17 Catherine Belsey and Jane Moore (eds) *The Feminist Reader: Essays in Gender and the Politics of Literary Criticism*, Basingstoke and London, Macmillan, 1989, p. 1.

18 Sarah Beckwith, 'A very material mysticism: the medieval mysticism of Margery Kempe', in David Aers (ed.) *Medieval Literature: Criticism, Ideology and History*, Brighton, Harvester, 1986, pp. 34–57; p. 36.

19 Elizabeth Fox-Genovese, 'Culture and consciousness in the intellectual history of European women', *Signs*, 1987, vol. 12. pp. 529–47. Fox-Genovese makes these points specifically in relation to the contradictory position on 'women's advance or decline' in the fifteenth and sixteenth centuries, apparent in Joan Kelly's stimulating and influential essays, 'Did women have a Renaissance?' and 'Early feminist theory and the *querelle des femmes*, 1400–1789' (reprinted in Joan Kelly, *Women, History, and Theory: The Essays of Joan Kelly*, Chicago, University of Chicago Press, 1984). In this latter essay Kelly, according to Fox-Genovese, 'implicitly identified the emergence of a coherent body of feminist thought in the very period that she had originally claimed was the seedbed of women's domestic confinement and the great downturn in women's status' (p. 533).

20 See Judson B. Allen with Theresa Anne Moritz, *A Distinction of Stories*, Columbus, Ohio State University Press, 1981; Judson B. Allen, *The Ethical Poetic of the Middle Ages*, Toronto, University of Toronto Press, 1982; and Paul Olson, *The Canterbury Tales and the Good Society*, Princeton, Princeton University Press, 1986. For comments on neo-Robertsonianism, see Patterson, op. cit. (1987), pp. 3–39; and David Aers, 'Rewriting the Middle Ages: some suggestions', *Journal of Medieval and Renaissance Studies*, 1988, vol. 18, no. 2, pp. 221–40; pp. 221–2.

21 See Alastair J. Minnis, *Medieval Theory of Authorship: Scholastic Literary Attitudes in the Later Middle Ages*, 2nd edn, Aldershot, Wildwood House, 1988, pp. 1–8; and Alastair J. Minnis and A. B. Scott with the assistance of David Wallace (eds) *Medieval Literary Theory and Criticism c. 1100–c. 1375: The Commentary Tradition*, Oxford, Clarendon Press, 1988.

22 On the subject of nation/national identity/gender, see Lesley Johnson, 'Imagining communities', Discussion Paper for *Imagining Communities: Medieval and Modern*, International Medieval Conference 1992, Centre for Medieval Studies, University of Leeds, Saturday 23 May 1992, pp. 1–12; pp. 6–9.

23 On gay and lesbian concerns in medieval studies see *Medieval Feminist Newsletter*, 1992, vol. 13, pp. 1–15. On men in medieval feminism, see *Medieval Feminist Newsletter*, 1988, vol. 6, pp. 16–17.

2 The Wife of Bath and the painting of lions

Mary Carruthers

In her Prologue, the Wife of Bath refers to the Aesopian fable of
the painting of the lion: the lion complains of a picture showing a
man killing a lion and suggests that if a lion had painted it the result
would have been different. Just so, says Alisoun, if women told tales
of marital woe to match those of the authorities represented in
Jankyn's book, they would show 'of men more wikkednesse/Than al
the merk of Adam may redresse'.[1] The moral of the fable expresses
an aspect of that general concern with the relationship of 'auctoritee'
to 'experience' which she announces in the first sentence of her
Prologue. Alisoun has often been characterised as attempting to do
away with authority altogether, as setting up a heterodox doctrine
of marriage based on female supremacy to replace the traditional
medieval view, sanctioned by the church fathers and by common
law, that wives should be humble, obedient and submissive to their
husbands in all things. But the Wife's understanding of the uses of
'auctoritee' is more complex than this analysis allows. Alisoun does
not deny authority when authority is true; she tells us straight off
that authority and experience agree on the great lesson 'of wo that
is in mariage'. She does insist, however, that authority make itself
accountable to the realities of experience. The fable of painting the
lion teaches that the 'truth' of any picture often has more to do
with the prejudices and predilections of the painter than with the
'reality' of the subject and that truthful art (and morality) must take
account of this complexly mutual relationship. In her prologue, the
Wife describes her own progress towards building a 'trewe' marriage
out of her experience and personality and uses her experience as
an ironic corrective both for the pronouncements of those clerics
and other authorities at whom she pokes fun in her prologue and
for the idealistic romancing in which she engages in her tale.

This paper first describes Alisoun's practical economic experience as a wealthy west-country clothier endowed with the property of her deceased spouses and then indicates how she uses this experience to counter and correct the ideal of subordinate wifehood painted by the 'auctoritee' of clerical writers like Jerome and of deportment-book authors like LaTour-Landry and the *ménagier de Paris*, who stressed the goal of 'gentilesse' prized by the wealthy bourgeoisie. Alisoun triumphantly shows in her prologue that economic 'maistrye' not only brings her the independence and freedom to love that the proscriptions of 'auctoritee' deny her but enables her to create finally a mutually nourished marital bond truer than any envisioned by the traditionalists. Then, having demonstrated the undeniable virtues of experience, Alisoun treats herself in her tale to a controlled flight of comic fantasy in the idealists' mode, demonstrating through parody, the literary instrument with which she typically corrects authority, her shrewd understanding of both the delights and the limitations of lion painting.

'Experience' is the first and most significant word in the Wife's prologue. Though obviously referring to the events of her personal life – to her five husbands, her cloth making, her love of travel – the word also includes a larger context, the experience of her whole social class, the bourgeoisie engaged in trade. It is in terms of this greater experience that we must understand what Alisoun means by 'maistrye'[2] and what her claim to marital sovereignty rooted in 'maistrye' would have meant to her peers.

Because property is the basis of that claim, the nature and legal standing of Alisoun's property are crucial considerations in understanding her prologue and tale. As a cloth maker in the west of England at this time, she was engaged in the most lucrative trade possible. By the late fourteenth century, the English wool trade had become as much a trade in finished cloth as it was in the raw wool itself,[3] and the cloth-making industry had entered the export markets, in addition to supplying domestic needs. There is every reason to believe that Alisoun's cloth making, which 'passed hem of Ypres and of Gaunt' (*GP*, 450), was big business. Manly thought that Chaucer was belittling the Wife in likening her skills to those of the great Flemish cloth makers,[4] but Chaucer's enthusiastic appraisal of her professional worth is no overstatement. The English cloth makers, thanks to protective legislation, were able to underprice their European competitors, to the point of contributing to a severe depression in Flanders, and thus to surpass the Flemish product in quantity as well as in quality.[5]

The Wife is not a weaver but a capitalist clothier,[6] one of those persons who oversaw the whole process of cloth manufacture – buying the wool, contracting the labour of the various artisans involved in manufacture, and sending bales of finished broadcloths off to Bristol and London for export. Women wool merchants and clothiers are common enough in the records of this period. They were usually widows, carrying on after their husbands' deaths, and some of them were very wealthy indeed.[7] The term 'cloth maker' refers to that person, the clothier, who manufactures cloth.[8] And to be a cloth manufacturer in the west of England in Chaucer's day was to be engaged in the trade in the manner I have just described, as its capitalist entrepreneur.

As early as the thirteenth century, English cloth manufacture was evolving from an urban-based, guild-monopolised trade to a rural-based 'domestic' industry, in which the clothier owned the material of manufacture throughout the stages of production.[9] In this shift from urban to rural lies the significance of Alisoun's dwelling 'biside Bathe'. Bath itself was an insignificant town throughout the Middle Ages, but the surrounding countryside of the Avon valley was an area of vigorous cloth production, whose clothiers took advantage of their proximity on the one hand to the wool-growing areas of the Cotswolds and Mendip Hills and on the other hand to the major port of Bristol.[10] Alisoun is no modest artisan. Her extensive travels at home and abroad are appropriate to her business as well as to her pleasure, and though she is provincial she comes from the richest of provinces.

In addition to the wealth she has garnered from wool, a good deal of property, including (most likely) the cloth business itself, has come to her from her husbands. Her legal title to this property is clear; she herself says that she gave it freely to Jankyn when she married him, and one cannot give what one does not own. Her claim is fully confirmed by the legal habits of her community. The customs of the bourgeoisie, customs that had the effect of law, gave propertied married women rights that were denied them by both the common law (which affected the rights of women whose property was held in manorial fiefs) and the canon law. Among the burgesses, married women retained the ownership and control of their property and could enter into contracts in their own names, their husbands having neither legal liability nor power of consent in such matters:

The common law was the custom of the King's Court, and an

outgrowth of feudal conditions which applied particularly to the larger landowners; for the upper classes of society its rules were no doubt appropriate, but it is only in the local customs of numerous cities, towns, and villages that we can see how different the life of the ordinary people was. In these customs, for example, we find that the position of the married woman was very different from that which the common law assigned her, the complete merging of her personality being obviously out of harmony with bourgeois habits. Local customs frequently keep the woman's property free from her husband's control, accord her liberty of contract (which was denied at common law), and even allow her to trade separately upon her own account.[11]

When custom conflicted with common law, the Court of Common Pleas tended to rule in favour of the custom.[12]

We can thus reasonably suppose that the Wife did indeed own in fee simple all the property her husbands had given to her and that she was accustomed to trade in her own name whether she was married or not. It was common for husbands to leave property to their wives without entail or other encumbrance and for the widow to be made executor.[13] From earliest times, the widow of a landed man had the right of dower, an automatic portion of her deceased husband's property.[14] By the fourteenth century, the dower was being replaced by jointure, property settled on the wife by the husband, usually as a condition of the marriage contract but sometimes at a later point in the marriage.[15] Alisoun is obviously aware of the importance of jointures and other property gifts:

> I wolde no lenger in the bed abide
> If that I felte his arm over my side,
> Til he hadde maad his raunson unto me;
> Thanne wolde I suffre him do his nicetee.[16]

This bald exchange may strike us as cynical, vulgar and immoral, but we must remember that by the standards common to her class Alisoun's behaviour is simply shrewd business. And since we may assume from her account that she was far too good a businesswoman to marry a man whose property was encumbered with children or other undesirable heirs, she has amassed a great deal of land and fee by the time we encounter her on the road to Canterbury.

It is within the context of her class and station that Alisoun makes her correction of traditional marriage teaching and teachers, including Jerome. The Wife's attitude towards her clerkly opponents should not be judged as primly as it often has been. She is not bitterly attacking them, for why should she attack a body of material so clearly removed (as the fathers themselves admit) from the lives of common wedded folk? She is not setting up a heresy, a counter-religion. To argue this is not only to disregard common pastoral doctrine and the customs of her class but to distort her own expressed intention and the tone of her debate.[17] 'Myn entente', she says, 'nis but for to pleye' (*WBP*, 198). She does not deny the celibate ideal its due; she merely points out its lack of domestic economy. A good wife should be thrifty, and only an imprudent household would set its board exclusively with gold and silver dishes (as Jerome himself said, echoing Paul).

A master of parody, Alisoun turns Jerome's words back on themselves, to his presumed discomfiture and to our delight. Jerome is one of those figures who open themselves up to such treatment, for the most intemperate of anti-feminist Christian satirists is a man best known in his private life for the circle of women disciples he collected, whose education he encouraged in a series of notably eloquent letters. It is the Roman period of Jerome's life, the period of Paula, Marcella, Eustochium, and the unfortunate Blesilla, that the Wife remembers especially about him, as her epithet for him, 'a clerk at Rome', indicates. And Alisoun is as exegetically skilled, as polemically successful, as Jerome would have wished any of his women friends to be; she has simply taken him at his word ('I do not condemn even octogamy')[18] and remarried all those times. Jerome was, moreover, a man so brilliantly vituperative that he constantly embarrassed himself. The *Adversus Jovinianum* got him into a great deal of trouble at the time it was written, so much so that his friend Pammachius withdrew from circulation and destroyed as many copies of the treatise as he could lay his hands on.[19] Jerome approved of this action, which he called 'prudent and friendly' in the letter of defence that he wrote to Pammachius.[20] The record of this controversy was not lost in the Middle Ages. In taking on Jerome as she does, Alisoun is not engaging in new sport but is making a rich joke at the expense of a notoriously ill-tempered saint's most notoriously ill-tempered work. The fate of Jankyn's book is the final turn of this excellent jest. For in burning the book that contains so much of the *Adversus Jovinianum*, Alisoun is simply consigning yet another copy of the treatise to the fate that Pammachius and Jerome himself ordered for it when it first appeared.

But Alisoun's most amusing darts are not necessarily her most important, for her primary attack in both the prologue and the tale is directed at a body of marital lore held commonly by her own class and articulated most fully in the deportment books written to foster 'gentilesse'. These books were designed to teach young girls how to be good wives, and the books that have survived[21] tend to stress wifely goodness more than wifely skills. They purport to be concerned with devotional instruction and morality, but as moral works they are curiously self-contradictory. Their morality tends to be 'gentility', manners and deportment only, and demonstrates a single-minded concern with domestic propriety. Yet they pretend also that social reward is unrelated to economic power, especially for women. They emphasise 'gentilesse', 'honour', 'worship', and 'prow', but in senses more appropriate to the Franklin, even to the Merchant, than to the Knight. It is this fuzzy 'morality' of the deportment-book writer that especially exercises the Wife in her early experiences with husbands and in her tale.

The two best-known deportment books are both French, and both were composed in the last thirty years of the fourteenth century, *The Book of the Knight of LaTour-Landry* (Caxton's translation of the original French work) and *Le Ménagier de Paris*, which has been translated as *The Goodman of Paris*.[22] The Knight of LaTour-Landry writes a beginning reading book for his young daughters, all of whom he expects will marry soon. The *ménagier* is instructing his young wife, aged fifteen:

> for your honour and love, and not for my service (for to me belongs but the common service, or less) since I had pity and loving compassion on you who for so long have had neither father nor mother, nor any of your kinswomen near you to whom you might turn for counsel in your private needs.[23]

Even though one of these writers is a gentleman and the other a burgess, their instructions are remarkably similar. And their books, like all such books for children, reflect more what the writers think marriage ought to be than what it is. In these works the husband is a father-god, all-knowing, all-powerful, generally benevolent, despotic; the child-wife's only task is to keep his honour and estate by practising absolute obedience. They exemplify biased lion painting at its worst. Yet sometimes they have their practical side. The *ménagier* has useful chapters on such matters as falconry, equine diseases, gardening, cooking, overseeing servants, and getting rid of household pests like fleas and flies. The knight's treatise lacks these lessons simply because he is writing for unmarried daughters rather than for a young bride who must cope immediately with the affairs of a large and unwieldy household, for the letters of the Paston women make clear that their daily responsibilities were just as burdensome as those of merchants' wives.

A wife acted as her husband's business partner and had to assume full responsibility for the conduct of his affairs when he was away, as medieval husbands with means often were. The *ménagier* and the knight are both particularly concerned that young girls understand a wife's obligation to care for her husband's honour and estate: to this end she must be patient, obedient and dutiful, especially in company, and she must not gossip or reprimand him publicly. The appearance of matrimonial unity was as important as the appearance of corporate unity is today, and for the same reasons. To teach this, the *ménagier* tells a tale that is revealing of the moral assumptions of his book. A merchant's wife ran off with a young man who promptly deserted her, and she was then forced by poverty into prostitution. Rumours of her fall reached the community where her husband lived. To dispel them, he dispatched her two brothers to fetch her home, decorated his house, and received her with great public display. He thus saved his wife's honour, says the *ménagier*, because it 'touched the honour of himself and his children' (pp. 184–6). The merchant was wise because in keeping his wife he kept his own estate.

A good wife is a wife who can keep her husband's good. She was frequently required to act for him in a legal capacity. Thus we hear of Margaret Paston holding a manor court while her husband was in London tending his legal affairs.[24] That formidable royal aristocrat, Lady Isabel Berkeley, while in London trying to keep herself out of the Tower, wrote to her husband:

> Sur your matter speedeth and doth right well, save my daughter costeth great good; At the reverence of God send money or els I must lay my horse to pledge and come hom on my feet: keep well all about you till I come home, and trete not without mee, And then all thinge shall bee well.[25]

With such discretionary power located in the wife, it was evidently essential that she be taught to respect her husband's social and economic estate as her own. And without such power, I would add, such injunctions would not be so important.

If the deportment books were content to teach that social behaviour was simply a practical area of domestic economy, wifely 'gentilesse' would get little quarrel from Alisoun. But they are not, of course, because their authors confuse manners and morals in a way that takes their writing into the realm of genteel fantasy. One of their morals is that among women virtue alone will be rewarded with success, a lesson that could not be further from the fact of most medieval marriages. LaTour-Landry begins his treatise with a tale of the king of England come to seek a wife among the three daughters of the king of Denmark. The eldest was lovely but coquettish, the middle one bold of speech, and the youngest meek, well-mannered and ugly. The king took the youngest because she was 'ferme in her estate, behaving, and of good maners' (*LaTour-Landry*, p. 17). His choice was against the advice of his friends, who warned him, significantly, that he would 'lose worship' if he did not choose the oldest, the heiress. It is a pretty tale, but it must be contrasted with the words of Stephen Scrope, writing around 1440: 'For very need I was fain to sell a little daughter I have for much less than I should have done by possibility.'[26] This is the same Scrope who, at fifty and 'disfigured in my person [by illness] . . . whilst I live',[27] was considered a fine match for twenty-year-old Elizabeth Paston.[28] The sale by parents of the rights to marry their children was a common practice among both gentry and bourgeoisie in the later Middle Ages.[29]

In view of such discrepancies between medieval theory and medieval practice, one must be careful about accepting the deportment books as authorities on what was actually anticipated in a medieval marriage. These books have much the same quality as modern books on dating etiquette for teenagers, which offer advice we truly know to be honoured more in the breach than in the observance. Occasionally, the writers themselves will admit the impracticality of what they appear to be counselling. At the end of his retelling of the Griselda story, the *ménagier* comments:

> And I, that have set the tale here merely to lesson you, have not set it here to apply to you, nor because I would have such obedience from you, for I am not worthy thereof, and also I am no marquis nor have I taken in you a shepherdess, and I am not so foolish, so overweening nor of so small sense that I know not well that 'tis not for me to assault nor to assay you thus, nor in like manner. . . . And excuse me if the story telleth of cruelty too great (to my mind) and above reason.
>
> (p. 137)

There can be no doubt that the Wife's behaviour, especially in her first marriages, is almost everything the deportment-book writers say it should not be. But not quite, for they would have had to approve, though perhaps grudgingly, her mastery of the practical

aspects of domestic economy and public 'honour'. She has chap-
erones and witnesses (however compromised), and though she
chides her husbands 'spitously', there is no evidence that she does
so in public. I rather hope that those ten-pound kerchiefs of hers
are out of date,[30] for it is more in keeping with the Wife's evident
economy to save and mend good stuff than to be constantly buying
the latest fashions. Her 'gites' are of scarlet, the choicest material.[31]
And, as she says, there are no moths or mites in her wardrobes.[32]

The practical bourgeois wife clearly contradicted the idealised
image of the subservient wife held up as a model by 'gentility' and
by the church. Yet the wit Alisoun directs at traditional marriage
lore, coming as it does from the rich experience of her class, should
not horrify her audience (though they may take exception to some
of it) because they would recognise the common truth of what she
is saying. Take for instance her ridicule of clerical teaching concerning the remarriage of widows. In fact, a rich widow was considered
to be a match equal to, or more desirable than, a match with a
virgin of property. A wealthy widow was considered a real find,
even for a family as landed as the Pastons. Edmund Paston writes:
'Her*e* is lately fallyn a wydow *in* Woorstede whyche was wyff to on
Boolt, a worstede marchaunt, *and* worth a m li [thousand pounds]'.[33]
The sole considerations are money and the inheritance rights of
issue from previous marriages. Thus Agnes Paston insisted that
Scrope reveal in full before any betrothal was arranged 'if he were
maried [to Elizabeth Paston] *and* fortuned to have children, if tho
children schuld enheryte his lond or his dowt*er* þe wheche is
maried'.[34] And Edmund Paston reassures his family concerning the
widow with the thousand pounds that she 'has but ij chylder*en*
whyche shalbe at þe ded*y*s charge'.[35] Nobody mentions the slightest
reservation about the morality of marrying widows. Nor do we find
such a lack of concern only among the practical Pastons. The Knight
of LaTour-Landry praises the piety of widows who do not remarry,
but it is clear that his expectations for his own daughters are quite
different:

> But, my faire doughters, take hereby a good ensaumple, that yef
> be fortune ye fall into a good marriage, and afterwardes God
> take youre husbondes from you, wedde you not ayen vnauisely
> for vain plesaunce, but werkithe bi the counsaile of youre true
> frendes.

(pp. 156–7)

And the *ménagier*, who is a very moral man indeed, clearly expects his young wife to marry again upon his death (pp. 42, 109).

As Alisoun knows from experience, the true fruits of marriage are described neither in Jerome nor in the deportment books but are set in the marriage bed. Its important spoils for her are neither children nor sensual gratification but independence.[36] Marriage is the key to survival, and that is what Alisoun seeks and finds. Her parents married her off when she was twelve, an early enough age to suggest either notable greed or straitened financial circumstances on their part.[37] The extent to which parents who were set on a marriage would go in order to break the will of a reluctant daughter is chillingly attested by the experience of Elizabeth Paston when her mother had bound her to the dreadful Scrope:

> sche hath son Esterne [this letter was written 29 June] þe most part be betyn onys in þe weke or twyes, *and* som tyme tywes on o day, *and* hir hed broken in to or thre places.[38]

After such treatment poor Elizabeth gave in and agreed to 'rewle hire to hym as sche awte to do' even though 'his persone is symple', though for other reasons the marriage finally fell through. It is difficult to imagine Alisoun's experience with husbands one through three as any better than the melancholy misalliances contemplated in the pages of the Paston letters. The lesson that Alisoun has learned is obvious: marriage is contracted for money, and the acquisition of money is equivalent to the attainment of honour, respect and independence. She alternately chides and flatters her old husbands into allowing her to walk about the town in her good clothes, but her freedom is hard earned:

> And therfore every man this tale I telle:
> Winne whoso may, for al is for to selle;
> With empty hand men may no hawkes lure.
> For winning wolde I al his lust endure,
> And make me a feined appetit –
> And yit in bacon hadde I nevere delit.
>
> (*WBP*, 419–24)

The root of marital 'maistrye' is economic control. The husband deserves control of the wife because he controls the estate; this is a fundamental lesson in the deportment books. As the *ménagier* says, a wife should behave according to her husband's desires, for he 'ought to be and is sovereign and can increase and diminish all' (p. 112). The logic is clear: sovereignty is the power of the purse.

This is not a spiritual doctrine but a property doctrine, based on the facts of a mercantile economy. Similarly, Alisoun realises that sovereignty is synonymous with economic control:

> They hadde me yiven hir land and hir tresor;
> Me needed nat do lenger diligence
> To winne hir love or doon hem reverence.
>
> (*WBP*, 210–12)

Her logic is neither unique nor shocking. For why did the king of England reward the youngest of Denmark's daughters with his rich person? For the reverence she did him, of course. Alisoun carries the lesson to its conclusion; once reverence is rewarded, the need for it is past.

Why Alisoun married her fourth husband is unclear from her prologue, but we may assume it had something to do with 'ricchesse', since Jankyn is the only exception she makes to this rule. Number four occupies her primarily as an occasion for remembering number five and her prime – the dances, carols, and entertainments that her money and her husband's absence on business allowed her to enjoy:

> Therfore I made my visitaciouns
> To vigilies and to processiouns,
> To preching eek, and to thise pilgrimages,
> To playes of miracles and to mariages.
>
> (*WBP*, 561–4)

A major part of her motive for desiring to hear sundry tales, to see and to be seen at these public occasions, was surely business, her own thriving cloth trade and her husband's as well. Yet it is clear that, by this point in her career, pleasure – even love – is a motive she is also free to entertain.

Alisoun is no simple acquisitive machine. Chaucer's brilliant stroke is to give her a streak of romance that blossoms in direct proportion to her accumulated wealth. Husband number four calls forth her fine lyricism 'Upon my youthe and on my jolitee' (*WBP*, 476). Her happiness at this stage in her life, however, can have little to do with the quality of that fourth marriage, which was as battle-ridden and woeful as any of the first three. What has changed for her is the degree of her financial independence. She waxes lyrical at this point in her life because she can now afford to; she has bought the freedom to 'daunce to an harpe smale,/And singe, ywis, as any nightingale,/Whan I hadde dronke a draughte of sweete win' (*WBP*, 463–5). The moral of this experience is not hard to draw:

independence of spirit blooms with economic independence, the freedom to give freely.

The full flower of Alisoun's awakened heart is her gift to Jankyn of the 'maistrye' of her property. She gives freely, consciously, as a token of perfect love, a sign of pure faith, a pledge of true 'gentilesse'. It is the extravagant gift of an extravagant sentiment, of 'love and no richesse', and it promptly gets her into the worst trouble of her woeful life. For her gesture does not inspire a corresponding generosity in him. Instead he proceeds to rob her of her independence and her will. Her one romantic excursion ends in a deafness symbolic of her failure to heed her own lesson: 'With empty hand men may no hawkes lure.' It is a lesson she will not forget again.

Jankyn provides the Wife her most painful encounter with traditional authority, and the terms of her ultimate success in her marriage to him express the full complexity of the truth of her experience. Jankyn believes in 'auctoritee', being too young to know that 'maistrye' derives not from an arbitrary schema, however ancient, but from that skill and knowledge which are acquired through experience and are respectful of the real intricacies of local custom and personality. He is not an eccentric; he is merely a very young man who has suddenly been given control of the entire estate of a formidable older wife and who feels understandably inadequate to the task.

Alisoun tells us that Jankyn 'sometime was a clerk of Oxenforde,/ And hadde laft scole and wente at hoom to boorde/With my gossib, dwelling in oure town' (*WBP*, 533–5). All that these lines indicate is that Jankyn is a local youth who had gone to university for a time (thus acquiring the title of clerk) and had left school to come home and get along in the world by means of his best assets, his legs. Fortunately, his landlady's best friend was a wealthy woman with an excellent record of outlasting husbands. It is unlikely that Jankyn, who had left Oxford before he was twenty, had completed any sort of degree, nor should we assume that he had any intention of doing so. The title 'clerk' implies nothing about the seriousness of his clerical vocation, student tonsure being a rite performed more often by the barber than by the bishop.[39] The names of married clerks and married masters occur regularly in Oxford records of the late fourteenth century, and their presence suggests strongly that secular influences were commonplace in certain faculties of the university, particularly in the arts, but also in medicine and, to some extent, in civil law.[40] The university was often the route of advancement for young men of Jankyn's class, who spent a few years in the arts curriculum preparing for careers without orders. The early registry books of Merton, Exeter and New colleges reveal the names of many students who came to Oxford during the late fourteenth century, stayed for three or four years without taking a degree, and then left their studies for worldly pursuits.[41] Jankyn's closest analogue is not the scholarly Clerk, but Nicholas; they are equally, and in the same ways, 'hende'.[42]

Jankyn, through his wife's indulgence, has been elevated to the status of a wealthy burgess. Such a responsibility presumably weighs heavy on the shoulders of so young a man, so recently discovered following the bier (probably for money) of a town notable.[43] And with all the cowardice and callousness of his years, Jankyn takes refuge in old authorities to proscribe the behaviour of his wife by reading to her every night from his 'book of wikked wives'. He is behaving not like a medieval cleric but like an inexperienced medieval husband, for the book is Jankyn's version of a deportment book, with the conventional age relationships of husband and wife hilariously, outrageously, reversed.[44]

Jankyn is all 'auctoritee' and no 'experience', and such a combination is dangerous, as Alisoun discovers from his behaviour. She learns more than this simple lesson, however. For in sentimentally relinquishing her estate to Jankyn, she gave away the basis on which she was able to make the gift in the first place, and her consciousness of the real importance of property to love is the complex truth that this final experience with Jankyn brings to her. She realises fully the foolishness of her momentary indulgence. That was a 'quainte fantasye', most untypical of her class. And I think that it is within the context of her misgiven gift that we should read her efforts to explain her aberrant heart:

I folwed ay my inclinacioun
By vertu of my constellacioun;
That made me I coude nought withdrawe
My chambre of Venus from a good felawe.

I loved nevere by no discrecioun,
But evere folwede myn appetit,
Al were he short or long or blak or whit;
I took no keep, so that he liked me,
How poore he was, ne eek of what degree.

(*WBP*, 621–4, 628–32)

The last line quoted, plus her earlier word 'discrecioun', provides the social context in which we should understand her excuses. The Wife is indeed grabbing at motives in these lines, but not out of an attack of ecclesiastical scruples. Her action in marrying the penniless Jankyn would have seemed the height of stupidity to all members of her class, and it is her sense of her extreme folly in the eyes of her neighbours, and in her own eyes as she looks back on the experience, that produces her self-apology. 'Allas, allas, that evere love was sinne!'[45] not only in the view of Jerome but in the light of all the practical wisdom of her class.

And then to compound the folly by giving her money away! Here no excuse will serve, and she attempts none:

> What sholde I saye but at the monthes ende
> This joly clerk Janekin that was so hende
> Hath wedded me with greet solempnitee,
> And to him yaf I al the land and fee
> That evere was me yiven therbifore –
> But afterward repented me ful sore:
> He nolde suffre no thing of my list.

> (*WBP*, 633–9)

Her last line is not the petulant comment of a spoiled child but the moment of truth for a generous master whose free gift has been abused by an ignorant apprentice. Love and economics have a proper relationship for women as well as for men; they are not unrelated concepts, whatever the writers of romances (and deportment books) may pretend. Ignorance of that lesson invites a destructive sentimentality that breeds marital tyranny. Alisoun realises simply that, without the sovereignty over herself that 'richesse' has brought her, she loses her freedom to love. 'Sovereinetee', 'maistrye', 'fredom', 'richesse' and 'love' are brought together as aspects of one whole truth at the end of her prologue.

And so the master resumes her 'maistrye'. As she takes back her property, she assumes the household sovereignty that her property right gives her:

> And whan that I hadde geten unto me
> By maistrye al the sovereinetee,
> And that he saide, 'My owene trewe wif,
> Do as thee lust the terme of al thy lif,
> Keep thyn honour, and keep eek myn estat',
> After that day we hadde nevere debat.

God help me so, I was to him as kinde
As any wif from Denmark unto Inde,
And also trewe, and so was he to me.

(*WBP*, 823–31)

She is true to Jankyn, keeping her honour and his estate, because
good business decrees that she be so – and because she has learned
to join business with her heart.

The Wife's tale should be understood in the context of her prologue rather than as a wishful alternative to it, for the story's utopian
simplicity of thought is severely qualified by the teller. Critics are
apt to take its sentimental idealism at face value, but I think that
this is an error, for though the Wife has been capable of sentimentality, she knows too much now to indulge herself in it seriously
again, even in a tale. Instead, she reveals her own fine comic understanding both of the delights of lion painting and of its essential
untruthfulness. Her tale gives full rein to the ideals of sentiment but
never lets us forget that they exist exclusively 'In th'olde dayes of
the King Arthour' (*WBT*, 1). It is her contribution to the exemplary
stories of the deportment books, for it is surely their ethos that the
Wife has especially in mind.

The tale teaches 'proper' marriage relationships. Only, of course,
it is an exemplum that turns the ideas of the male deportment-book
writers upside-down – and, viewed from that angle, they seem comic
indeed. The *ménagier*, articulating the sentiments of men of his class,
states that the husband ought to be, and is, sovereign because he
can increase and diminish all. On the contrary, Alisoun demonstrates, the wife ought to be sovereign because it is she who can
increase and diminish all, through her magical powers. Her tale is
strongly akin to the deportment-book stories in both method and
substance; it is askew only in gender. It shares with them the voice
of the all-wise older counsellor, the aristocratic milieu, the concern
with virtue (that of the younger person being counselled especially),
the emphasis on gentility, the showpiece exemplum against gossip,[46]
and the digressive, informal manner of storytelling. The chief difference between them, besides the obvious one of sex roles, lies in
intention. The deportment-book writers do not often seem aware of
the problems of truth that are inherent in the exemplary genre, the
painting of lions and hunters, but Alisoun clearly is. The result is a
significant difference in tone. The one is solemn and hortatory, the
other not so. The Wife of Bath's tale is funny. That is a crucial point
to remember.

The double sense of what constitutes gentility that we see in the instructions of the deportment-book writers is the Wife's starting point and the fulcrum of her jest.[47] The old hag and the rapist-knight understand 'gentilesse' in different ways. She sees it only as an inner, moral quality, and he defines it solely in terms of birth and class. The hag expresses the deportment books' idealised view of 'gentilesse' and the knight a practical, class-based version. The knight believes that gentlemen can do whatever they want to anybody – except marry penniless old hags – without losing their 'gentilesse'. His class consciousness is much in evidence. 'Allas', he cries, 'that any of my nacioun/Sholde evere so foule disparaged be' (*WBT*, 212–13), and he objects that the hag is 'comen of so lowe a kinde' (*WBT*, 245). He is simply articulating the practical marriage standards of gentlefolk: one can marry up or across but never down, certainly not without a great deal of money to offset the match.

This is not the way genteel people ought to argue, however, and the old hag will have none of such reasoning. She takes up the young criminal's objections in their proper order, treating the most serious at greatest length. And that, of course, is 'gentilesse', which she takes to mean innate moral worth. Her teaching on the subject could come straight out of a deportment book, particularly from a tale such as the one about Denmark's daughters: 'Heer may ye see wel how that genterye/Is nat annexed to possessioun.... For gentilesse cometh fro God allone' (*WBT*, 290–1, 306).

The next most important subject is money, and again the hag takes the genteel position: 'The hye God, on whom that we bileve,/ In wilful poverte chees to live his lif' (*WBT*, 322–3). This is also a deportment-book lesson, exemplified in the tale of poor Griselda in the *ménagier*'s book. But though Griselda was rewarded for her poverty with a princely hand, the real-life chance of any poor and lowly girl being so advanced for her morals alone was inconceivably small. Age and looks are the last items on the hag's agenda, as well they should be, for in the light of true virtue only an idiot (or an imperfect human being) would care about such attributes. But the old hag is kind in the end. As she tells her browbeaten bridegroom: 'sin I knowe your delit,/I shal fulfille youre worldly appetit' (*WBT*, 361–2).

The story of the magical hag and the rapist, though it has superficial analogies to Alisoun's experience with Jankyn, also has crucial differences. Economic power is banished from the tale and replaced by fairy magic. But the relationship of economics to love is a real one, as Alisoun has proved in her prologue 'with muchel care and wo'. In the tale, however, the hag's magic turns her into a gentleman's dream at the mere casting up of a curtain. She rewards the youth's pledge to let her 'chese and governe as me lest' by honouring his pleasure, just as every good deportment-book heroine should. The hag is a benign despot, who smiles over the wallowings of ordinary mortals in a world in which she knows all the answers and controls all the options. And, as in all deportment books, the benignity of her despotism requires the absolute subservience of her mate.

The hag's intelligence is limited in ways that Alisoun's is not. Her magic serves as a blind for her, relieving her of the need to test her propositions in 'experience'. She argues positions that Alisoun has long rejected, especially when she denies any importance to 'possessioun'. The obtuseness bred by her insulation from experience parallels the knight's moral stupidity. Herein lies a major difference between the Wife's lion and the lions portrayed by the writers of deportment books. The Wife's tale is not just a piece of special pleading. Its real seriousness lies precisely in its refusal to succumb to the blandishments of 'th'olde dayes of the King Arthour'.

It is an easy temptation to sentimentalise the Wife for telling the tale she chooses. That she does so instead of relating the cruder *Shipman's Tale*, however, is Chaucer's respectful gift to the acuteness of her intelligence, not to the pathos of her emotions. Having mastered through 'tribulacion' the harsh economics of marriage, Alisoun sought the reward of her demonstrated skills in a sentimental attachment to Jankyn and discovered that marital bliss is really based on economic power after all. The shrewdness that this experience taught her does not desert her in her tale. Rather, painting her own lion becomes an occasion for her to reveal the sentimentality, the romance, involved in any idealistic painting.

The Wife does not identify herself with the lion she paints, the old hag. The hag argues deportment-book virtues, and her magic is certainly showy. But, as Alisoun knows, the truly magical element of the tale is not the hag's transformation, not the bliss issued in by the husband's submission to his wife's tyranny, but the 'parfit joye' of their marriage even though she is old and come of low kindred. Unlike Alisoun, magical hags do not thrive 'biside Bathe'. And thriving Alisoun is, for though one critic sees her as a figure of 'aged lust' dancing 'over the grave',[48] the fiftyish Wife is hardly a candidate for a tombstone. Alisoun herself states, in a fine housewifely metaphor, that the flour of her beauty is gone and only the bran is left – yet Our Lord refreshed many a man with barley bread.

To see the Wife as the ugly old crone of her tale, devastated by the loss of youthful bloom, is to sentimentalise her well beyond the bounds of the text. Her portraitist describes her as fair of face, and there is no reason to doubt him.

Practicality and shrewdness are surely not enough to get Alisoun into heaven, as she immediately tells us, but neither should they condemn her to hell. Purgatory is the state she is most familiar with from the trials of her marriages; yet we know from Dante that purgatory is characterised by kindness and hope as well as by pain. The Wife's cheerful acceptance of a lowly place in the Lord's vineyard invigorates and infuriates those pilgrims who attempt to answer her and who, in pointing to her self-confessed shortcomings, manage not to disarm the strength of her practical concord with her world and time but to reveal the weakness of their own understanding. For lion painting is dangerous sport, apt to redound badly upon the artist unless she is conscious of the underlying game, and that knowledge Alisoun shares with very few of her fellow pilgrims.

AFTERWORD

When I first wrote this essay, I remember thinking of it essentially as a modest gloss on some of the 'local habitation' – the fourteenth-century English accents – within Chaucer's literary character of the Wife of Bath, of a sort that should have been done years before, as it had been for pilgrims like the Knight, the Friar, the Prioress and the Pardoner. I never anticipated that it would cause controversy. How wrong I was. Within a few weeks of its appearance, I received two letters to which the editor of *PMLA* asked me to respond, one of which accused me of the fatal error of believing that the Wife was 'a real person' and the other of making her into a 'hero' – an Economic Woman, instead of the 'emblem of human carnality' which all knowledgeable medievalists, including my correspondent, knew her to be. I replied in due course, the correspondence was published, and there – for a time – the matter rested.[1]

But it has become clear in the dozen years following its publication that this essay struck a raw nerve among Chaucerians, not because it made the Wife a 'real' woman, but because it insisted that Chaucer had created in her a fiction whose power was a quality that I enjoyed.[2] My essay did not judge her severely, and that choice on my part seems to have disappointed a number of subsequent critics, for whom I have, in the words of one, delineated much too 'nice', too 'liberal', a Chaucer.[3]

The debate about the Wife of Bath has modulated during the late 1970s and 1980s from 'what sort of Woman is Alisoun of Bath?' to 'What sort of feminist is she?' The answer has remained much the same: she is negative and disruptive. A year after my essay was first published, D. W. Robertson added more detail to my characterisation of the fourteenth-century rural west-country cloth industry in which Chaucer so firmly situates the Wife in her *General Prologue* portrait, but he still insisted that her chief function in the *Tales* was iconographic, a horrifying gloss on the negative figure of the 'bondwoman' of Galatians.[4] Essays from the late 1970s by feminists – such as those by Arlyn Diamond, Hope Weissman, and Sheila Delany[5] – concluded that she was a poor excuse for a feminist, one who couldn't see beyond the misogynistic discourse (whether clerical or bourgeois-capitalist) that held women in check by reducing them to a hostile Other. Her 'independence' was a sham: one essayist wrote of her 'inability to recognize [herself], or the woman [she] know[s] . . . in this figure compounded of masculine insecurities and female vices as seen by misogynists'.[6] Sheila Delany condemned her from within the framework of Marxist historiography as one who had thoroughly internalised bourgeois capitalism and was therefore doomed to incorrect responses and failed solutions.

Two essays from the early 1980s, both by men taking a feminist position, came to the same sorrowful conclusions. Lee Patterson, like Hope Weissman before him, called her a verbal transvestite, who 'remains confined within the prisonhouse of masculine language'.[7] Marshall Leicester concluded that her strong 'public' polemicism was continually undermined by a 'private' sub-text that revealed her 'experiential interests' in 'making room for the possibility of love in the patriarchal world by giving women space to be responsible partners'.[8] And during that same decade, Louise Fradenburg produced a sophisticated Marxist psychoanalysis of the Wife's tale as an expression of the contradictions of early-modern bourgeois capitalism, concluding that it showed the regressive fantasies of a privatised self, while admitting, uneasily though honestly, that in the end the Wife seemed to escape from the constraints of such ideological analysis.[9]

I was, and remain, troubled by all these analyses, as various as they are and as persuasive as they are about some aspects of the experience someone might have while reading those texts that Chaucer called, collectively, 'the Wife of Bath'. I am troubled because in their various ways each writer wants to deny or restrain the one quality which Chaucer deliberately gave to this character in abundance, and that is power. Power is not simply a matter of 'individual freedom', but a public matter of how one acts towards others, whether in social institutions like marriage, or on social occasions, like telling stories to a group of listeners, either fictional or actual. Indeed, in the case of the Wife, this power seems to have asserted itself immediately over both the fictional pilgrims and the actual audience of the work, including her own author, for she is interrupted twice, and cited both in the Merchant's Tale and in Chaucer's *Envoy to Bukton* as a voice that requires response.

The power which the Wife has is power *as a fiction*, power to engage the imagination and emotions of readers. The economic wealth, the independence of spirit and opinions that Chaucer uses to characterise her are *metaphors* for this fictive power, the only kind of 'real' power that a text can have. This takes me once again to the question of the 'reality' of the Wife of Bath, although I must say that I am neither comfortable nor patient with those critics who make much of this matter (when was the last time they read Sidney's *Defence of Poetry*?) because, for the most part, I think they have misrepresented what I said about Chaucer's fictional character and also that they misunderstand more fundamentally (and sometimes perversely) how a literary creation may be said to 'be'.

I shall start with a simple observation: the statement that 'the Wife of Bath never existed' is not interchangeable with the statement that 'there is no Wife of Bath'. They can be identical statements *only* if all senses of 'is' and 'exist' are defined strictly to mean 'in physical actuality independent of Chaucer's text'. And when they are so defined, the question-begging nature of the statement that 'there is no Wife of Bath; there is only Chaucer's text' should become apparent. Readers who are not merely tilting at strawmen but who find themselves genuinely surprised to learn that the Wife of Bath and Chaucer's other characters 'never existed' have taken too trustingly the assurance of Chaucer's narrator that he is a mere reporter of others' tales. I myself have found it hard to credit that any scholarly critic who had studied and written about literature at any time after 1950 would actually take such a position seriously – but I was wrong again.

I have just had the interesting experience of reading at one sitting D. J. Wurtele's essay on 'The problem of [the Wife of Bath's] fifth husband', the most recent episode in *The Case of the Homicidal Wife*, and Sheila Delany's essay on 'Strategies of silence in the Wife of Bath's recital', two essays that appear to be at opposite ends of the theoretical spectrum, and yet share a common assumption: that only things existing extra-textually, outside literature and fiction, can be said to 'be'.[10] 'Roadside realism' and 'socialist realism' have in common a belief that literature 'is not' except in reference to some extra-literary 'referent'. Wurtele and others who are constructing the 'case history' of the Wife and her husbands start from an assumption (stated or not) that Chaucer's descriptions *report information* about an extra-literary reality that must be filled in from 'gaps' in the text. But Delany also wants to fill in the gaps left by Chaucerian 'silences', gaps that she believes refer transparently to Chaucer himself, a male poet of the court of Richard II. Delany would deny that what Chaucer wrote 'is' at all: as she says, she uses the phrase 'Wife of Bath' in her essay only for the sake of convention. She more properly should call the Wife, Delany says, *'The Canterbury Tales* III. 1–1264'.[11] Chaucer's textual 'Wife', in Delany's view, only records information by what the text both does and does not say about the poet's (politically incorrect) opinions.

'Roadside realism' and 'psychological realism' were both supported by the notion of a 'timeless' quality in art. 'Socialist realism' substitutes for this an idea of timeless politics, revealed in 'metahistorical' patterns of struggle against dominance, whether colonialism, capitalism or patriarchy. But I cannot see that we have gotten very far if we substitute for the notion of Universal Art the notion of Universal Politics. All varieties of Realism, it seems to me, regard literature either as (incomplete) reportage or as (incorrect) propaganda: in either case, however, only that which is Real 'is', extra-textually so. This is a logical trap that leads to the dismissal of poets altogether – as Plato demonstrated quite some time ago.

What Realism seems most uncomfortable with is a rhetorical view of literary texts as a 'common place' where successive generations of readers meet in an imaginary, ongoing dialogue, where the words which readers hear or see, in a famous saying of Isidore of Seville, 'recall the voices of those who are not immediately present to us' (*Etymologiae* I.3). These voices can be those of people who actually lived or they can be fictional characters: their ontological status doesn't matter, because the ontology of the text (the only 'is' it has) is embodied in the *reader*, who re-members what it calls forth in her. This is the effect of the 'power' that I am discussing in this afterword and that I find most intriguing about the literary character called the Wife of Bath. It goes without saying that when I locate the 'embodiment' of the Wife's 'power' in a reader, I am also emphasising its 'occasional', time-and-place-bound quality.

What is extraordinary about the Wife's power is that she keeps it; no effective effort is made in the poem to restrain or squelch it. In this respect, Chaucer treats her differently from the other powerful voice of the pilgrimage, the Pardoner, who is first reduced to silence by Harry Bailly and then constrained by the Knight. The Pardoner loses his power – Chaucer has seen to that. But this is not true in the case of the Wife. She continues to *bother*, to exert an effect on others as long as *The Canterbury Tales* remains a social fiction – that is, until the authoritarian voice of the Parson, invoking an extra-textual Reality, seeks to transform the pilgrimage world at the end. And, Parson or no Parson, she retained a powerful imaginative life for her author, and apparently for his audience – to say nothing of the six hundred years of readers since.

Power is always troubling to those who are subjected to it, even when we may understand the need for it. And female power is particularly troubling, because we – men and women both – are unused to it, except in a circumscribed world like home or elementary school. The best way to deal with what we do not recognise, a category that still includes assertive female power, is not to hear it, or to channel it 'properly' – that is, through a man.

The Wife of Bath is not channelled through any male; rather she forces male voices to do her bidding. Whatever we may think of this 'rape' of the male (and it certainly makes for bad feminism), it is an unrestrained expression of power. I don't think transvestism is the issue to focus on, for that is just another way of saying that the Wife doesn't behave as she 'ought'. Rather I think her seizure of power is more compellingly, and interestingly, related to the masculine violence which runs as a motif through both the Wife's prologue and tale. This relationship has begun to be sketched out in a sophisticated analysis by Carolyn Dinshaw.[12]

Modern readers often want the powerful to be also good, especially the female powerful, for we are more used, in both literature and life, to be disappointed by male power-wielders. At least we want women to be understanding, and to be 'role-models' whom we can emulate without too many complications and reservations. But these are desires that readers bring in response to the Wife's powerful performance, and which, I think, they have condemned her for not satisfying. There is no doubt in my mind that 'the Wife of Bath' is no feminist, whether pre-, proto-, retro- or anti-. I never thought she was. Nor do I doubt for a minute that neither she nor her creator were good Marxists. And she is certainly no liberal, nor is she a good Christian. Saying these evident things about her, however, does not, it seems to me, tell us much, except by way of example of how different readers with differing opinions have chosen to 'make up' a character in their own image.

I certainly do not fault that readerly need to respond to her, because I think that it is exactly what Chaucer intended, or rather, what his text 'intends'. The Wife's Prologue and Tale are often described as 'performance', a word which properly defines the rhetorical nature of all her tale-telling. A rhetorical performance is above all a social occasion, a speaker and an audience meeting within a text, and the occasion is intended to generate the active participation and response, through ear and eye (inner ear and eye when we read silently), of the audience.

This assumption about the social, and hence ethical, nature of literature was a commonplace of ancient pedagogy, carried over into medieval culture. In the sixth century, Gregory the Great spoke of the texts of Scripture as a sort of mirror, 'in which we see our own beauty, our own ugliness'.[13] He was defining an active, participatory experiencing of the text – not asking the reader to be 'informed' by it in the way that a recipe-book informs us about how to roast a duck, but to be 'formed' within the text in the way that seeing ourselves in a mirror helps to form our selves. Responding to it, feeling compelled to 'answer' the Wife, is an essential part of the ongoing process of engaged, social (and – since one theme of the text is power – also political) response to this pilgrim story-teller which Chaucer invites from us.

The newness of Chaucer's Wife as a literary text lies in the fact that such power has been given to a female voice, without any effort on Chaucer's part to shut her up. Here the comparison with the Pardoner is again instructive, for he is silenced *within the text itself*. The impulse to shut the Wife up comes from readers, whom she variously frightens, repels and attracts, as we variously respond to her power. No other of the Canterbury pilgrims, to judge by the centuries of response we have, has so exercised people. In that respect, the Wife best fulfils the premise of the *Tales* as an occasion for tale-telling. Individual readers will continue to try to constrain her, to close her off either negatively or positively, but I think we should recognise that such closure comes from us, the audience, and we shall probably have no more success at it than her fictional audience did.

NOTES

1 *The Wife of Bath's Prologue*, 701–2; hereafter cited in the text as *WBP*. All textual references to the *Canterbury Tales*, cited parenthetically by abbreviation, are to E. T. Donaldson (ed.) *Chaucer's Poetry*, 2nd edn, New York, Ronald, 1975.

2 The *MED* glosses of 'maistrye', 'maister' and 'maistress(e)' make it clear that in Middle English 'mastery' connotes skill and the authority or control deriving from superior ability, rather than the idea of simple dominance devoid of merit or skill.

3 Eileen Power states that in 1310–11 English wool exports totalled 35,509 sacks, virtually all of raw wool, whereas in 1447–8, exports totalled 21,079 sacks, of which 13,425 were cloth: see *The Wool Trade in English Medieval History*, London, Oxford University Press, 1941, p. 37. A chart showing the growth in cloth exports in relation to those of raw wool for the period 1350–1540 indicates that in the last decade of the fourteenth century cloth and wool exports were equal for the first time: see E. M. Carus-Wilson, *Medieval Merchant Venturers*, 2nd edn, London, Methuen, 1967.

4 J. M. Manly, *Some New Light on Chaucer*, New York, Holt, 1926, p. 229.

5 Carus-Wilson, op. cit., pp. 239–62, esp. pp. 259–60. See also Power, op. cit., p. 101; May McKisack, *England in the Fourteenth Century*, London, Oxford University Press, 1959, pp. 356–7; and T. H. Lloyd, *The English Wool Trade in the Middle Ages*, Cambridge, Cambridge University Press, 1977, pp. 315–16. It is worth noting that by the time of Richard II royal cloth purchases were virtually all from English clothiers dealing in English cloth, though in the reign of Edward II such purchases had been mainly of foreign-manufactured cloth. Flemish cloth, which dominated early in the century, disappeared almost completely from the royal accounts by the 1330s (Carus-Wilson, op. cit., p. 242, n. 3).

6 Carus-Wilson, op. cit., p. 262. See also Eileen Power, *Medieval Women*, ed. M. M. Postan, Cambridge, Cambridge University Press, 1975, p. 67.

7 Carus-Wilson, op. cit., pp. 92–4. See also Power, *Medieval Women*, op. cit., pp. 56–7, and Sylvia Thrupp, *The Merchant Class of Medieval London*, 1948; rpt. Ann Arbor, University of Michigan Press, 1962, pp. 169–74.

8 *MED*, s.v. 'Cloth', def. 8(a). Manly believed that the Wife was a weaver, a member of a guild of weavers in the suburb of St Michael's *juxta Bathon* 'biside Bathe'. But Chaucer does not say that she is a weaver, let alone a guild member. Alisoun's trade follows a newer organisational pattern than the one of which Manly was apparently thinking. A cloth maker is a manufacturer of cloths, the person responsible for the production of broadcloths or half-cloths, those units of regulated size in which woollen material was produced and sold. The organisation of the industry in the west counties at this time placed that responsibility in the hands of the clothier, not of the artisans who performed the various tasks leading to the final product. While it is true that the phrase 'maken cloth' can be used in a restricted sense (as in *Piers Plowman*, B. v. 215–16 and B. vi. 13–14) to refer, respectively, to the activities of weaving and spinning, Langland specifies in these lines exactly which cloth-

making activity he intends. When the phrase is used without such quali-
fiers, it refers to the general manufacture of cloth, as Chaucer makes
clear by his reference to 'hem of Ypres and of Gaunt', the Flemish
manufacturer-merchant-exporters whom the Wife and her peers have
now surpassed. See, in addition to the citations in *MED* and *OED*,
s.v. 'Clothmaker', the usages quoted by E. Lipson, *A History of the
Woollen and Worsted Industries*, London, Black, 1921, pp. 44, 112 and
by Thrupp, op. cit., p. 272; and the remarks of Kenneth G. Ponting, *The
Woollen Industry of South-West England*, Bath, Adams and Dart, 1971,
pp. 19–20.

9 E. Lipson points out that the clothier-entrepreneur is a figure distinctive
to the west-country cloth trade: *A Short History of Wool and its Manufacture*, Cambridge, Mass., Harvard University Press, 1953, pp. 68–73.
Carus-Wilson argues that a rudimentary capitalist entrepreneurial system
was a feature of English cloth production from at least the early thirteenth century, even in the cloth towns of the north and east, which
were then the centre of manufacture (op. cit., pp. 211–38). See also E.
Miller, 'The fortunes of the English textile industry in the thirteenth
century', *Economic History Review*, 2nd ser., 1965–6, vol. 18, pp. 64–82,
and Ponting, op. cit., pp. 7–20.

10 Carus-Wilson, op. cit., pp. 4–9, and Power, *Wool Trade*, op. cit., p. 47.
The factors that led to the change from urban- to rural-dominated cloth
manufacture in England are examined in Miller and in Carus-Wilson
(op. cit., pp. 183–210). On Bristol as a fourteenth-century port, pre-
eminent in the wool trade at mid-century, third behind London and
Southampton at its end, see J. W. Sherborne, *The Port of Bristol in
the Middle Ages*, Bristol, Bristol Historical Association, 1965, pp. 9–11.
Ponting suggests that in the late fourteenth century much west-country
cloth was shipped from London, Bristol never regaining the domination
it had enjoyed earlier (pp. 15–16).

11 Theodore F. T. Plucknett, *A Concise History of the Common Law*, 5th
edn, London, Butterworth, 1956, p. 313. On the trading rights of married
women see Mary Bateson, *Borough Customs*, Selden Society Publications, no. 18, London, Selden Society, 1904, pp. 227–8. A representative
entry is the following from Torksey, dated 1345: 'Item dicunt quod
mulier mercatrix respondebit cuicunque et debet responderi sine viro
suo et potest amittere et recuperare.' Accounts of these rights are given
in A. Abram, 'Women traders in medieval London', *Economic Journal*,
1916, vol. 26, pp. 276–85, and in Power, *Medieval Women*, op. cit.,
pp. 53–9. Margery Kempe describes her ventures in the brewing and
milling trades, undertaken with her own money and against her husband's wishes: S. B. Meech (ed.) *The Book of Margery Kempe*, Early
English Text Society, OS 212, London, Oxford University Press, 1940,
pp. 9–10. On the property rights of bourgeois married women, see Mary
Bateson, *Borough Customs*, Selden Society Publications, no. 21, London,
Selden Society, 1906, pp. 102–8. In 1327, the mayor and bailiffs of Oxford
wrote to the mayor and bailiffs of London for their confirmation of a
judgement that recognised a wife's right 'to give and sell to whom she
will' of her own property. In 1419 a London customal states, 'ne le
baroun ne poet my deviser les tenementz de droit de sa femme, ne lez

tenements queux le baroun et sa femme ount joynetement purchacés'. John Kempe exacts a promise from his wife, Margery, to pay off all his debts before he will agree to a vow of connubial chastity; this incident strongly suggests that he had no right to use her property as he chose (*Book*, op. cit., pp. 24–5).

12 In one interesting case from 1389, the Court of Common Pleas bowed to local custom in ruling that a husband was not liable for the debts of his wife incurred during her trading (Plucknett, op. cit., pp. 313–14). On the respect of common law for local custom, see N. Neilson, 'Custom and the common Law in Kent', *Harvard Law Review*, 1924, vol. 38, pp. 482–98.

13 See H. S. Bennett, *The Pastons and their England*, 1922, rpt. Cambridge, Cambridge University Press, 1968, p. 59. See also F. J. Furnival (ed.), *Fifty Earliest English Wills*, Early English Text Society, OS 78, London, Oxford University Press, 1882, esp. the following, from a codicil to the will of Stephen Thomas of Lee (1417): 'More wryt y nough[t] vnto yow, bot þe holy trinite kepe yow now, dere and trusty wyf . . . wer-for I pray ȝow, as my trust es hely in ȝow, ouer alle oþere creatures, þat this last will be fulfyllet, and all odere that I ordeynd atte home, for all þe loue þat euer was betwen man and woman' (pp. 40–1).

14 Plucknett, op. cit., pp. 566–8. See also Cecile S. Margulies, 'The marriages and the wealth of the Wife of Bath', *Mediaeval Studies*, 1962, vol. 24, pp. 210–16. Unfortunately, Margulies confined her argument to dower right under the common and canon law only and overlooked the crucial area of town and village customary laws. A similar argument (and error) was made by Thomas A. Reisner in 'The Wife of Bath's dower: a legal interpretation', *Modern Philology*, 1973–4, vol. 71, pp. 301–2.

15 Plucknett, op. cit., pp. 568, 586. The importance of jointure to a woman's security in all classes may be judged by Margaret Paston's continuing efforts to marry her daughters or, failing that, to introduce them into worthy households; 'for I wuld be right glad', she writes of one of them, '*and* she myght be proferrid be mariage or be servyce so þat it myght be to here wurchep and profight': Norman Davis (ed.) *Paston Letters and Papers*, vol. 1, London, Oxford University Press, 1971, no. 186 [30 June 1465]. The Pastons belong to a different class of the newly rich than does Alisoun, for their wealth was in manorial land rather than in trade. Agnes married William Paston I (1378–1444) in 1420 and died in 1478; Margaret married John Paston I (1421–66) in 1440 and died in 1484. Though one must evidently exercise caution in using the Paston letters as evidence of the customs and opinions that prevailed more than seventy years earlier, there is no reason to dispense entirely with the rich picture of marriage they furnish, provided that their contents can be corroborated by evidence contemporary with Chaucer. For the reader's convenience I have provided the dates of probable composition assigned by Davis to each of the letters I quote. A recent analysis of some of the Paston material is Ann Haskell's 'The Paston women on marriage in fifteenth-century England', *Viator*, 1973, vol. 4, pp. 459–71.

16 *WBP*, 415–18. The *OED*, s.v. 'Ransom', indicates that the word during this period always carried the meaning of a money or a property fine, except in the specific context of Christ's ransom (his life) for the redemp-

tion of humankind. Chaucer uses the word six times; once in the Parson's tale to mean Christ's sacrifice and elsewhere to mean a monetary fine, as it does in each of its four occurrences in the *Knight's Tale* and as it does here in the Wife's prologue. Alisoun exacts a fine from her husbands for their freedom of access to her body.

17 Recent criticism has at last rescued the Wife from charges of religious heresy in regard to her frank admission of pleasure in married sex. Among medieval pastoral theologians a majority opinion held that pleasure in married sex was at worst a venial sin, and a minority even considered that it was no sin at all; the canonists believed that it was possible to contract a valid marriage from the motive of fulfilling sexual desire as long as no effort was made to prevent conception. This theological background has been examined most recently by Henry A. Kelley in *Love and Marriage in the Age of Chaucer*, Ithaca, N.Y., Cornell University Press, 1975, esp. pp. 245–61. See also E. T. Donaldson, 'Medieval poetry and medieval sin', *Speaking of Chaucer*, New York, Norton, 1970, pp. 164–74. On the orthodoxy of the Wife's theology, see Donald R. Howard, *The Idea of the Canterbury Tales*, Berkeley, University of California Press, 1976, pp. 248–51.

18 Indeed Jerome did 'not condemn even octogamy' twice in his writings: *Adversus Jovinianum*, I, 15, J. P. Migne (ed.) *Patrologiae Cursus Completus, Series Latina* [hereafter, *PL*] Paris, 1844–64, vol. 23, p. 23, and *Epistola XLVIII seu liber apologeticus ad Pammachium, pro libris contra Jovinianum*, ch. 9 (*PL*, vol. 22, p. 499).

19 On the controversy during which Jerome was nearly condemned for heresy because of what he appeared to be saying about marriage in the *Adversus Jovinianum*, see the biography by Jean Steinmann, *St. Jerome*, trans. R. Matthews, London, Chapman, 1959, pp. 216–27. Anne Kernan refers to this controversy in relation to the Wife of Bath ('The archwife and the eunuch', *English Literary History*, 1974, vol. 41, pp. 1–25). See also the remarks of E. T. Donaldson, 'Designing a camel', *Tennessee Studies in Literature*, 1977, vol. 22, pp. 1–16.

20 *Epistola XLIX ad Pammachium*, ch. 2 (*PL*, vol. 22, p. 511).

21 Eileen Power details the sources of this material (*Medieval People*, 8th edn, London, Methuen, 1946, p. 184). An example in English verse is 'How the good wife taught her daughter', in F. J. Furnivall (ed.) *The Babees Book*, Early English Text Society, OS 32, London, Oxford University Press, 1868, pp. 36–47.

22 Thomas Wright (ed.) *The Book of the Knight of LaTour-Landry*, Early English Text Society, OS 33, London, Oxford University Press, 1906. All my references to this work are to this edition. J. Pichon (ed.) *Le Ménagier de Paris*, Paris, Société des Bibliophiles Français, 1846. All references are to the English-language version, Eileen Power (trans.) *The Goodman of Paris*, New York, Harcourt, 1928.

23 Power, *Goodman*, op. cit., p. 43.

24 Davis, op. cit., vol. 1, pp. 188–9 [July-Aug 1465].

25 Sir John Maclean (ed.) *John Smyth's Lives of the Berkeleys*, II, Gloucester, Bristol and Gloucestershire Archaeological Society, 1833, pp. 62–3. Lady Isabel was the eldest daughter of Sir Thomas Mowbray; the letter was written in 1447.

26 James Gairdner (ed.) *The Paston Letters*, 1904; rpt. New York, AMS, 1965, vol. 1, p. 155. The quotation is from a letter of Scrope, part of a collection in the British Museum relating to Sir John Fastolf, Scrope's stepfather and Paston's benefactor.

27 ibid., vol. 1, p. 154.

28 The arrangements are described by Elizabeth Clere, Agnes Paston's niece (Davis, op. cit., vol. 2, no. 446 [no later than 29 June 1449]). Cf. Agnes's own thoughts on the subject, written to her son John with a warning for haste, because 'S*er* Herry Ynglows is ry3th besy a-bowt Schrowpe for*e* on of his do3thter*es*' (Davis, op. cit., vol. I, no. 18 [no later than 1449]).

29 Scrope himself had been bartered shockingly by his stepfather; see Gairdner, vol. 2, no. 97. On the practice of selling marriage rights, see Bennett, op. cit., pp. 28–9; it is condemned in Walter W. Skeat (ed.) *Piers Plowman*, London, Oxford University Press, 1886, C.xi.256–7: 'for thei 3eueth here children/For couetise of catel and conynge chapmen'.

30 Manly says they are old-fashioned (op. cit., p. 230). D. E. Wretlind has argued, however, that hats with large kerchiefs were making a comeback at Queen Anne's court ('The Wife of Bath's hat', *Modern Language Notes*, 1948, vol. 63, pp. 381–2), but Howard points out that large hats were the contemporary rural fashion (op. cit., p. 105, n. 32).

31 *OED*, s.v. 'Scarlet', and see Carus-Wilson, op. cit., p. 218, n. 4; scarlet may often have been dyed red, but the word at this time was a technical term for a type of fine cloth of any colour.

32 LaTour-Landry would have approved: 'a good woman shulde arraie her after her husbandes pusaunce and hers, in suche wise as it might endure and be meinteyned' (op. cit., p. 67).

33 Davis, op. cit., vol. 1, no. 398 [probably after 1480].

34 ibid., vol. 1, no. 446.

35 ibid., vol. 1, no. 398. Ecclesiastical easiness concerning the remarriage of widows is attested by a letter of the late fourteenth century from Roger Kegworthe, a London draper, to Robert Hallum, one of the most distinguished churchmen and canonists of the period. Kegworthe asks Hallum to help him arrange a marriage with an eligible widow, 'de bone conversacioun et poet ore bien expendre par an quarrant marcz', who is being actively courted also by the Marshall of the Hall of the Archbishop of Canterbury (M. D. Legge (ed.) *Anglo-Norman Letters and Petitions*, Anglo-Norman Text Society, vol. 3, Oxford, Blackwell, 1941, pp. 118–19).

36 Two commonly held assumptions about the Wife of Bath deserve comment, because they have crept into the realm of 'facts' about her without a shred of evidence to support either one. The first is that she is childless, the second that she is 'oversexed'; indeed the first has led to the second, for, being childless (so the argument runs), she has no right to any sexual encounter, and therefore any sex is 'oversex' for her. But we do not know whether or not the Wife has children; we know only that she does not say so. There is no reason to attribute any significance to her silence. Chaucer's concern is wifehood, not motherhood. Wifehood and motherhood were not linked concepts at this time, as they are today,

for wives had little to do with the nurture of their children (see, e.g., Bennett, op. cit., pp. 71–86). The books of deportment, while covering every conceivable concern of wifehood, never mention the bearing or nurturing of children. The 'problem' of the Wife of Bath's children is of exactly the same sort as the most famous of literary non-problems: 'How many children had Lady Macbeth?' and it deserves to be consigned to the wastebasket of critical inquiry for the same reasons. It is simply not a question we can legitimately ask of this text, because the text provides us with no basis for an answer.

37 Twenty was a common age for marrying. Margery Kempe was twenty 'or sumdele mor' when she married (*Book*, op. cit., p. 6); the daughter in the *Reeve's Tale* is twenty; Elizabeth Paston (born c. 1429) was nearly twenty when her mother began to bargain in earnest for her marriage. The *ménagier*'s wife, however, was only fifteen when he wrote his treatise for her, and Thrupp says that the daughters of London merchants in this period usually married at about seventeen (p. 196).

38 Davis, op. cit., vol. 2, no. 446.

39 Charles E. Mallet, *A History of the University of Oxford*, 1924, rpt. New York, Barnes and Noble, 1968, vol. 1, pp. 151–2. Mallet suggests that university undergraduates could be as young as fourteen; in 1386, however, Oxford petitioned to have the minimum age raised to sixteen (J. A. W. Bennett, *Chaucer at Oxford and at Cambridge*, Toronto, University of Toronto Press, 1974, p. 72, n. 2). The arts course leading to the bachelor's degree took at least four years to complete, but many students took longer. See representative careers catalogued in A. B. Emden, *A Biographical Register of the University of Oxford to 1500*, London, Oxford University Press, 1957–9, passim.

40 The title 'magister' was used for a master of arts or a doctor in another faculty or – grudgingly, especially at Oxford – for a bachelor of arts (Emden, op. cit., vol. 1, pp. xv–xvi). By my rough count in the *Register*, there were at least a dozen married arts masters at Oxford in the last half of the fourteenth century; there were married physicians and a few married bachelors of civil law who also held Oxford degrees. Edmund Stonor reported, c. 1380, that his nephew was studying grammar in the establishment of a married master at Oxford ('magister et ejus uxor') (Charles L. Kingsford (ed.) *The Stonor Letters and Papers*, London, Camden Society, 1919, vol. 1, p. 21, Camden Society Publications, 3rd ser., vols 29–30).

41 The conclusion that many who entered Oxford did so without expecting to pursue clerical careers is supported from a number of sources. A count based on Emden's *Register* of students and masters between 1350 and 1410 reveals a steady 30 per cent who did not proceed to orders; this percentage is undoubtedly too low, since most of the sparse records containing information about the subsequent careers of Oxford graduates are ecclesiastical. As Emden observes, 'Even more elusive, of course, are the many hundreds of Oxford clerks who never qualified for a degree at all, and who passed from Oxford into secular as well as into clerical employment. The exceptionally full records of New College point to the conclusion that at all times during the medieval period the number of undergraduates who never proceeded to any degree was large' (op.

cit., vol. 1, p. xviii). Sylvia Thrupp points out that London merchants of the fourteenth and fifteenth centuries were ambitious to achieve educational polish through university training (op. cit., pp. 159–61). The paternal concern of Clement Paston (d. 1419) is typical: a 'good pleyn husband' himself (according to a fifteenth-century biographical account; see Davis, op. cit., vol. 1, pp. xli–xlii), he sent his son William (b. 1378) to university, thereby starting his family's fortunate rise, and succeeding generations of Pastons followed his example. One of Richard FitzRalph's charges against the friars (made in a sermon of 1357) was that 'very many of the common people' feared that the friars at Oxford were taking advantage of youthful students and pressing them too soon into orders; see Mallet, op. cit., vol. 1, p. 75, n. 2, which also refers to a university ordinance of 1358 forbidding the friars from admitting students under eighteen. The concern of the common people in 1357 is echoed a century later by Margaret Paston, who cautions her son Walter, a clerk at Oxford, 'that he benot to hasty of takyng of orderes þat schuld bynd hym till þat he be of xxiiij yere of agee or more. . . . I will loue hym bettere to be a good seculare man þan to be a lewit prest' (Davis, op. cit., vol. 1, no. 220 [probably 18 January 1473]).

42 The pun on 'hende' is noted by Donaldson in 'Idiom of popular poetry in the Miller's Tale', *Speaking of Chaucer*, op. cit., p. 17.

43 The custom of paying mourners to ensure a good turnout at one's funeral is amply attested in contemporary wills. Alisoun may not have wasted money on a fancy tomb, but both her honour and her estate would have required a decent funeral for her husband.

44 Alisoun calls the book a 'book of wikked wives', but this is yet another instance of Chaucer's standard joke, wherein books of good behaviour are perceived to be books of wicked behaviour, because they are more often crowded with examples of the awful ends of evil-doers than with the rewards of the just. The classic examples are the Man of Law's remarks on Gower and the exchange between Alcestis, the God of Love, and the poet in the prologue to the *Legend of Good Women*. Robert A. Pratt has demonstrated the accessibility at Oxford of the sources of Jankyn's book; one would expect an inexperienced young man whose head is still full of the university to draw on just such bookish stuff in seeking to counsel his wife ('Jankyn's book of wikked wyves', *Annuale Mediaevale*, 1962, vol. 3, pp. 5–27.

45 *WBP*, 620. Francis L. Utley reminds us that the Wife's use of the word 'love' in this proverb 'must not be shrugged aside as mere ignorance or bias'; indeed it makes the proverb in her mouth a complex and ironic statement different in meaning and emphasis from the traditional sentiment, attributed by medieval preachers to the laity, that 'lechery is no sin' ('Chaucer's way with a proverb: "Allas! allas! that evere love was synne" ', *North Carolina Folklore*, 1973, vol. 21, pp. 98–104.

46 Both the *ménagier* and the Knight of LaTour-Landry tell versions of the same cautionary story about gossip, a story as intriguing in its own way as that of Midas' ears. 'Wol ye heere the tale?' A squire tells his wife that he has laid two eggs, enjoins her to secrecy, and by the time the tale has made its way back to his ears, he is supposed to have laid a

whole basketful (*LaTour-Landry*, op. cit., pp. 96–7, and *Goodman*, op. cit., pp. 182–3).

47 An interesting analysis of class consciousness in the Wife's tale has been made by Dorothy Colmer in 'Character and class in the Wife of Bath's Tale', *Journal of English and Germanic Philology*, 1973, vol. 72, pp. 329–39.

48 B. F. Huppé, *A Reading of the Canterbury Tales*, Albany, State University of New York Press, 1964, p. 127.

Notes to Afterword

1 *Forum* Correspondence from R. M. Jordan, W. I. Wimsatt and M. J. Carruthers, *PMLA*, 1979, vol. 94, pp. 950–3.

2 In a talk given in October 1988 at the University of California, Los Angeles, Elizabeth Kirk developed the idea that, in the Wife, Chaucer was 'empowering' a marginalised Other. Peggy Knapp has argued recently that the Wife's theme is 'control of discourse, *auctoritee*': see Peggy Knapp, 'Alisoun of Bathe and the reappropriation of tradition', *The Chaucer Review*, 1989, vol. 24, pp. 45–52; p. 46.

3 Sheila Delany, 'Strategies of silence in the Wife of Bath's recital', *Exemplaria*, 1990, vol. 2, pp. 49–69; p. 54. Reprinted in Sheila Delany, *Medieval Literary Politics: Shapes of Ideology*, Manchester and New York, 1991, pp. 112–29.

4 D. W. Robertson, Jr, ' "And for my land thus hast thou mordred me?": land tenure, the cloth industry, and the Wife of Bath', *The Chaucer Review*, 1980, vol. 14, pp. 403–20.

5 Arlyn Diamond, 'Chaucer's women and women's Chaucer', in A. Diamond and Lee R. Edwards (eds) *The Authority of Experience*, Amherst, University of Massachusetts Press, 1977, pp. 60–83; Hope P. Weissman, 'Antifeminism and Chaucer's characterizations of women', in George Economou (ed.) *Geoffrey Chaucer*, New York, McGraw-Hill, 1976, pp. 93–110; Sheila Delany, 'Sexual economics, Chaucer's Wife of Bath, and *The Book of Margery Kempe*', *Minnesota Review*, 1975, NS 5, pp. 104–15; reprinted in Sheila Delany, *Writing Woman*, New York, Schocken, 1983, pp. 76–91; reprinted in this volume, pp. 72–87.

6 Diamond, op. cit., p. 68.

7 Lee R. Patterson, ' "For the Wyues love of Bathe": feminine rhetoric and poetic resolution in the *Roman de la Rose* and the *Canterbury Tales*', *Speculum*, 1983, vol. 58, pp. 656–95; p. 682.

8 H. Marshall Leicester, 'Of a fire in the dark: public and private feminism in the *Wife of Bath's Tale*', *Women's Studies*, 1984, vol. 11, pp. 157–78; p. 173.

9 Louise O. Fradenburg, 'The Wife of Bath's passing fancy', *Studies in the Age of Chaucer*, 1986, vol. 8, pp. 31–58.

10 D. J. Wurtele, 'Chaucer's Wife of Bath and the problem of the fifth husband', *The Chaucer Review*, 1988–9, vol. 23, pp. 117–28; Delany, 'Strategies of silence', op. cit.

11 Delany, 'Strategies of silence', op. cit., p. 46.

12 Carolyn Dinshaw, *Chaucer's Sexual Politics*, Madison, Wisconsin and London, University of Wisconsin Press, 1989.
13 Gregory the Great, *Moralia in Job*, II, 1, in J. P. Migne, *Patrologia Latina*, Paris, 1844–64, vol. 75, p. 553. I have written at length on medieval reading and the idea of text in *The Book of Memory*, Cambridge, Cambridge University Press, 1990.

3 Engendering pity in the *Franklin's Tale*[1]

Felicity Riddy

Let us suppose that Chaucer's mother, Agnes, could read. It is not impossible, since she was married to two substantial London merchants and was the heiress of another,[2] and if we are to look anywhere for literate women in the fourteenth century (outside the nunneries) it must be among members of the aristocracy and the urban elites. Presumably someone told stories to her son when he was a small boy and taught him to read; why not his mother?[3] And if she could read – or even if she did not read herself, but arranged for books to be read to the household – what sort of books would they have been? One surviving book which, it has been suggested, was the property of a wealthy London merchant is the Auchinleck manuscript, compiled in the 1330s;[4] it is just as likely, it seems to me, to have been read by a merchant's wife or widow.[5] The texts it contains are almost entirely in English, and although it must have been an extremely expensive volume to produce, the Auchinleck manuscript belongs – with its romances and female saints' lives – to an unlearned, story-telling culture. Its stories are about knights and ladies, princes and princesses, but they are not courtly or sophisticated in the way that *Troilus and Criseyde* and the *Confessio Amantis* are. By the 1380s upper-class mores had developed a mode of expression in English that was not available fifty years previously.

Among the contents of the Auchinleck manuscript are three of the five surviving English *lais* that predate the *Franklin's Tale*, Chaucer's own example of the genre. Indeed, it has been suggested that Chaucer may have known the Auchinleck manuscript itself, or a collection very like it,[6] and may have drawn on some of its contents for *Sir Thopas* and for the Franklin's prologue, which seems to echo the Auchinleck prologue of *Lai le Freine*. In *Sir Thopas* Chaucer burlesques the tail-rhyme romances his mother may have read, exposing their uncourtliness in particular.[7] In the *Franklin's Tale* he treats the English *lais* that his mother may have read quite differently; instead of mocking their lack of polish he assimilates the genre into courtly culture, using it to address the shifting social divisions of the late fourteenth century. The direct and understated lyric intensity of the Auchinleck *lais* is transformed in the *Franklin's Tale* into the more fashionable and sophisticated emotionalism of the courtly *plainte*.[8] This is an apparently natural transformation, since *lai* and *plainte* were already associated in French[9] and since anyway the *lai* began its literary life in the hands of Marie de France as a courtly genre. It looks as if, with the *Franklin's Tale*, the English *lai* has, like Agnes Chaucer's son, simply found a place at court. The transition, however, from the context of the Auchinleck manuscript to the context of the *Canterbury Tales*, is not simple, and has gender as well as class implications. Specifically, in moving upmarket the *lai* creates new problems for its women readers.

If Agnes Chaucer, or the poet's sister Katherine Manning, or perhaps the round-cheeked Rosamounde to whom Chaucer addressed a *balade*, ever read the *Franklin's Tale*, they cannot have placed it in the intellectual milieu recently argued for it, of late medieval classicism, because as women they were excluded from that kind of learning.[10] Dorigen's voice cannot, for them, have represented the discourses of scholastic *quaestio* or Boethian commentary.[11] Nor do I think – for the same reasons – that they would have immediately located the tale's themes in the contemporary 'nobility debate' or read it as a Dantean exploration of the 'relation between the letter and the spirit, the literal and the metaphoric'.[12] Rather they, like many of its early male readers, would have related it to what was called 'norture': polite upbringing, good manners, gentle breeding. It is 'norture', after all, that links the *Franklin's Tale* with the *Squire's*, which precedes it in most of the best manuscripts.[13] In the headlink the Franklin interprets the Squire's sentimental rhetoric ('So feelyngly thou spekest, sire' (676))[14] as an example of 'gentil' utterance which not only creates a world of refined and extravagant sensibility within his tale but simultaneously confirms its teller's social standing. Listening to the Squire makes the Franklin anxious about his own son, who would rather talk to people of low birth 'Than to comune with any gentil wight/Where he myghte lerne gentillesse aright'(693–4). The Franklin's anxiety is well founded: in a period of social mobility, which the history of Chaucer's own family neatly illustrates,[15] the 'gentil' man is made as well as born. Along with a particular station in life goes the necessity that he acquire the social skills and virtues, including ways of talking, which demarcate the boundaries of that station.[16] On the other side of the divide separating gentle from non-gentle are all the heterogeneous lower-class groups in rural society for which late fourteenth-century officialdom lacked a consistent terminology: peasants, serfs, villeins, free tenants, cottars, *cultores*, labourers, husbandmen and yeomen.[17] It is hardly surprising that Chaucer should make the spokesman for social demarcation a man on the margin: a franklin, one of that indeterminate group which seems, in the earlier fourteenth century at least, to have straddled the boundary between gentle and non-gentle and whose gentility by the 1390s was still not entirely secure.[18] The Franklin as narrator is in effect the creation of his tale's 'gentil' discourse; he is not a character in his own right, or a study in social climbing, but the product of a pun. The tale embodies a myth of aristocracy in which certain moral attributes – including, crucially, the attribute of 'fredom' – are translated into social skills and annexed by the upper classes, especially by upper-class men, as a means of self-definition. And so the tale about 'fre' men is told by a free man,[19] a man who is *francus*, a franklin, and holds land in freehold.

The fact that Chaucer has made the spokesman for gentility a father anxious about his own son and envious of another's has the effect of embedding the *Franklin's Tale* in the discontents of patriarchy and its problems of self-perpetuation. Moreover it suggests what the narrative will bear out: that 'gentillesse' has to do with relations between men. If the Franklin is envious of the Squire, the Host resents them both. His cry of 'Straw for youre gentillesse' (695) sounds like a challenge to the boundaries which sustain the Franklin's precarious social identity, but in fact provides the occasion for reaffirming those boundaries. The Franklin's poised and studiedly civil reply is a gesture available only to those with power, a smooth put-down which demarcates the closed circle of the ensuing narrative: on the outside the rude Host; on the inside the Franklin and the 'olde gentil Britouns' from whom his 'laye', it is claimed, descends. The genre chosen by Chaucer for the *Franklin's Tale* is a means of defining the latter's social standing in a competitive masculine world. Excluded with the Host from the closed circle are the urgent contemporary challenges to degree that had sent mobs into the streets of London only a dozen years or so before this story was written; included are the 'gentil' men who were in the process of becoming gentlemen in the last decades of the fourteenth century.[20]

In 'gentil' discourse 'fredom' or 'fraunchise', along with the 'trouthe' and 'pitee' with which the tale also engages, are elements in a class myth. A fifteenth-century rhyme brings these key terms together, making both their social and gender implications clear:

> In whom is trauthe, pettee, fredome, and hardynesse,
> He is a man inheryte to gentylmene.
> Off thisse virtues iiij. who lakketh iij.,
> He aught never gentylmane called to be.[21]

'Hardynesse', boldness, is not at issue in this tale, but the other three all are: 'fredom' and 'trouthe' famously so, 'pitee' less explicitly. Pity as a social virtue sanctifies hierarchy, since it is predicated on the difference between higher and lower, or between weaker and stronger: it is a mode of relationship with one's inferiors.[22] Men's pity for women – Theseus's pity for the Theban ladies, for example, at the beginning of the *Knight's Tale* – conforms to the traditional gender hierarchy, but female pity for a man – the 'wommanly pitee' which the lover requests from the lady in courtly lyric – necessarily entails a reversal of that hierarchy since the man must place himself beneath the woman in order to receive her pity. Nevertheless his self-abasement is not feminising, but is rather, as I shall argue, a means of self-definition in relation to other men; both pitying and being pitied are, for men, positions of power.

The same is not true for women. Representing the female as a figure of pathos is a commonplace of courtly fictions, but its familiarity should not obscure the fact that it is a masculinist strategy which, as Mary Wollstonecraft sees in her *Vindication of the Rights of Woman*, is, in its trivialisation, close to contempt.[23] The courtly pity evoked for Dorigen trivialises her in ways that Wollstonecraft would have found familiar: at lines 815–28 she is represented as utterly incapacitated by the absence of her husband. At line 847 we are told that while he was away she used to walk on the shore or 'sytte and thynke':

> But whan she saugh the grisly rokkes blake
> For verray feere so wolde hir herte quake
> That on hire feet she myghte hire noght sustene.
>
> (859–61)

The narrator's phrase – 'grisly rokkes blake' – is echoed in Dorigen's own protest a few lines later at 'thise grisly feendly rokkes blake': both voices, his and hers, are part of a continuity of feeling speech. The rocks are represented as physical, and it is precisely because they are so that Dorigen makes her rash oath. Nevertheless,

Dorigen's 'feendly' suggests that they are supernatural rather than natural, and thus may not be resistant in the way that physical things are in the world of *fabliau*: in the *Miller's Tale* the door to Nicholas's room has to be broken down, and when John falls from a tub in the roof he breaks his arm. Arveragus's ship is not wrecked as his wife fears it will be, nor is there any danger of that happening in this tale. Her terrors are part of its way of constructing feminine experience as subjective, as issuing from the mind and coloured with intense and extravagant emotion. Dorigen's subjective relation to the external world is a reflection of the narrator's relation to her: the pathos of her situation is created by his 'gentil' style, and she is herself the object of extravagant courtly feeling, of the 'pitee' that 'renneth soone in gentil herte', as Chaucer says on four occasions.[24] The narrator's pity for Dorigen is a hallmark of the gentility of his tale, and it enfeebles and in the end marginalises her. The initially bold attempt she makes at lines 865–93 to confront the problem of evil collapses into intellectual helplessness and she tearfully leaves 'disputison', or logical argument, to (male) clerks; her 'compleynt' at lines 1355–1456, in which she presents herself as sexual victim (and which derives, ironically enough, from Jerome's anti-feminist *Ad Jovinianum*) is so long that it invites – and has received – the traditional criticism about female garrulousness.

The pathos of the male characters is created in a different way and has a different effect, relieving them of responsibility for Dorigen's extraordinarily distasteful sexual predicament. Aurelius's suffering is familiar from the courtly *plainte*, which constructs the lover as an object of pity; his address to Dorigen at lines 967–78 represents her as a superior being with the power of life and death over him as he sues to her in agony for mercy. In courtly fictions the 'gentil' man is defined by his capacity to hold off, to refrain from consummation, while he endlessly beseeches pity. According to the myth of aristocracy, the ability to substitute eloquence for intercourse is what marks 'gentil' men off from peasants, who are, as the twelfth-century writer Andreas Capellanus puts it in his *De Amore*, 'impelled to acts of love in the natural way like a horse or a mule, just as nature's pressure directs them'.[25] The 'gentil' man's sexual deferral can go on for years: Aurelius is in love with Dorigen for over two years before speaking directly to her and then waits another 'two yeer and moore' before organising the removal of the rocks.[26] Not, of course, that he is silent all this time: deferral is given voice in the other vehicles of courtly utterance, in the 'layes,/Songs, compleintes, roundels, virelayes' (947–8) that he composes. It follows that if the man's 'gentillesse' depends on his not having intercourse but on speaking feelingly of love, then the woman must be unavailable; she has to be represented as 'daungerous' – as hard-heartedly unyielding – in order to allow him his status. The man's role as courtly lover is compromised by a woman who is promiscuous or even forward.[27] The woman's value to the man – her function in his self-represen-tation – therefore rests on her chastity, which the plot is required to maintain. Dorigen can only play a passive role in the story (which is not, in the end, even her story); the Alisouns of the *Miller's Tale* and the *Wife of Bath's Prologue* have no place in this kind of narrative. Dorigen has to reject Aurelius's advances as she does in order to be a prize worth having; we know that she will not submit to him because if she did he would not want her. And this is of course how the tale develops, acting out the imperatives of the masculine fantasies which are represented by the courtly style.

In the thirteenth-century *Roman de la Rose*, which is a primary source for the conventions of the French courtly *plainte*, the Daunger of the beloved – that is, her aloofness, her unwillingness to yield to the lover – is represented allegorically as a peasant with a club. Although this symbolism may at first seem perverse, the courtly *plainte* reveals why it should be so. The complaining lover, as I have said, requires the lady to refuse him; the imploring and pitiable stance created for him simultaneously creates her pitiless-ness. If 'pitee renneth soon in *gentil* herte', then it follows that pitilessness is the attribute of the 'villein', of the non-gentle. In fact Love in Chaucer's *The Romaunt of the Rose* (a translation of part of the *Roman de la Rose*) helpfully makes clear that this is the case: 'Thise vilayns arn withouten pitee,/Frendshipe, love, and al bounte' (2183–4). The way in which *Roman* and *Romaunt* represent the mercilessness of the beloved woman as a peasant's revolt – as an attack by a dangerously aggressive 'cherl' armed with a club[28] – confirms my earlier observation that pity is predicated on hierarchy: the converse of pity is the world-upside-down. It also exposes the problem created for the male by the handy-dandy game that courtly discourse plays with power. The woman's sexual disdain, her power to withhold herself, is an affront to the male–female hierarchy, which is expressed symbolically as an affront to the social hierarchy. The image of the woman as threatening peasant points to an area of anxiety, to a male sense that the ritualised reversals of courtly experience – which are engineered by him – are nevertheless at the same time humiliating and dangerous.

Some of the tale's ambivalence towards Dorigen may have its

roots in the problems raised for courtly fictions by the male lover's need for the woman to be inaccessible. The odd backing-off of the plot obviously stems from this – the way in which it does not move forward to a sexual climax as the Miller's, Shipman's and Merchant's tales do – and so does the way in which its attention shifts from Dorigen to the men. The action has to stop short of her 'queynte' (genitalia), which is an element in the discourse of a *fabliau* like the *Miller's Tale* but not of courtly *lai*. And because it is this kind of story, the narrator is able to reassure the company about what will happen when Arveragus tells Dorigen that she must keep her promise to Aurelius:

> Paraventure an heep of yow, ywis,
> Wol holden hym a lewed man in this
> That he wol putte his wyf in jupartie.
> Herkneth the tale er ye upon hire crie.
> She may have bettre fortune than yow semeth;
> And whan that ye han herd the tale, demeth.

> (1493–8)

The Host and the others of the pilgrims – and the audience beyond the text – who stand outside the charmed circle of 'gentillesse' need to be reassured that the conventions of courtly literature will preserve Dorigen from sexual exploitation. She is the creation of a feeling speech which represents women as causing men infinite suffering by refusing to grant them their favours – favours which, once granted, would make them not worth the male's extravagant claims for pity in the first place. Both sexes are caught in a complicated double bind, and perhaps we can see this as the trap that Dorigen believes she is in at line 1341, when she finds the rocks have moved. The trap is obviously the trick that has been played upon her by their moving, but it may also be seen as the trap created for the courtly lady by a plot that apparently requires her to give herself to a lover.

The trap affects the courtly lover as well as the lady, of course. Casting the woman in the role of sexual victim, obliged to have intercourse against her will, has the effect for the man of representing him as a rapist, a male role that is clearly incompatible with the myth of aristocracy which, I have been arguing, this kind of courtly fiction serves. Dorigen's 'compleynt' at lines 1355–1456 does just this. Momentarily she speaks as if she were in a different kind of story, as if she were one of the heroines in *The Legend of Good Women*, for example; she identifies herself, in fact, with Lucrece, whose story is told there. It is a tricky point in the narrative for both of the men: Aurelius is dangerously close to being a déclassé bounder like Tarquinius, and Arveragus to a ridiculous cuckold from a *fabliau*. The narrative's courtly tone is maintained, in part at least, by the way the action is made to hinge on the appeal to 'trouthe'. When she meets Aurelius on the way to the garden where she must give herself to him, Dorigen seems barely capable of understanding the courtly imperative – the need to maintain 'trouthe' at all costs – that is compelling her there:

> And he saleweth hire with glad entente,
> And asked of hire whiderward she wente;
> And she answerde, half as she were mad,
> 'Unto the gardyn, as myn housbonde bad,
> My trouthe for to holde – allas, allas!'

(1509–13)

This is probably the point at which the tale's masculinity is most apparent. If Arveragus and Aurelius are to be preserved from contempt, Dorigen's revulsion from what she has been ordered to submit to in the name of an aristocratic abstraction can only be represented as madness.[29] The terms of the tale will not allow her to dissent rationally at this point. She is permitted an affecting madness, however, so that her distress may provide the occasion for the show of 'pitee' on the part of Aurelius that will save her and at the same time define him as a gentleman: Aurelius 'in his herte hadde greet compassioun/Of hire and of hire lamentacioun/And of Arveragus, the worthy knyght' (1515–17). The *raison d'être* of Dorigen's humiliation turns out to be to permit a display of 'gentillesse' on the part of the men. This, it seems, it what the narrator means when he urges his audience to trust the tale.

Aurelius's compassion indicates to the reader versed in 'gentil' codes that here is a young gentleman who, unlike Tarquinius, is not going to betray his class. Arveragus's 'grete gentillesse' reminds Aurelius that 'fro his lust yet were hym levere abyde/Than doon so heigh a cherlyssh wrecchednesse/Agayns franchise and alle gentillesse' (1522–4). He is held back 'fro his lust' because to yield to it would be 'cherlyssh': a 'cherl' is a serf, a villein or a peasant.[30] To have intercourse with her would be the action of Andreas Capellanus's farmer. When Aurelius later tells the philosopher-magician what has happened, he reveals quite bluntly not only the masculine nature of this 'gentillesse', but also the power structure on which 'pitee' and 'fredom' rest:

That made me han of hire so greet pitee;
And right as frely as he sente hire me
As frely sente I hire to hym ageyn.

(1603–5)

This moment harks back to much earlier in the poem, when Dorigen
had first rejected Aurelius, asking him 'What deyntee sholde a man
han in his lyf/For to go love another mannes wyf,/That hath hir
body whan so that hym liketh?' (1003–5). This last line alludes to
the conventional contemporary teaching on the sexual obligations
of marriage, the marriage 'debt', which gives either partner rights
over the other's body.[31] Here it is not mutual, however; Dorigen's
rights over, or desire for, her husband Arveragus are not given (as
they might be) as a reason for her rejection of Aurelius. Instead she
represents herself simply as an object available, at whim, to her
husband's pleasure; Aurelius cannot have her body because it
belongs to Arveragus. It is the nearest the 'queynte' comes to enter-
ing the tale's discourse and looks momentarily like a challenge to
'gentillesse'. Nevertheless the effect of this speech turns out not
to be subversive; rather it makes Dorigen collude in the tale's
underlying view of her sexuality as property which the men propose
to pass backwards and forwards between them in order to establish
their status.

Dorigen's definition of herself as 'another mannes wyf' does not
mean, though, that she is simply wrapped up as a sexual parcel, since
her wifehood also opens up more problematic issues of freedom and
power. The point is often made that Arveragus' commands to Dorigen when he discovers her promise to Aurelius ('Ye shul youre
trouthe holden, by my fay!' (1474), 'I yow forbede, up peyne of
deeth . . .' (1481)) seem to contradict the terms of the agreement
made between the two of them at the beginning of the tale. Arveragus is presented initially as a courtly lover, defined as such by his
servitude and suffering. As a mere knight he is, moreover, lower
than Dorigen in social status, as lines 735–7 reveal. Once they marry,
their relationship becomes paradoxical. Privately, as the object of
his courtly devotion, she is superior to him, and they agree that he
will continue to treat her as a lover should: 'hire obeye, and folwe
hir wyl in al,/As any lovere to his lady shal' (749–50). In public,
however, as 'her housbonde and hir lord' he retains the sovereignty
due to a husband 'for shame of his degree' (752): because to do
otherwise would dishonour him. And so in lines 753 and 758 she
treats him as her superior, addressing him with 'ful greet humblesse'

and promising to become his 'humble trewe wyf', where before he
had shown her 'meke obeysaunce'.

This handy-dandy presentation of the sovereign lady who is a
humble wife and the obedient lover who is his wife's lord is frequently read as a version of idealised reciprocity, as a 'solution' to
the questions of authority raised in the other stories of the marriage
group.[32] But the language of courtly fictions, for which notions of
hierarchy and status are the *raison d'être*, can only express reciprocity in terms of power: there is no escape from higher and lower
or from service and sovereignty. Moreover the agreement between
the two of them is undercut as soon as it is made, when higher and
lower turn out to be masculine and feminine:

> Heere may men seen an humble, wys accord;
> Thus hath she take hir servant and hir lord –
> Servant in love, and lord in mariage,
> Thanne was he bothe in lordshipe and servage.
> Servage? Nay, but in lordshipe above,
> Sith he has bothe his lady and his love;
> His lady, certes, and his wyf also,
> The which that lawe of love acordeth to.

(791–8)

The last four lines of this passage change the rules of the paradoxical
game being played with degree, withdrawing its challenge to patriarchy and making clear that it is only a game, by suggesting that
the male lover's servitude is not really 'servage' at all but another,
in fact superior, kind of lordship: this seems to be the meaning of
lines 795–6: 'Servage? Nay, but in lordshipe above,/Sith he has bothe
his lady and his love.' This, though, is no more than is to be expected,
given that the sexual politics of the tale is established by a language
in which the 'meke obeysaunce' of the lover to his lady is treated
as part of a courting ritual and his 'humblesse' as an aspect of
charm. As the story proceeds, the inescapable implications of the
language in which reciprocity has been defined close in on Dorigen.
When Arveragus later orders her to give herself to Aurelius, apparently violating the terms of the agreement between them about
matters of love, he is in fact simply exercising the reserved powers
of the male which he had never surrendered. Women may, as the
narrator says, 'desiren libertee,/And nat to been constreyned as a
thral' (768–9), but there is no freedom for them between 'lordshipe'
and 'servage' when one turns out to be masculine and the other
feminine. This is made clear in the speech in which Aurelius reveals

to Dorigen that the rocks have moved. It is introduced by his approaching her with the lover's subservience, apparently relinquishing masculine authority for feminine abasement: 'And whan he saugh his tyme, anon-right hee,/With dredful herte and with ful *humble* cheere,/Salewed hath his *sovereyn* lady deere' (1308–10, my italics). But alongside this abject strain goes another, threatening and assertive, revealed in his use of imperatives: 'Avyseth yow'; 'Repenteth yow'; 'Dooth as yow list.' These are the aggressive syntax of power. The speech is another version of reciprocity: Aurelius now is both 'in lordshipe and servage', both master and slave. He has her in his power, but courtly discourse masks this fact; indeed it is essential that it should. If he just took her, she would not be the 'sovereyn lady' whose status confirms his own. That her sovereignty confers no real power on her is clear from the nature of the service – sexual submission – she is going to be required to perform. The pleasing paradoxes of the opening lines now look hollow indeed.

The sexual politics of the tale is presented, and therefore often read, as if sealed off from contemporary life by the *lai*'s traditional setting in the remote and pagan past. Legendary history here is like the love garden which is the locus of the central action: the paradisal no-place made by the 'craft of mannes hand so curiously' (909), which replicates both the self-containedness and masculinity of courtly fictions and the closing of the circle of 'gentillesse' whose interests those fictions serve. Nevertheless, as the ambivalence of the social status of the class of franklins in fourteenth-century England makes clear, 'gentillesse' is not in fact a closed circle, any more than the language of the tale can be self-contained. The opposition between 'lordshipe' and 'servage', between being 'free' and being 'thral', reaches out beyond the story to social structures which were being challenged and tested in Chaucer's own lifetime. The Franklin's remark that 'Women, of kynde desiren libertee,/And nat to been constreyned as a thral;/And so doon men, if I sooth seyen shal' (768–70) is not true of sexual politics only. One of the demands of the Peasants' Revolt was that the oppositional categories of free and thrall be dissolved. The governing classes saw – or thought they saw – only too clearly that their own continuance rested on the distinction between thraldom and freedom. For them the prospect of the dissolution of the boundaries between lord and villein was apocalyptic.[33] And, of course, one group in particular whose very existence depended on this distinction was the franklins, who were defined by their free status.

It is not surprising that the final strategy of the *Franklin's Tale* should be to shift away from Dorigen, and the issues of 'fredom' and 'servage' that her predicament raises, back to the competition among the men which was established in the headlink. This shift is a means of recontaining the disruptions that courtly discourse has brought into being, the threats to hierarchy that women and peasants pose. At the end of the tale there is an attempt to reclaim 'fredom' as a class- and gender-exclusive social skill, the noble generosity which is one of the defining attributes of the gentleman. Lower-class dissent from the assumptions of 'gentillesse' had already been raised by the Host and dismissed before the tale had begun. Now it is the women's turn to be silenced and contained. The Franklin's final, knowing question – 'Which was the mooste fre, as thynketh yow?' (1622) – refers only to the male characters in his story and is addressed only to the 'Lordynges' among his listeners, recreating that closed circle of male gentility.[34] Responding to the tale's interrogative ending seems to be part of a language game that the women pilgrims are expected to watch but not to play. The ending, though, is at best ambivalent: on the one hand it attempts to impose a certain kind of reading on the tale by returning to the themes of the headlink, presenting it as a *demande d'honneur* and locating it in masculine court culture. On the other hand, the fact that the question is left open invites dissident readers to provide their own answers or indeed to engage in a dialogue with the tale. Among these may be numbered, perhaps, the Agnes Chaucers, Katherine Mannings and Rosamoundes of the fourteenth century – the female readers whom the Franklin ignores – who, like many of their modern counterparts, may not have agreed that women are to be pitied and that only men are 'free'.

NOTES

1 I am very grateful to the editors of this volume for suggesting many improvements to my essay.
2 Chaucer was born in the early 1340s. His father, John Chaucer, is recorded from 1337 on as citizen and vintner of London. In 1349 Agnes Chaucer inherited various properties formerly owned by her uncle Hamo de Copton, citizen and moneyer of London. In 1366, after John Chaucer's death, Agnes married another London vintner, Bartholomew Chappel. See Martin H. Crow and Clair C. Olson (eds) *Chaucer Life-Records*, Oxford, Oxford University Press, 1966, pp. 4, 6–7.
3 For mothers as teachers, see Claire Cross, ' "Great reasoners in Scripture": the activities of women Lollards', in Derek Baker (ed.) *Medieval Women*, Oxford, Blackwell, 1978, pp. 359–80. At a higher social level, Walter of Bibbesworth wrote his *Tretiz de Langage* in the mid-thirteenth

century for a noblewoman, Dyonise de Mountechensi, to use in teaching French to her children. The popularity of the image of St Anne teaching the Virgin to read from the thirteenth century on is often regarded as reflecting actual practice.

4 National Library of Scotland, Advocates 19.2.1. See the facsimile, ed. D. Pearsall and I. C. Cunningham, London, Scolar Press, 1979.

5 See Caroline Barron, 'The golden age of women in medieval London', in *Medieval Women in Southern England, Reading Medieval Studies*, 1989, vol. 15, pp. 35–58: 'London widows could also draw up testaments in which they disposed of quite considerable sums of money, plate jewellery, furnishings and, on occasion, books' (p. 43). Her evidence, though, is mostly fifteenth century; little is known about the literacy of merchants' wives in the mid- to late fourteenth century.

6 Five pre-Chaucerian English *lais* survive: *Le Freine, Sir Orfeo, Sir Dégarre, Emaré* and *Sir Landeval*. The first three are in the Auchinleck manuscript, while the other two are in fifteenth-century vernacular miscellanies catering to similar tastes. (I exclude Thomas Chestre's *Sir Launfal, Sir Gowther* and *The Erl of Tolous*, which were probably all written in the late fourteenth century and so do not certainly predate the *Franklin's Tale*.) For the possibility that Chaucer knew the Auchinleck manuscript, see Laura Hibberd Loomis, 'Chaucer and the Auchinleck MS: Thomas and Guy of Warwick', in *Essays and Studies in Honor of Carleton Brown*, New York, New York University Press, 1940, pp. 111–28, and 'Chaucer and the Breton lays of the Auchinleck MS', *Studies in Philology*, 1941, vol. 38, pp. 14–33. For evidence of the popularity of French *lais* in England in the thirteenth century, see G. Brereton, 'A thirteenth-century list of French lays and other narrative poems', *Modern Language Review*, 1950, vol. 45, p. 40–5.

7 Many of the jokes in *Sir Thopas* seem to be at the expense of old-fashioned, provincial or lower-class diction and tastes. In Jean d'Angoulême's fifteenth-century manuscript of the *Canterbury Tales* (Bibliothèque Nationale, fonds angl. 39), *Sir Thopas* is cut short after only two stanzas, which suggests that for either Jean or his source the in-jokes no longer had any point.

8 A number of Chaucer's lyrics are courtly complaints (e.g. *The Complaint unto Pity, A Complaint to his Lady, The Complaint of Mars*) which draw on the conventions of the French *plainte*. Chaucer also uses the complaint as an element in larger structures: in the speeches of the Man in Black in *The Book of the Duchess*, of Troilus in *Troilus and Criseyde*, of the falcon in *The Squire's Tale*, etc. See W. A. Davenport, *Chaucer: Complaint and Narrative*, Cambridge, D. S. Brewer, 1988.

9 In OF *lai* was a lyric or song, or a short narrative poem. Both senses are retained in ME (see *MED, lai* n. (2), (a) and (b)). The thirteenth-century list of French *lais* printed by Brereton (see n. 6 above) includes *La pleinte vavayn* (Gawain?) and *La pleynte meliaduc* (Tristan's father in the prose *Tristan*), presumably because *lai* and *plainte* are both understood as lyric utterances. In Chaucer's usage 'lay' (= lyric) and 'compleynt' are often associated; see *The Book of the Duchess*, 463 and 471; *Merchant's Tale*, 1881; *Franklin's Tale*, 947–8.

10 It is, unfortunately, not likely that Agnes Chaucer could have read the

Franklin's Tale, since she was probably dead by 1381; see Crow and Olson, op. cit., p. 9. Evidence on Chaucer's sister Katherine Manning is late but plausible; ibid., pp. 2n., 288 and n., 512. Rosamounde is the dedicatee of Chaucer's *balade* 'To Rosamounde'.

11 My colleague A. J. Minnis argues this in his 1986 Chatterton Lecture on Poetry, 'From medieval to Renaissance? Chaucer's position on past gentility', *Proceedings of the British Academy,* 1986, vol. 72, pp. 205–46. See pp. 208 and 209–12. The scholastic *quaestio,* as a method of argumentation employed in a system of higher education open only to men, is in this sense masculine. Trevet's Latin commentary on Boethius is aimed at an academic (and thus male) readership; when he wrote a chronicle for Edward I's daughter Mary, who was a nun, he used French.

12 For the 'nobility debate' (whether nobility is a matter of birth or virtue) see Minnis, op. cit.; for letter and spirit, see R. A. Shoaf, 'The *Franklin's Tale*: Chaucer and Medusa', *Chaucer Review,* 1986, vol. 21, pp. 275–90.

13 An exception is the Hengwrt MS, in which the order of the tales is anomalous.

14 All quotations from Chaucer's works are from Larry D. Benson, *et al.* (eds) *The Riverside Chaucer,* 2nd edn, Oxford, Oxford University Press, 1988, and are cited by line number.

15 Chaucer's son, Thomas, the vintner's grandson, was 'not only a wealthy landed gentleman with large holdings in Oxfordshire, Hampshire and Buckinghamshire, but also a public official who had a long and distinguished career'. Thomas's daughter, Alice, became the duchess of Suffolk (Crow and Olson, op. cit., p. 544).

16 See the discussion by Christopher Dyer in *Standards of Living in the Late Middle Ages: Social Change in England c. 1200–1520,* Cambridge, Cambridge University Press, 1989, pp. 13–14, of the gradations of English society in the late fourteenth century. Dyer observes of the late medieval aristocracy (his term for nobility and gentry considered as a group) that 'the aristocrats themselves were acutely conscious of their special qualities. They hoped that their hallmark was their gentle behaviour, expressed by their generous and courteous treatment of others' (p. 19). Although Dyer does not make this explicit, 'gentle behaviour' must include speech. His remark about 'generous and courteous treatment of others' has obvious relevance to the ideological construction of 'fredom' and 'pitee' in the *Franklin's Tale.*

17 See Dyer, op. cit., p. 14 and esp. p. 22, from which this list of terms is taken.

18 See Nigel Saul, 'The social status of Chaucer's Franklin: a reconsideration', *Medium Aevum,* 1983, vol. 52, pp. 10–26, which corrects aspects of Henrik Specht, *Chaucer's Franklin in the 'Canterbury Tales',* Copenhagen, Publications of the Department of English, University of Copenhagen, 10, 1981.

19 The word 'free' is used in more than one sense within the tale itself: at lines 745 and 767 'free' means 'unconstrained', 'at liberty', while at line 1605 'frely' and line 1622 'fre' mean both 'generously', 'generous' and 'nobly', 'noble'. That 'free' (meaning 'generous') is a class term is clear from the fact that actions which are described as 'free' are also 'gentil' (i.e. well-bred): cf. the narrator's 'Thus kan a squier doon a gentil dede/

As wel as kan a knyght' (1543–4) and the philosopher's 'Everich of yow dide gentilly til oother' (1608). A classless equivalent of 'free' is provided by 'large', the primary meaning of which (according to *MED*, 'large' adj. 1a (a)) is 'munificent, open-handed'. Chaucer uses it occasionally to denote a specifically aristocratic generosity (cf. 'Largesse' in the *Romaunt of the Rose*, 1150ff.) though more often of openhandedness in general. Unlike 'free', 'large' does not shade into 'noble' but, as the other meanings listed in *MED* show, in the opposite direction.

20 *MED* shows that 'gentil man', meaning 'one of noble or gentle birth', occurs from the turn of the thirteenth century, though most of the occurrences are from the late fourteenth century on. The term seems to have this generalised sense in Chaucer's usage and continues to be used of both nobility and gentry in the fifteenth century. (See *MED*, 'gentil-man' n. 1 (a)). Nevertheless, 'gentilman' has apparently also acquired a more specific meaning as a designation of a particular rank in society by 1384, 'when Richard II granted to one of his servants a pension of $7\frac{1}{2}d$ a day "to enable him to support the estate of a gentleman to which the king has advanced him"' (quoted from *Calendar of Patent Rolls, 1381–5*, p. 72, by Chris Given-Wilson, *The English Nobility in the Late Middle Ages*, London, Routledge & Kegan Paul, 1987, p. 70.) Immediately after the Statute of Additions of 1413, which required a defendant in certain kinds of legal proceedings to give his 'state, degree or mystery', 'gentilman' is used to designate the lowest rank of the gentry, below esquire and above yeoman. According to F. R. H. Du Boulay, the first English gentleman so designated was Robert Erdeswick of Stafford, 'gentilman', indicted in 1414 ('The first gentleman', *The Listener*, 30 October 1958, pp. 687–9). *MED*'s earliest occurrence is dated 1416: 'Thomas Bekeryng, gentilman'. The place of gentlemen in the social hierarchy was clear enough by around 1420 for Lydgate to speak in the *Troy Book* of 'Many worthi knyghte,/And many squier, and many gentil man' (1388–9). The linguistic evidence suggests, then, that this group, who seem to have displaced or swallowed up the franklins, were moving into place in the last decades of the fourteenth century and were well established by the second decade of the fifteenth. For an excellent discussion of the implications of the term, see D. A. L. Morgan, 'The individual style of the English gentleman', in Michael Jones (ed.) *Gentry and Lesser Nobility in Late Medieval Europe*, Gloucester and New York, Alan Sutton, 1986, pp. 15–35.

21 Quoted in *MED*, gentil-man n. 2, from T. Wright and J. O. Halliwell (eds) *Reliquiae Antiquae*, 2 vols, I, London, Wm Pickering, 1841 (repr. New York, A. M. S. Press, 1966), p. 252. In these lines the apparently universal term 'whom' (= whomsoever) turns out to be gender-specific; that is, it only refers to men. I suggest in n. 28 that 'trouthe' (which, as Aurelius tells Dorigen, is 'the hyest thyng that man may kepe') is similarly gendered. More work should be done on courtly discourse as apparently universal but in fact gendered, and the problems that this creates for the construction of feminine subjectivity. For an excellent discussion of some of these issues, see Maria Black and Rosalind Coward, 'Linguistic, social and sexual relations: a review of Dale Spender's *Man Made Language*', in Deborah Cameron (ed.) *The Feminist*

Critique of Language: A Reader, London and New York, Routledge, 1990, pp. 111–33.

22 Douglas Gray, 'Chaucer and "pité" ', in Mary Salu and Robert T. Farrell (eds) *J. R. R. Tolkien, Scholar and Storyteller*, Ithaca and London, Cornell University Press, 1979, pp. 173–203, comments that 'There is . . . invariably a close connection (in Chaucer's poetry) between *pité* and *gentilesse*, nobility of soul. The two are almost inseparable; it is as if wherever there is true *gentilesse* there will be *pité* and vice versa' (p. 179). Although I agree with these remarks in general, I do not accept Gray's blanket interpretation of 'gentilesse' as 'nobility of soul'; in the *Franklin's Tale*, at least, 'gentilesse' is the 'nobility of soul evinced by people of free status' and the 'pitee' associated with 'gentilesse' is a class virtue.

23 See Mary Wollstonecraft, *Vindication of the Rights of Woman*, ed. Miriam Brody, Harmondsworth, Penguin Books, 1982. Chapter 5 is devoted to 'Writers who have rendered women objects of pity, bordering on contempt'. Wollstonecraft is scathing about Baroness de Stael's claim that Rousseau, when he presents women 'with all the *charms, weaknesses, virtues,* and *errors* of their sex', respects their persons. 'The master', Wollstonecraft comments, 'wished to have a meretricious slave to fondle, entirely dependent on his reason and bounty; he did not want a companion whom he should be compelled to esteem' (p. 204).

24 *Knight's Tale*, 1761; *Squire's Tale*, 479; *Merchant's Tale*, 1986; *Legend of Good Women*, Prologue F, 503.

25 P. G. Walsh (ed.) *Andreas Capellanus on Love*, London, Duckworth, 1982, Bk I, ch. 11, p. 223. Andreas Capellanus was probably associated with the court of Champagne in the 1180s, though the nature of the association is unknown.

26 In *The Book of the Duchess* the narrator's (?) love sickness has lasted 'this eight yeer', and The Man in Black's second wooing is at least a year ('another yere', 1258) after the first. In the *Knight's Tale* seven years pass before Palamon is released from prison and fights Arcite over Emily; the tournament is fixed for fifty weeks later; Palamon finally marries Emily 'certeyn yeres' (2967) after Arcite's death.

27 In *Sir Gawain and the Green Knight* the fact that the Lady takes the sexual initiative ensures that Gawain cannot maintain his traditional identity as courtly lover. In *Troilus and Criseyde*, Bk 3, Chaucer brilliantly surmounts the difficulties presented to him by the need to balance the requirement of the plot that the couple should have intercourse against maintaining the courtly tone of the narrative. His use of Pandarus ensures that neither Troilus nor Criseyde has to take the sexual initiative.

28 Cf. *The Romaunt of the Rose*, fragment 2:

> With that sterte oute anoon Daunger,
> Out of the place were he was hid.
> His malice in his chere was kid;
> Full gret he was and blak of hewe,
> Sturdy and hidous, whoso hym knewe . . .
> I durst no more there make abod
> For the cherl, he was so wod,

> So gan he threte and manace,
> And thurgh the haye he did me chace.
>
> (3130–4; 3159–62)

29 That 'trouthe' in the sense of fidelity to one's given word is a (masculine) aristocratic abstraction seems to be borne out by the promise made by Edward, duke of York in 1405 that he would, if need be, pay his troops himself: 'on my trouthe and as y am a trewe gentilman' (cited by Morgan, op. cit., p. 17, from *Rotuli Parliamentorum*, V, p. 608).

30 See *MED*, *cherl* n. 1 (c) and 2. By extension it means 'a person lacking in refinement, learning or morals; boor, ignoramus', and is a common term of abuse. The myth of aristocracy constructs the nobleman as well-born, generous and courteous and the peasant as base, boorish and villainous.

31 See the *Parson's Tale*, 939: 'Another cause [of marital intercourse] is to yelden everich of hem to oother the dette of hire bodies, for neither of hem hath power of his owene body'.

32 Mary Wollstonecraft quotes the strikingly similar arrangement that Rousseau proposes in *Emile*: 'Emilius, in becoming your husband, is becoming your master, and claims your obedience. Such is the order of nature. When a man is married, however, to such a wife as Sophia, it is proper he should be directed by her. This is also agreeable to the order of nature. . . . You will long maintain the authority in love, if you know but how to render your favours rare and valuable. It is thus you may employ the arts of coquetry even in the service of virtue, and those of love in that of reason.' Wollstonecraft calls these paradoxes 'unintelligible' and asks whether the surest way to make a wife chaste is really 'to teach her to practise the wanton arts of a mistress, termed virtuous coquetry' (op. cit., pp. 187–8). A recent defence of the paradoxes of the Arveragus–Dorigen relationship is made by Jill Mann in *Geoffrey Chaucer*, Hemel Hempstead, Harvester Wheatsheaf, 1991, pp. 111–20.

33 According to the writer of the *Anominalle Chronicle*, at his confrontation with Richard II at Smithfield in May 1381, Wat Tyler demanded that

> no lord should have lordship in future, but it should be divided among all men, except for the king's own lordship . . . And he demanded that there should be no more villeins in England, and no serfdom nor villeinage, but that all men should be free and of one condition.

Richard acceded, but these demands were repudiated by Parliament in November, in terms that are revealing:

> They (that is to say, the prelates, lords and commons) prayed humbly to our lord the king that as these letters of manumission and enfranchisement had been made and granted through coercion, *to the disinheritance of themselves and the destruction of the realm*, they should be wiped out and annulled by the authority of this parliament.

See R. B. Dobson (ed.) *The Peasants' Revolt of 1381*, 2nd edn, London, Macmillan, 1983, pp. 164–5 and 329–30; my italics. According to Dobson, the *Anominalle Chronicle* was written by a member of the king's entourage. He was possibly acquainted with Chaucer, who was, as far as is known, in London at the time of the Revolt. On the night of 12 June 1381 the Aldgate, above which Chaucer lived, was opened to admit the men of Essex into the city. (See Dobson, pp. 220 and 225.)

34 It does not seem feasible to argue that 'Lordynges' is not gender-specific. *MED*, 'lording(e)' n. 7 (a), defines it as 'a term of polite address used by persons of humbler station to their superiors; by poets, minstrels, or storytellers to readers or audience; sir; – usually pl.'.

4 Sexual economics, Chaucer's Wife of Bath and *The Book of Margery Kempe*

Sheila Delany

Few individuals in the Middle Ages occupy our attention as commandingly as two women – one fictional, one real – from the decline of that era. One is Chaucer's Dame Alice, the Wife of Bath; the other is Margery Kempe, the fifteenth-century gentlewoman from Lynn, author of the first autobiography in English. Both women were curiously 'modern', inasmuch as both were of the middle class; both travelled extensively in Europe and the Middle East; both were of an independent and robust nature; both preferred the autobiographical mode; and both were deeply concerned with sexuality, though from different perspectives: the one to enjoy, the other to renounce.

Chaucer's portrayal of the Wife of Bath shows an acute awareness of what I am here calling 'sexual economics': the psychological effects of economic necessity, specifically upon sexual mores. The Wife of Bath belongs to the petty bourgeoisie; she is a small-time entrepreneur in the textile trade, which, already by the thirteenth century, had come to dominate the English economy and its international trade. From her suburb of St Michael's juxta-Bathon, Dame Alice is in no position to rival the great textile magnates of her time; she remains a middle-sized fish in a small pond, though, as Chaucer remarks with some irony:

> Of clooth-makyng she hadde swich an haunt,
> She passed hem of Ypres and of Gaunt.
>
> (*General Prologue*, 447–8)[1]

The theme that Chaucer develops in Dame Alice's revelation of her marital history is that her sexuality is as capitalistic as her trade. For her, God's commandment 'to wexe and multiplye' (28) bears fruit not in children, but in profit: marriage settlements and land inheritances from her husbands, together with everything she can wring from them by nagging and manipulation. The old image of copulation as the marriage debt Alice wrenches round to her own point of view by asserting that her husband must be 'bothe my dettour and my thral' (155), adding the notion of an exploitative social relationship. She goes on to claim the profit motive as the basis for marital harmony:

> But sith I hadde hem hoolly in myn hond,
> And sith they hadde me yeven al hir lond,
> What sholde I taken keep hem for to plese,
> But it were for my profit and myn ese?
>
> (211–14)

The cynical conclusion to which Alice's experience leads is also phrased in the imagery of commerce:

> Wynne whoso may, for al is for to selle;
> With empty hand men may none haukes lure.
> For wynnyng wolde I al his lust endure,
> And make me a feyned appetit.
>
> (414–17)

Her strategy in marriage is based on the economic principle of supply and demand:

> Forbede us thyng, and that desiren we;
> Preesse on us faste, and thanne wol we fle.
> With daunger oute we al oure chaffare;
> Greet prees at market maketh deere ware,
> And to greet cheep is holde at litel prys:
> This knoweth every womman that is wys.
>
> (519–24)

Thus the Wife of Bath has thoroughly internalised the economic function of the bourgeoisie in reducing quintessentially human activity – love and sexuality – to commercial enterprise. She understands that as a woman she is both merchant and commodity: her youth and beauty the initial capital investment, and her age – the depreciation of the commodity – a condition against which she must accumulate profit as rapidly and therefore as exploitatively as possible.

In evaluating the Wife of Bath, however, we must also recognise the degree to which such internalisation of capitalist method is a defensive strategy against the special oppression of women in a society whose sex and marriage mores were thoroughly inhumane.

Alice can inherit land and engage in business, but she can exercise no control over the disposition of her body. Her first marriage to a rich but impotent old dotard took place when she was twelve: not Alice but her parents or guardians would have invested this choice piece of sexual capital for the sake of social standing and a profitable settlement – just as we see the Miller of the *Reeve's Tale* expecting an advantageous match for his virginal Malkin, until the goods are damaged by Alain the clerk. The potential horror of a January–May match Chaucer graphically details in the *Merchant's Tale*; nor was it, in Chaucer's time and later, by any means an uncommon practice for girls (and, less frequently, boys) to wed at an early age. It was not only parents who profited from the marriage of their offspring but also the legal guardian, who held the custody or wardship of the marriageable person in return for a fee or tax upon marriage: a form of feudal privilege conferrable by the king. In 1375 Chaucer, as king's esquire, was granted custody of the lands and marriage of the heirs of Edmund de Staplegate, himself heir of a wealthy Canterbury merchant; the grant was worth £10 in its time (probably close to £25,000 today). Thus Chaucer himself, as well as many of his friends involved in similar transactions, made substantial profit on the marriage market.[2]

In fact, Alice's alternatives were few and unattractive, for outside the convent there was little room in medieval Europe for the single woman. Religious, social and parental authority combined to urge acceptance of a profitable match, however repulsive personally. From one point of view, therefore, it is the Wife of Bath's personal triumph to have adapted with such success to the institutions of her day: to have found pleasure and even, towards the end of her life, some peace of mind. This is not, of course, the last word on Dame Alice. From the doctrinal point of view she is spiritually impoverished, and Chaucer's condemnation of her sexual economics represents in small his critique of the competitive, accumulative practices of the medieval bourgeoisie at large.

In real life, though, such triumphant adaptation to the reality principle can scarcely have been the rule. Medieval society took its toll, whether in murder, infanticide, suicide, insanity or daily misery, as surely as modern society continues to do. Unfortunately, the realities of sexual economics are usually such as to bankrupt the investor, who is also commodity. Margery Kempe, as much as Alice of Bath, is of the bourgeoisie, but Margery's internalisation of her class ethos brings no profit and large loss. Not five husbands but only one; not happily childless but perennially pregnant (she

had fourteen offspring); not flinging herself into a life of venerean
hedonism, but guilt-ridden and full of ambivalence about sex, fasci-
nated by and loathing it at once; not rejoicing in the permissive
behests of a kindly god, but sacrificing herself to the continual
remonstrances of a strict, authoritarian Jesus, with visions, crying
fits and trances. In order to understand the differences between the
fictional and the real versions of sexual economics, we will need to
know something about Margery Kempe's specific environment and
also about the general development of capitalism in the fifteenth
century.

Let us begin with the specifics, by placing Margery Kempe in her
social milieu. The exact dates of her birth and death are not known,
but they can be safely estimated at about 1373 and 1438.[3] Her home
was Lynn, Norfolk – Bishop's Lynn, as the city was called, after
its ecclesiastical overlord, the Bishop of Norwich.[4] Because of its
strategic location at the mouth of the River Ouse, and its function
as the only port for the trade of seven shires (especially the Scandi-
navian trade), Lynn had by the thirteenth century established itself
as one of the richest and most important commercial cities in
England. It was also one of the staple towns for wool, that is,
one of certain few designated towns where wool could be officially
weighed, taxed and shipped.

These two distinctive features, an ecclesiastical overlord and a
thriving commercial base, meant that in Lynn, class struggle took
on an even sharper and more protracted character than in most
other English towns. For the effort of the upper bourgeoisie to gain
political control of the city and establish its independence of the
feudal aristocracy was met by more than the usual resistance. As
A. S. Green points out:

> Prelates of the Church professed to rule with a double title, not
> only as feudal lords of the soil, but as guardians of the patrimony
> of St. Peter, holding property in trust for a great spiritual
> corporation. . . . Leaning on supernatural support for deliverance
> from all perils, it could the better refuse to discuss bargains
> suggested by mere political expediency.[5]

Such spiritually sanctioned intransigence led to many confrontations,
both legal and physical. It is possible that as a child Margery witnessed the riotous expulsion of the bishop in 1377 by the armed
populace of Lynn.[6]

It is important that we not misjudge Margery by viewing her
through eighteenth-century spectacles. During the eighteenth

century, such individualistic religious enthusiasm as Margery's was practised largely by the lower-middle-class and proletarian members of dissenting sects. Though we may see Margery as a forerunner of later developments, she remained nonetheless an orthodox Catholic and member of the upper bourgeoisie of Lynn. Her father, John Brunham, was, she tells us, 'mayor five times of that worshipful borough, and alderman also many years'.[7] Brunham's year-long terms as mayor ran from 29 September 1370–1, 1377–8, 1378–9, 1385–6 and 1391–2. He was elected from and by a governing body of twenty-four jurats, all named for life terms from the guild merchant, or professional association of the wealthiest merchants of the town; in Lynn it was called the High Guild of the Trinity. When he was not mayor, and sometimes even concurrently, Brunham served in other important public offices: as coroner, justice of the peace, member of Parliament, and chamberlain (one of four burgesses elected annually as financial officers of the city). Margery's husband also belonged to the upper ranks of the bourgeoisie, who, by their wealth, qualified for the name of burgess (in contrast to the lower bourgeoisie and artisans, who, as *inferiores*, were excluded from municipal government). Though John Kempe was not as consistently in the public eye as Brunham, he was also one of the first citizens of Lynn and was elected chamberlain in 1394.

In a passage that recalls the Wife of Bath's status-conscious love of finery (*General Prologue*, 448–52), Margery recounts 'her pride and pompous array' as a daughter of what Henri Pirenne has called 'the urban patriciate':

> for she wore gold pipes on her head, and her hoods, with the tippets, were slashed. Her cloaks also were slashed and laid with divers colors between the slashes, so that they should be the more staring to men's sight, and herself the more worshipped.
>
> (p. 12)

To become even richer – 'for pure covetousness and to maintain her pride', as the author puts it – Margery went into business for herself: first brewing, 'and was one of the greatest brewers in the town for three years or four, till she lost much money' (p. 13), then into grinding corn, with two horses and a hired employee, until that enterprise failed as well. Yet these ventures by no means impoverished Margery. She remained a rich woman despite her business losses, more solvent than her husband, apparently, for when Margery asked her husband to remain chaste he countered her by asking her to pay his debts (p. 31). Still later, the records of Lynn give notice of a Margeria Kempe being admitted to the Trinity Guild.

In brief, then, Margery Kempe was what the Wife of Bath would have liked to be: socially prominent and well-to-do, a member of one of the most prominent families in one of England's richest towns. It is with a grain of salt, then, that we must take R. W. Chambers's somewhat patronising remarks about 'poor Margery',[8] even if we do not take 'poor' in its economic sense. Yet, of course, there is a kernel of truth in Chambers's epithet, inasmuch as what he was responding to – and what I suspect we respond to even more sympathetically – is the quality of personal agony in Margery's book. Margery's spiritual autobiography is, according to Chambers, disappointing and even 'from certain points of view, painful'. It is not a book of devotion; we are constantly aware of Margery in relation to her society; and it is the peculiar quality of her religious experience – unsatisfying for Chambers, fascinating for us – that is so inadequate an instrument of transcendence.

We learn nothing of Margery's childhood – an omission to be regretted by psychoanalytic critics and social historians alike. The book opens with the fact of Margery's marriage at the age of twenty. Her first pregnancy occurred 'within a short time, as nature would'. Both pregnancy and labour were difficult, and during the pregnancy she was 'ever hindered by her enemy, the devil', so that she often did penance by fasting and prayer. After the birth of her child she 'went out of her mind', because of fear of damnation, for a period of eight months, during which time she suffered diabolical hallucinations. She was kept from suicide only by being bound night and day. Her remission came spontaneously with a vision of Jesus, who, clad in a mantle of purple silk, sat by her bed and said, 'Daughter, why hast thou forsaken me and I forsook never thee?' (p. 11).

The next twenty-five years were an amalgam of worldly and religious experience: her business ventures, her prideful array, the temptation to adultery with a close friend who rejected her after he had made the initial advance, the bearing of fourteen children, and several serious illnesses including dysentery. Interspersed with these worldly concerns were visions of paradise; conversations with Mary and Jesus and SS. Peter, Paul and Catherine; auditory, olfactory and other sensory hallucinations with religious import; diabolical fantasies of men (including priests) showing her their genitals; revulsion against 'fleshly communing' with her husband and repeated efforts to persuade him to abstain from sexual intercourse; travels to local and foreign shrines; and, in Jerusalem, the onset of what came to be her best-known trait, her 'crying', the uncontrollable sobbing and shouting that overcame her at moments of religious intensity, especially through pain and sorrow in contemplation of the Passion of Christ.

Eventually John Kempe was won over to the chaste life and took up separate residence in order to avoid gossip. In old age John fell downstairs in his own house, suffering a head injury that left him senile and incontinent. With characteristic split attention to physical detail and spiritual values, Margery describes their pathetic last years together:

> Then she took home her husband with her and kept him years after, as long as he lived, and had full much labour with him; for in his last days he turned childish again, and lacked reason, so that he could not do his own easement by going to a seat, or else he would not, but, as a child, voided his natural digestion in his linen clothes, where he sat by the fire or at the table, whichever it were; he would spare no place.
>
> And therefore was her labour much the more in washing and wringing, and her costage in firing; and it hindered her full much from contemplation, so that many times she would have loathed her labour, save she bethought herself how she, in her young age, had full many delectable thoughts, fleshly lusts, and inordinate loves to his person.

It is easy enough to say, then, that the remarkable *Book of Margery Kempe* gives us a social reality that Chaucer could neither observe firsthand nor sympathise with if he saw. As a man, as a devout Catholic, as a highly placed civil servant and courtier, as a poet in the continental courtly tradition, he could scarcely be expected to see the bourgeois woman in other than the conventional doctrinal and literary terms. Chaucer shows us one version of the internalisation of mercantile capitalism, the commodification of sexuality, but his neat schema is far too simple. The analogy between sexual and economic realms is engaging, in part because of its simplicity, and it helps Chaucer to expose what from the courtly point of view constitute the 'vices' of the bourgeoisie. Yet Margery's story shows that the bourgeois woman was far less likely to be a successful entrepreneur in her domestic life than she was to be an exploited worker; as Friedrich Engels remarked, 'Within the family the husband is the bourgeois and the wife represents the proletariat.'[9] Of course, Margery is far from being literally a proletarian, but the function of Engels's metaphor is to call attention to the special oppression of women in class-structured society. It may be difficult to see Margery as an oppressed person when she is wealthy and seems to hold her own so well. Nonetheless I want to suggest that her book is precisely a document of the special oppression of women in early capitalist society. Despite her class position, and to some extent because of it, Margery is exposed to and has internalised the most damaging aspects of bourgeois society.

This is not to negate the significance or validity of other approaches to the book. Hope Emily Allen, first editor of the text, showed its indebtedness to the continental tradition of 'feminine mysticism', especially to the works of St Bridget of Sweden (who died in 1373 and was canonised in 1391, and whose chapel Margery visits in Rome), and Blessed Dorothea of Prussia.[10] Admittedly this tradition offered Margery a vocabulary and a form for the expression of her own experience, but it offers no understanding of the genesis of that experience. Nor is a psychoanalytic approach fully adequate to the task of explaining Margery and her book. Everyone agrees that she was 'neurotic'; Allen's diagnosis emphasises hysteria, and to this we may add post-partum psychosis, wish-fulfilment, infantile regression and reaction formation as obvious neurotic syndromes revealed in the book. Yet because psychoanalysis generally omits the social factor in the development of neurosis, suspending the individual in artificial isolation, it cannot provide a real understanding of neurosis, which is not, after all, an answer but the very thing to be explained. Both source study and psychoanalytic criticism must be supplemented with a methodology that places the individual in a social context and also provides as full as possible a definition of 'social context'. By placing Margery Kempe in time, place and class, I have merely provided some of the data necessary to such an effort. I have not gone beyond the phenomena of history to the laws of history, nor have I dealt with the question of how Margery's internalisation of the ethos of early capitalism is manifested in her book. I now want to focus on three aspects of the book that help us to address those problems. They are the author's constant awareness of money, her perception of herself as property, and the alienated quality of her relationships.

The transition from feudalism to capitalism during the later Middle Ages was the transition from an economy based on use value to one based on exchange value. The feudal manor produced goods (mainly agricultural) that were used or else exchanged for other goods. Feudal dues were generally paid in labour or in kind, and the manor's surplus was used by its producers or its owners. In such an economy money was not a prime necessity, and while it was never wholly absent in the earlier Middle Ages, it played a very limited role in the economy of Europe. The development of industry and of mercantile capitalism meant that goods were no longer being produced for immediate use, but rather for sale in domestic and foreign markets; they were to be exchanged not for other goods but for money. Money could be accumulated, then reinvested for profit or lent at interest; large fortunes could be rapidly made; the big bourgeoisie could subsidise kings and impoverished aristocrats, buy titles and estates, and successfully compete with the feudal aristocracy for political power. Serfs and villeins left the manor to become free workers and artisans in the towns; those remaining began to demand the commutation of feudal dues and taxes and the establishment of money wages – in other words the abolition of feudalism, as in the English rebellion of 1381, the Bohemian Taborite rising of 1420, and the Peasant Wars in Germany during the first part of the sixteenth century. It was a lengthy process, which Marx and Engels characterise in their famous sentences from the *Communist Manifesto*:

> The bourgeoisie, wherever it has got the upper hand, has put an end to all feudal, patriarchal, idyllic relations. It has pitilessly torn asunder the motley feudal ties that bound man to his 'natural superiors', and has left remaining no other nexus between man and man than naked self-interest, than callous 'cash payment'.[11]

With Margery Kempe, one is kept constantly aware of the 'cash nexus'; it pervades her consciousness as it pervaded her world, part of every human endeavour and confrontation. No one is immune from money consciousness. From lowest to highest we see everyone pinching pennies, whether his own or someone else's: even the Archbishop of York squabbles over the fee to be paid Margery's escort (p. 167). Jesus denounces such concern for lucre (p. 209), but it is nonetheless the backdrop to Margery's religious devotion. The economics of pilgrimage is laid before us almost as prominently as its spiritual motivation. Thus we learn of the public financial settlement that Margery made before embarking for the Holy Land; of her expenditures for food, wine, bedding, lodging and transportation; of the groat she paid a Saracen to bring her to the Mount where Jesus fasted forty days; of wage negotiations with the humpbacked Irishman who became Margery's servant. We hear continually of her fear of being robbed and her anxiety at being delayed in Rome because of insufficient funds, and are as relieved as she when gold finally arrives – proof that God is with her. With account-book scrupulosity Margery registers every gift, whether alms, cloth for a dress, or payment for her stories. Perhaps the most revealing single passage is the conversation in which Margery asks Jesus to be her executor:

> Lord, after thou hast forgiven me my sin, I make thee mine executor of all the good works that Thou workest in me. In praying, in thinking, in weeping, in going on pilgrimage, in fasting, or in speaking any good words, it is fully my will, that Thou give Master N. [Margery's confessor] half of it to the increase of his merit, as if he did them himself. And the other half, Lord, spread on Thy friends and Thine enemies, and on my friends and mine enemies, for I will have but Thyself for my share.
>
> Daughter, I shall be a true executor to thee and fulfill all thy will; and for the great charity that thou hast to comfort thy fellow thou shalt have double reward in heaven.
>
> (pp. 26–7)

It is a spiritual economics as schematic as anything produced by the Puritans: good deeds and prayer the commodity, transferable and administered by Jesus (with the legal/psychological pun on 'will'), invested in Master N. and other projects, and producing an enviable profit in heaven of 100 per cent.

Yet despite this profound awareness of money, with Margery we are far from the aristocratic acceptance of wealth as a natural thing, or from the aristocratic virtue of largesse and the continual circulation of goods that is so prominent a feature of the courtly romance. On the contrary, the dominant tone of her concern is anxiety: the fear of loss of money or goods and the fear of being unable to provide for herself. This anxiety reflects not only Margery's personal experience of business failure but also that of her class, whose fortunes depended on speculation and investment and were therefore always subject to loss. This anxiety appears especially in her ambivalent attitude towards poverty. Margery views poverty as a spiritually glorifying condition, and she yearns in the Franciscan manner to imitate the poverty of Jesus. Yet once she is moneyless, moving among the common people of Rome without the security and social advantages conferred by wealth, she is deeply frightened.

And indeed this was the paradox of wealth for the medieval woman: that it created and destroyed at once. The creative power of money is that it compensates for the deficiencies of nature. The ugly person can buy a beautiful mate; the stupid person can buy intelligent employees; the bad person is honoured for his or her social position.[12] Thus money creates socially, and Margery is created a valuable piece of property, a good match for the burgess John Kempe and with a social position entirely unrelated to her desires or talents. Yet it is precisely as a piece of valuable property that Margery is most profoundly destroyed, for she can never attain full humanity while she has no power to dispose of herself as she pleases. Like any medieval woman, Margery is born the property of her father; on her marriage this right is transferred to her husband. While she is owned by someone else, she remains alienated from herself – and I am using the verb 'alienate' here in its original sense: to transfer the rights of ownership to another person.

Early in the book, Margery recounts an incident that poignantly reveals her understanding of this impotence. After her first vision of paradise, she urges her husband to continence. Yet having no right of property over her own body, Margery must endure legal rape when persuasion fails:

> She said to her husband, 'I may not deny you my body, but the love of my heart and my affections are withdrawn from all earthly creatures and set only in God.'
>
> He would have his will and she obeyed, with great weeping and sorrowing that she might not live chaste. . . . Her husband said it was good to do so, but he might not yet. He would when God willed. And so he used her as he had done before. He would not spare her.
>
> (p. 16)

Like the Wife of Bath, Margery is free to own property, run a business, and enter a guild, but she is not free to dispose of her person. Oppressed within her class, she participates in the economic advantages of the class but not in the full range of personal freedom extended to the bourgeois man. The incident recounted above reminds us that rape – *raptus* – sometimes means theft: here, the theft of one's person. It is not, of course, only Margery's husband who is guilty of this most fundamental form of theft, but the laws of religion and society that gave a husband authority over that piece of valuable property, his wife. And it is not only Margery who is victimised by these laws, but John as well, who is forced into the unpleasant choice of abusing his wife or abusing himself. For he cannot be divorced; neither can he find a normal sex life elsewhere. Luckily for Margery, though, her husband was the complete bourgeois: more committed to his needs than to those of his wife, but even more committed to financial than to physical necessity. Thus, when Margery offers to pay his debts, John finally agrees to let her take the vow of chastity (p. 32). In this way Margery, like any serf, buys manumission from her lord: the human property whose service she removes has its price.

Margery is as alienated from spiritual selfhood as she is from physical, for without her husband's consent she cannot obey the urging of her soul to go on pilgrimage. Luckily John Kempe grants his wife permission to go. Her confessor, too, has the right to deny permission and is angry that she does not ask. Yet even in her travels, Margery has only jumped out of the frying pan into the fire, for she is as plagued with fear of rape throughout her journey as she is with fear of theft; indeed, on one occasion she is threatened with rape and only narrowly manages to dissuade her assaulter.

The alternatives were few in medieval society for the woman who resented the alienation of self. One was violence against the most immediate oppressor, the husband, and it has recently been suggested that the Wife of Bath availed herself of this alternative in disposing of her fourth husband.[13]

We may read a thinly veiled death-wish against her husband when Margery has a vision in which Christ promises to slay him.[14] But more often the internalisation of oppression led to self-inflicted punishment, which, as mortification of the flesh, brought the social advantage of ecclesiastical approval. Thus, in the Middle English translation of the *Vita* of the French mystic Marie d'Oignies, we read, 'And for she [Marie] hadde not openly power of hir owne body, she bare prively under hir smok a fulle sharpe corde, with the whiche she was girded ful harde.'[15] Margery, too, internalises the special oppression of women through self-inflicted punishment. Not only is she continually obsessed with the desire to die, but she practises fasting, waking and other forms of asceticism, and also wears a hair shirt under her clothes every day for several years.

With substantial limitation on her personal freedom, the medieval bourgeoise remained far more dependent than her husband on personal relationships for a sense of fulfilment. Yet even in this realm Margery seems to find little to sustain her. Her children are never mentioned as a source of stability, security or comfort, with the exception of one son whom Margery converts from a profligate life. Likewise, there is no reference to Margery's relation with her parents. It is through her marriage that we get some sense of what 'normal' family relations were like. Though Margery wore a hair shirt for several years, her husband never knew about it, even though, as the author emphasises, 'she lay by him every night in his bed and wore the haircloth every day, and bore children in the time' (p. 17). Plainly, the absence of intimacy and communication seems as awful to Margery as it does to us.

Now John Kempe was not a cruel or an evil man, nor does Margery accuse him of monstrosity: he neither beat her nor had her put away as insane nor denounced her publicly. He was distressed by his wife's eccentricity, though more, it seems, because it interfered with his sex life than for any other reason. Yet considering the measures at his disposal and the social standards of the time, John Kempe was a fairly reasonable man. He was, of course, a very busy man, extremely concerned with profit and loss, getting and spending, office and status: we have already seen that while he could not be persuaded to live chastely, he could be bribed to do so. A busy man, too, was Margery's father, five times mayor of Lynn, and doubtless no less money-minded than John Kempe. Even the clergy emerge from Margery's moral account-book as busy, ambitious, and often greedy. This, then, is the normal world in which Margery moves. Its normalcy is grotesque, not unlike our own, and its relationships are often deformed and dehumanised. In such a world, Jesus is the only male authority figure who is neither busy nor ambitious but always available and ready to love. Thus Jesus becomes ideal father, promising 'all manner of love that thou covet-est', and ideal husband as well, united with Margery in mystical marriage (p. 112) and demanding only virtue.

Though Karl Marx knew nothing of Margery Kempe, his remarks on religion read as if tailor-made for her:

> Religious distress is at the same time the *expression* of real dis-tress and the *protest* against real distress. Religion is the sigh of the oppressed creature, the heart of a heartless world, just as it is the spirit of a spiritless situation. It is the opium of the people.[16]

Religion is Margery's way of asserting her ownership of herself, of overcoming alienation while simultaneously providing the most poignant testimony to that alienation. It is also her way of projecting into mental reality the loving relationships so fervently desired and so glaringly absent from her domestic life. One could also say that Margery discovered a way to use the system against the system – a way to leave home, travel, establish a name for herself, and mean-while remain both chaste and respectable. Religion became her way of combating the special oppression of women, which she in no way understood as oppression, though she suffered and rebelled against its experiential weight.

Compared with Margery Kempe, the Wife of Bath capitulated, consenting to the abuse of her sexuality but turning it to personal profit. Hers is the bureaucratic mentality, and it is she who, with her ethos of 'making it in a man's world' and 'beating the man at his own game', seems familiar enough to us now. But even Alice cannot really beat the man at his own game, nor can Margery really opt out of an abhorrent social system, and neither capitulation nor abstention recommends itself as a viable alternative to us. Instead, as Marx goes on to say immediately after the lines I have quoted above,

> The abolition of . . . the illusory happiness of the people is required for their real happiness. The demand to give up the illusions about its condition is the demand to give up a condition which needs illusions.

It is not the bourgeoisie that can, or ever could, create 'real happiness' for women any more than it can or could for society at large. What we see in Chaucer's Wife of Bath and in Margery Kempe are two strategies doomed to failure precisely because the capitalism they internalised was still immature. The social conditions did not yet exist for the emancipation of women any more than for the emancipation of the English rural and urban workers whose strategy in 1381 could also only lose. Factory labour, the industrial revolution, finance capital and imperialism – these laid the basis for the full emancipation of women and men from exploitative relations of production and property. They created the worldwide proletariat that can replace the institutions of bourgeois society with those of socialism. We no longer have to make the choices that Margery Kempe did. Significant personal freedom is available to us, in education, productive labour and sexuality. To be sure, our freedom is far from complete, nor can it be complete while exploitative relations of property and production continue to exist. But we are able now to address ourselves to the problem of full and genuine liberation, and to do so is the most important task we are freed for. To undertake that task moves us from the world of religion to that of politics: the struggle to destroy 'a condition which needs illusions' and to create one in which illusions have no place.

NOTES

1 Chaucer quotations are from F. N. Robinson, *The Works of Geoffrey Chaucer*, 2nd edn, Boston, Houghton-Mifflin, 1957. Robinson notes that 'the reputation of the cloth made in Bath was not of the best'.

2 On marriage settlements in fourteenth- and fifteenth-century England, see Paul Murray Kendall, *The Yorkist Age*, New York, W. W. Norton Co., 1962, ch. 10; Edith Rickert, *Chaucer's World*, New York, Columbia University Press, 1948, ch. 2; H. S. Bennett, *The Pastons and their England*, Cambridge, Cambridge University Press, 1922, ch. 4.

3 A chronology of Margery Kempe's life and times, together with the evidence for these dates, is provided in the edition by S. B. Meech and Hope E. Allen, Early English Text Society, OS 212, London, Oxford University Press, 1940, vol. 1.

4 Only with the Reformation was the city's name changed to King's Lynn. For much of the following information about Lynn, I am indebted to Alice S. Green, *Town and Life in the Fifteenth Century*, 2 vols, London, Macmillan, 1894.

5 Green, op. cit., vol. 1, pp. 277–8.

6 Nearly a century later, feelings still ran high. Richard Dowbigging's account of a confrontation between the bishop and the mayor of Lynn concludes: 'And so then the Bishop and his squires rebuked the mayor of Lynn, and said that he had shamed him and his town forever, with much other language, etc. . . . And so at the same gate we came in we went out, and no blood drawn, God be thanked.' Item 200 in John Warrington (ed.) *The Paston Letters*, Everyman edition, 2 vols, London, Dent, 1924, no. 752.

7 For the convenience of readers not familiar with Middle English I have taken quotations from the modernised edition of W. Butler-Bowden, London, Jonathan Cape, 1954.

8 Butler-Bowden, op. cit., Introduction, pp. xx.

9 F. Engels, *The Origin of the Family, Private Property, and the State*, New York, International Publishers, 1942, pp. 65–6.

10 See H. E. Allen's 'Prefatory note' and textual notes to Meech and Allen, op. cit.

11 Karl Marx and Friedrich Engels, *Manifesto of the Communist Party*, in *Collected Works*, London, Lawrence & Wishart, 1976, vol. 6, pp. 486–7.

12 On the creative power of money see Karl Marx, 'The power of money in the bourgeois society', in *Economic and Philosophic Manuscripts of 1844*, Moscow, Foreign Languages Publishing House, 1961, pp. 136–41.

13 Beryl Rowland, 'On the timely death of the Wife of Bath's fourth husband', *Archives*, 1972, vol. 209.

14 'I shall suddenly slay thy husband', Meech and Allen, op. cit., p. 27. In the manuscript a marginal note inserts after 'slay' the phrase 'the fleshly lust in'. This scribal insertion seems gratuitous, and especially unjustified in view of the contents of the next chapter. There Margery's husband poses a conundrum: if he were forced under pain of death to 'commune naturally' with Margery, would she consent, or see him killed? Her answer: 'I would rather see you being slain, than that we should turn again to our uncleanness', Meech and Allen, op. cit., p. 30. A few lines

further on, Margery says, 'I told you nearly three years ago that ye should be slain suddenly.' Clearly, she is speaking of her husband's life, not his lust. Meech also believes that the emendation is 'quite wrong'.

15 See Meech and Allen, op. cit., p. 261.
16 From the introduction to Marx's *Contribution to the Critique of Hegel's Philosophy of Right*, in *Marx and Engels on Religion*, New York, Schocken Books, 1964. Italics in original.

5 Mysticism and hysteria: the histories of Margery Kempe and Anna O.

Julia Long

In the humiliation of God, she sees the dethronement of man, inert, passive, covered with wounds, the crucified is the reverse image of the white, bloodstained martyr exposed to wild beasts, to daggers, to males, with whom the girl has so often identified herself; she is overwhelmed to see man, man-God has assumed her role. She it is who is hanging on the tree, promised the splendour of the resurrection.[1]

(Simone de Beauvoir)

Hysterics suffer mainly from reminiscences.[2]

(Freud)

The roles of mystic and hysteric are important in the history of women's experience, and both find a focal point in the figure of Margery Kempe, a woman born in the late fourteenth century, responsible for the earliest known piece of autobiographical writing in English.[3] Traditionally, Kempe's claims to mystical experience have been largely dismissed, both by clerics in her own time and in much of the criticism that followed the discovery of the book in 1934.[4] Her status has been generally relegated from that of a mystic to one suffering from more material symptoms, such as 'heart condition, or some other sickness'[5] or a 'hysterical personality organisation'.[6] This has not gone unnoticed among still more recent critics,[7] and Sheila Delany rightly points out that her neurosis or hysteria is 'not after all, an answer but the very thing to be explained'.[8] In other words, the levelling at Kempe of terms like 'hysteric', or indeed 'mystic', is meaningless unless we start to examine the specificities of her history and behaviour, and also develop an informed awareness of the ways in which these terms have been and are used.

This frequent labelling of Kempe as an hysteric provides an

interesting context in which to explore her book in conjunction with the study of the history of Bertha Pappenheim, Breuer's 'Anna O.'. The case of Anna O. is the first case study in Freud and Breuer's *Studies on Hysteria*, and indeed, before later work revealed her identity as Bertha Pappenheim, Anna O.'s identity to the reading public was solely that of an hysteric, a patient of Breuer.[9]

Pappenheim's social world is of course very different from that of Kempe, and any understanding of the two histories must take into account the specificities of the societies in which they lived. Recent studies which focus on the social context and material conditions of Kempe's existence have greatly enhanced our understanding of her book, because they insist on a social dimension which is inscribed in the text but not usually addressed, or addressed as if it were a troubling aspect which impedes, rather than enables, Kempe's mystical experiences.[10] However, the concern of this essay is why both Margery Kempe and Bertha Pappenheim should be labelled with the same term in spite of such enormously differing circumstances, in spite of their very different stories. What is it about their respective behaviours that earns this verdict? And what do the histories of these two individuals tell us about the patriarchal powers with whom they were interacting and, indeed, conflicting – namely, the medieval clergy and nineteenth-century psychoanalysts? This essay will explore remarkable continuities in their two histories, and the parallels in their behavioural patterns and strategies for survival, whilst in no way trying to assert that the experiences of the two women can be considered to be at all 'the same'.

Firstly, I want to acknowledge the pioneering roles played by Kempe and Pappenheim by stressing their places at the origins of a genre and of a system of thinking respectively – roles that have not always been fully recognised. Kempe has been credited with writing the first known autobiography in English – remarkable in that she was a woman, all the more remarkable in that she was illiterate.[11] Kempe herself describes the struggles involved in the production of her book in the 'proem': she was dependent on the goodwill and courage of the various priests who had undertaken to set down her story. That such sympathetic scribes existed does not alter the fact that the Church maintained its power by striving to maintain a monopoly on religious writings and teachings. Also, of course, as a woman Kempe was going directly against the Pauline doctrine that women should not preach. The book itself, therefore, not only relates many challenges and conflicts between Kempe and the Church; in its very existence it is a challenge to the Church's

power, and we should not underestimate her achievement in producing it.

Similarly, Pappenheim is located at 'the origins', not of a genre,
but of a system of thinking – psychoanalysis. History 'naturally'
credits physicians for medical breakthroughs, but sometimes patients
themselves are instrumental in pioneering an advance, and none
more so than Anna O., who actually invented the 'talking cure' that
is so much a part of psychoanalysis and therapy today.[12] Of course,
just as we only have access to Kempe's story through her scribe, we
only have access to Pappenheim's story through the writing of Josef
Breuer: it is his choice, his selection, his interpretation that determine what we read. The production of both texts lay in the hands
of the male authority, a cleric and an analyst respectively. Similar
problems of authenticity therefore apply in both cases – both histories have been mediated by men.[13] But the facts of the existence of
these two histories, both pioneering, both paradoxically produced
by, and in many ways in conflict with, the patriarchal powers of
their day, already shed some light on the struggles of the two women
at their respective centres.

Margery Kempe was born around 1373 in Lynn, a thriving commercial town in Norfolk and one of the richest in England. Her
father was a prominent member of the upper bourgeoisie of Lynn,
and had been mayor five times; the man she married, John Kempe,
was of the same class, although a lesser figure. Margery bore fourteen children in the course of her marriage, although there is little
mention of her family in her book, which is overwhelmingly concerned with detailing her religious experiences, her conversations
with Christ, her pilgrimages and her clashes with those around her.
The lack of presence of her family (except her husband, inasmuch
as his presence affects her relationship with God) is significant
in revealing Kempe's concerns and priorities. Hers is a spiritual
autobiography, with an express purpose – that 'sinful wretches . . .
may have great solace and comfort for themselves, and understand
the high and unspeakable mercy of our sovereign Saviour Jesus
Christ'.[14]

Margery Kempe's book opens with the birth of her first child,
shortly after her marriage when Kempe is around twenty years old
'or somewhat more'. The pregnancy is difficult and the birth trau-
matic. Kempe's struggles are not merely physical but also mental –
the physical sickness acts as a catalyst for her need to confess 'a
thing on her conscience which she had never revealed before that
time in all her life'. Apparently she is loath to confess this thing,

but in her pain and distress the devil comes to her and says that she must confess or she will be damned:

> Therefore, after her child was born, and not believing she would live, she sent for her confessor, and said before, fully wishing to be shriven of her whole lifetime, as near she could. And when she came to the point of saying that thing which she had so long concealed, her confessor was a little too hasty and began sharply to reprove her before she had fully said what she meant, and so she would say no more in spite of anything he might do. And soon after, because of the dread she had of damnation on the one hand, and his sharp reproving of her on the other, the creature went out of her mind and was amazingly disturbed and tormented with spirits for half a year, eight weeks and odd days.[15]

In *Mystic and Pilgrim: The Book and World of Margery Kempe* Clarissa Atkinson suggests that Kempe is here suffering from 'post partum psychosis', a severe form of post-natal depression.[16] Such an explanation is possible since we have available to us today a vocabulary of medicine and psychoanalysis that has established such concepts as 'psychosis'; they are part of what we consider to be possible in the range of human experience. Such a diagnosis, however, reveals something of the problems of negotiating texts such as Kempe's book which have a complex status, having been received as an empirical historical document, 'literature', women's history and so forth. The problems of interpreting such a text depend on the tools the reader has for interpretation, the grid through which the reader receives the text, which is in turn dependent on the vocabulary available due to the intellectual traditions which inform the reading of, for instance, feminist or psychoanalytic theory.[17] Kempe herself, of course, was an interpreter of her own life, with the tools and traditions available to her, and she offers a quite unequivocal explanation of the cause of her madness – the fact that she is caught between the fear of damnation and the fear of her confessor's 'sharp reproving': damned if she does, damned if she doesn't. Let us look at this scene in the context of late medieval Christianity, when confession was an extremely important religious sacrament as the doctrine of the Church was based on the process of sin, guilt and absolution. Through penance, the sinner is forgiven and returns to a 'state of grace'. Obviously, the power of the confessor in this sacrament is formidable, being in a position to determine the sinner's spiritual state. Much literature was produced concerning the ritual of penance:

The contemporary Church ... recognized in penance a means of extending its hegemony, and thus, in the fourth Lateran Council, it promulgated legislation requiring periodic confession of all souls. The penitential manuals disseminated in the wake of this legislation sought to increase the authority of the confessor by a twofold process: by emphasising his instrumentality in dispensing forgiveness and by establishing him as a scientist of the soul.[18]

These penitential manuals listed and described all manner of sexual activities and were intended to establish whether one had committed certain sins, by acting as a guide for the priest. However, such manuals were, of course, extremely ambivalent and no doubt held considerable fascination for the celibate priest! It is quite possible that by arousing sexual feelings in the confessor, for which he felt shame, the manuals also served as an instrument via which he projected his own guilt onto the sinner and was consequently more harsh than was 'necessary': 'intended to instruct, the rhetoric could also be deployed by individual confessors to constrict the spirits in their care'.[19] The confessional situation is strikingly similar to that of analysis – the 'professional' authority controlling the situation, the sinner or patient revealing what would be taboo to discuss outside this context. Both religious confession and psychoanalysis serve to legitimate discussion of sexual desire, and both transform the terms of this into the appropriate jargon. The phenomenon of transference in psychoanalysis therefore seems equally possible in the confessional situation. Of course, as I indicated above, there are problems involved in the use of vocabulary from one tradition to describe the situation of another, and so there are problems involved in applying the term 'transference' here.[20] Nonetheless, in both analysis and confession there exists a particular set of historical circumstances which gives authority to one group over the other; indeed, in the process of these two events the power relationship is reinforced. That such circumstances should result in a particular psychoanalytic phenomenon seems to me quite likely.

For the reader interested in attempting a psychoanalytic reading of *The Book of Margery Kempe*, then, the scene with her confessor at the beginning of the book is highly significant. If, according to Freud, 'hysterics suffer mainly from reminiscences', the guilt that Margery is carrying, and vainly trying to repress, is a key factor in her ensuing madness and as such invites speculation as to the nature of the great sin she has committed. The power of the confessor is also revealed – once he is 'a little too hasty', in reproving her he has the power to cause her to fall into insanity. His harshness may well be the result of the projection dynamic that the confession situation seems to encourage, as mentioned above with regard to penitential manuals. That the relationship between the priest and female confessors was a particularly delicate one is indicated by John Myrc's early fifteenth-century *Instructions for Parish Priests*, which includes confessional etiquette for priests hearing the confessions of women. As Mary Flowers Braswell notes, '[t]he author of *Instructions for Parish Priests* obviously expected confessors to hear heinous admissions from females, since no other group of penitents is singled out for such consideration'.[21] Kempe's relationship with the priest, then, may well have been complicated by the fact that she was a woman. Of course, we can only be speculative about this episode, having so little information available, but this much is evident: this initial act of confession is the first record of Kempe's often problematic encounters and relationships with religious authorities.

The sickness into which Kempe falls manifests itself in terrifying hallucinations of devils and torments which articulate taboos, forbidden desires antithetical to her role as a good Christian daughter, wife and mother:

> and in this time she saw, as she thought, devils opening their mouths all alight with burning flames of fire, as if they would have swallowed her in, sometimes pawing at her, sometimes threatening her, sometimes pulling her and hauling her about both night and day during the said time. And also the devils called out to her with great threats, and bade her that she should forsake her Christian faith and belief, and deny her God, his mother, and all the saints in heaven, her good works and all good virtues, her father, her mother, and all her friends. And so she did.[22]

As this passage indicates, Kempe's sickness is terribly destructive – she slanders 'her husband, her friends and her own self' and suffers suicidal and self-destructive impulses, biting her own hand 'so violently that the mark could be seen for the rest of her life' and tearing at the skin near her heart, so that in the end she is 'tied up and forcibly restrained both day and night so that she could not do as she wanted'.[23] She is caught up in a vicious circle of sickness and restraint: if her madness is a sign of her rebellion against her role (as indicated by its nature – revealing violent feelings towards herself, her beliefs, her family), it leads to her being even more constrained – forcefully and literally. Kempe has need of a way out from this destructive circularity, and her need for transcendence is satisfied in the form of Jesus Christ, who comes as an all-merciful figure, a Saviour, with the words 'Daughter, why have you forsaken me, and I never forsook you?'[24] In the figure of Christ, Kempe finds the comfort she has been seeking, and after many trials, including failed business enterprises and the temptation to commit adultery, she devotes her life to God in a very public and quite spectacular fashion. Although I do not wish to concentrate on Kempe's attempts to set up first as a brewer, then as a mill-owner, these enterprises do show her considerable energy and self-confidence. She is not a 'victim' who turns to a 'saviour' for rescue but one who very actively participates in the construction of her own life and destiny. Of course, when the businesses fail and she returns, humbled, to Christ, she rejects the self who took pride in such ventures, but she displays similar single-mindedness and courage of her convictions in her spiritual life and pilgrimages.

Bertha Pappenheim was born in 1859 in Vienna, the third of four children (she had two older sisters and a younger brother). As Dianne Hunter describes, she received an 'education typical for girls of her class and family position', speaking perfect English, reading French and Italian, and having the accomplishments of embroidery and lacemaking, as well as learning horse-riding.[25] Pappenheim's education, however, finished with school, and after this she led an extremely monotonous existence. Breuer noted that she was 'markedly intelligent', possessing a 'powerful intellect which would have been capable of digesting solid mental pabulum and which stood in need of it'.[26] The monotony of her existence led to habitual daydreaming, the creation of a 'private theatre' – a habit which Breuer considered a precondition of her illness.

In July 1880, when Pappenheim was twenty-one years old, her father (of whom, according to Breuer, she was 'passionately fond') fell ill with a 'peripleuritic abscess'.[27] Pappenheim devoted herself to the care of her father to such an extent that it took a toll on her own health. Her symptoms became so bad that she could no longer continue her role as carer:

> During the time Bertha Pappenheim nursed her father, she stopped eating. Her weight loss was such that she was forbidden to continue her nursing duties. She had also developed a cough which resembled her father's. At this point, Dr Breuer was called in for the first time. Over the next three months, a very complex

hysteria developed. Pappenheim suffered rigid paralyses of her arms and legs, paresis [partial or incomplete paralysis] of the neck muscles, headaches and somnambulism. First her right arm, then her right side, then her entire body suffered contracture. She was intermittently deaf. She had a convergent squint and severe, inexplicable disturbances of vision. She had temper tantrums during which she would throw things about the room, tear the buttons off her bedclothes, and grow distressed when relatives appeared. . . . [She] experienced a profound disorganisation of speech and, for some time, total aphasia.[28]

Let us consider, then, this collapse alongside the experience of Margery Kempe. Both are young women, around the same age – one an obedient daughter, the other a newly married wife. In Pappenheim's circumstances she is relatively powerless to make subjective choices or have any degree of control over her own life (Kempe, as has been noted, was able to start her own business, but at this point – newly married and a mother for the first time – it is quite likely that she was experiencing a diminished sense of her own selfhood and subjectivity). The sickness in both cases unleashes terrible feelings of violence towards their own families, feelings which have no place to be expressed in the status quo. In both cases, too, the sickness effects a role reversal from carer (mother, nurse) to one in need of care; at the same time the sickness negates the question of agency – the families cannot accuse Margery or Bertha of rejecting their familial duties, for it is the sickness itself which prevents them from carrying them out: the sickness itself is the agent. The hysteria/sickness can therefore be seen as a significantly passive form of rebellion against the roles they were either forced into or felt obliged to adopt (note that Pappenheim is 'forbidden' to continue her duties – her daughterly devotion is therefore not called into question). Even if Pappenheim consciously contributes to her illness by ceasing to eat, it is a particularly passive form of agency, and in cases of anorexia nervosa the question of conscious choice in eating or starving is far from straightforward.

In fact, the sickness initiates for both an escape from the binds of family life and offers possibilities of an alternative existence, in which both can pursue more freedom and control than would have been possible in their actual families.[29] However, such an escape is necessarily incomplete, fraught with contradictions, and achieved at an incredibly painful cost in damage to the self. For this 'passive resistance' involves in its very nature a negation of the self, demonstrated by both in violently self-destructive impulses and best illustrated through the common area of fasting and anorexia.

In Pappenheim's case we recognise a fairly typical instance of anorexia nervosa: an intelligent yet constrained young woman using her body as a site of resistance and rebellion, refusing to develop and fit into the role that has been ascribed to her. But the phenomenon of anorexia, widely recognised and documented as it is today, did not arise in a vacuum, and I want to explore its connections with religious fasting, of the type undertaken by Margery Kempe. The idea of religious fasting has its roots in the notion that to denigrate or punish the flesh is to elevate the soul, thus encompassing a strong element of self-punishment which is also evident in anorexia. For Kempe, religious fasting is part of her self-chastisement and expression of her revulsion at her physicality, sexuality, at the 'inordinate love' between herself and her husband and the 'great delight that each of them had in using the other's body'.[30] For Kempe, sexuality becomes 'so abominable to her that she would rather, she thought, have eaten and drunk the ooze and muck in the gutter than consent to intercourse, except out of obedience'. As the last phrase shows, Kempe is caught between two masters, God and her husband, a trap that she attempts to resolve by encouraging and praying for her husband to be chaste. She does great 'bodily penance', undertaking much fasting and long vigils and wearing a hair-shirt.

This, of course, is not purely idiosyncratic behaviour on Kempe's part – there is a strong tradition of fasting as part of religious practice. But it is significant that it is a practice that held great appeal for women, especially the female continental mystics of the late Middle Ages, for whom denigration of the flesh was a central part of religious experience. Caroline Walker Bynum's essay 'Fast, feast and flesh: the religious significance of food to medieval women' is very instructive on this subject, and I shall focus on her analysis with regard to Margery Kempe.[31] Bynum points out that food itself played a strong ritualistic role in medieval Christianity:

> Food was not only a fundamental material concern to medieval people; food practices – fasting and feasting – were at the very heart of the Christian tradition. A Christian in the thirteenth and fourteenth centuries was required by Church law to fast on certain days and to receive communion at least once a year. Thus the behaviour that defined a Christian was food-related behaviour.[32]

Not only were food and fasting crucial in medieval spirituality, but they were, as I have indicated, 'in the period from 1200 to 1500... more prominent in the piety of women than in that of men'.[33] Bynum's analysis includes an important cultural explanation as to why the connection between female piety and food specifically was so strong, arguing that 'food was important to women socially. In medieval Europe (as in many countries today) women were associated with food preparation and distribution rather than food consumption. The culture suggested that women cook and serve, men eat.'[34] Women's social role also proscribed other manifestations of piety – Bynum observes that, for instance, 'women who wished to follow the new poverty and begging ... were simply not permitted either by their families or by religious authorities to do so'.[35]

Following Bynum's argument, however, it is evident that this cultural explanation is not wholly adequate:

> This issue of control is, however, more basic than this analysis suggests. Food-related behaviour was central to women socially and religiously not only because food was a resource women controlled but also because, by means of food, women controlled themselves and their world.[36]

In the tradition of Christian doctrine, women are taught to feel shame for their physicality and sexuality since these qualities were instrumental in the Fall, and Eve uses her womanliness to tempt Adam. In the Fall, female sexuality and food are strongly connected – Eve offers Adam the 'forbidden fruit' and their pleasure in eating it results in shame; at the same time, Eve's body is very much aligned with the apple (it is a commonplace in literature to describe the female form in images of fruit) – her body is the object of Adam's temptation as much as the apple. Food and female sexuality are therefore represented as the two great factors that will lead a man into sin, and the shame a woman feels as a result of this connection means that the idea of chastising the flesh is far more central to women than to men. As Bynum argues:

> Moreover, in controlling eating and hunger, medieval women were also explicitly controlling sexuality. Ever since Tertullian and Jerome, male writers had warned religious women that food was dangerous because it excited lust. Although there is reason to suspect that male biographers exaggerated women's sexual temptations, some women themselves connected food abstinence with chastity and greed with sexual desire.[37]

For Margery Kempe, too, there is a strong connection between food and sexuality. In chapter 3 we see an example of a woman unable to practise her piety in the way that she desires: she wants to abstain from sexual relations with her husband and instead is forced to endure years of marital rape:

> He would have his will with her, and she obeyed with much weeping and sorrowing because she could not live chaste.[38]

She therefore turns to the religious practices that are available to her – fasting, vigils, long hours of attendance at church and wearing a hair-shirt. It seems that for Kempe these practices are not only a manifestation of her devotion to God, but also a self-punishment for her sexuality, even though her sexual relations with her husband are, at this point, entirely against her will.

She finally manages to negotiate an agreement with her husband concerning these practices in chapter 11. At this point they have been chaste for eight weeks and John Kempe is obviously unhappy with both his wife's fasting and her sexual abstinence:

> 'Margery, grant me my desire, and I shall grant you your desire. My first desire is that we shall still lie together in one bed as we have done before; the second, that you shall pay my debts before you go to Jerusalem; and the third that you shall eat and drink with me on Fridays as you used to do.'
>
> 'No, sir', she said, 'I will never agree to break my Friday fast as long as I live.'
>
> 'Well', he said, 'then I'm going to have sex with you again.'[39]

Here Kempe clings to her fasting as the area which her husband cannot control – she knows that even if she does not agree to have sex with him, she will be forced to anyway. An agreement is reached after she prays to Christ for guidance and he allows her to break her fast as long as her husband cooperates with her desire for sexual abstinence:

> For my beloved daughter, this was the reason why I ordered you to fast, so that you should the sooner obtain your desire, and now it is granted you. I no longer wish you to fast, and therefore I command you in the name of Jesus to eat and drink as your husband does.[40]

Margery's fasting then has here served an enabling role, allowing her to escape the bounds of marital sexual relations, and she succeeds in reaching an agreement with her husband to this effect. Through the chastising of her own flesh, she gains a greater freedom to pursue the religious life she wants. For Pappenheim, too, it seems likely that her anorexia is linked to her sexuality, in the sense that through starvation she can deny herself a woman's body, and along with this the identity of woman and all that encompasses in terms of lack of power, lack of privilege and lack of control. However, within the concept and reality of fasting/anorexia, we find again the paradox of escape or transcendence through self-destruction: the realm of control is limited to the woman's body, and involves punishment rather than nurturing. As both Kempe's and Pappenheim's cases make clear, though, the control of the body through fasting can enable women to achieve a greater social control through the effect that it has on others. In this sense, the woman's body becomes a site of language, a signifier on which struggles for power are enacted. I shall now turn to the issue of language and the body as a means of communication.

I have been concerned in this essay with the struggles of Kempe and Pappenheim over identity: sickness as an escape from prescribed roles, the search for transcendence and an alternative existence. I shall now concentrate on a fundamental aspect of identity – language – and examine the ways in which both Kempe and Pappenheim attempt to create a space in which to gain a voice, or to forge new ways of speaking. I want to explore the possibility that both Pappenheim's 'hysteria' and Kempe's 'mysticism' originate from the need of women to create illusions, or self-deceptions, in order to speak under patriarchy. Since, in patriarchal discourse, woman is posited as the 'other', the mirror via which man defines his own identity, a woman attempting to enter the realm of patriarchal discourse as a speaking subject is forced to employ strategies to escape this position and gain a voice that will be acknowledged and recognised.[41] For Kempe, the way is through an identification with Christ's Passion, an identification which enables her to find a voice. As in the case of fasting, she doesn't do this in a vacuum; a tradition exists:

> The phenomenon of female mysticism was widespread in the late Middle Ages. From the thirteenth to the fifteenth centuries it was women who were more likely to be mystics than men, and it was women who encouraged and propagated the most distinctive aspects of late medieval piety – devotion to the human Christ as lover, husband and infant, devotion to the Eucharist in a form of piety which insists on the physical as a legitimate means of access to the spiritual.[42]

In medieval mysticism, two 'routes' were available via which the mystic could aspire to mystical union with God – the 'via negativa' and the 'via positiva'.[43] The way of negative mysticism is based on the idea of seeking access to God through absence – the aspiring mystic is engaged in a process of self-emptying, of getting rid of all human experience and images which will obscure knowledge of God. This type of mysticism is generally privileged as superior to positive mysticism, the latter involving the search to know God through human imagery and analogy; the Incarnation is the natural centre of this type of mysticism. It is this type of mysticism which 'insists on the physical as a legitimate means of access to the spiritual',[44] and it is this form of mysticism that Kempe adopts. It seems to me a particularly suitable way of getting around the problems of her own physicality: fasting is a means of subduing, punishing, attempting, to be rid of her flesh – identifying with Christ's Passion is a way of legitimating, of 'reinstating' physicality but in a 'higher' form that can be reconciled with her religious beliefs – no longer to be enjoyed by her husband but as an essential part of her aspirations to be close to Christ. Even her sexuality can be incorporated into her mysticism, as is evidenced by her recording of her sublimated sexual relations with Christ, where she locates sexuality in the realm of the soul, although using the most material, most physical terms:

> Therefore I must be intimate with you, and lie in your bed with you. Daughter, you greatly desire to see me, and you may boldly, when you are in bed, take me to you as your wedded husband, as your dear darling. . . . Therefore you can take me boldly in the arms of your soul and kiss my mouth, my head and my feet as sweetly as you want.[45]

To the fourteen-times pregnant Kempe, a great advantage of this sublimated sexuality is that it will not result in conceiving another child.

It is not surprising, then, that Kempe, for whom issues of sexual desire and physicality are such a problem, should identify so closely with Christ on a very physical level, to the extent of physically enacting his Passion. However, the fundamental problem at the heart of this identification is once again self-abnegation: Kempe paradoxically gains a 'presence' through her own 'absence'. She is allowed a voice only inasmuch as she claims Christ is speaking through her. Her own presence is immaterial; she is legitimate only as a vessel for God.

The difficulties for women in gaining a voice in patriarchal discourse took a very specific form in late medieval Christianity, where the teachings of St Paul were used as an authority to stop women from preaching. Kempe therefore posed a great threat to clerics who, as I have mentioned, considered they had a monopoly in the area of spiritual guidance and who were deeply paranoid about any threat to this monopoly. This threat is evident from the fact that she was often arrested and charged with Lollardy: since Kempe's religious practices and pilgrimages were antithetical to Lollard beliefs, it is obvious that the charges were more indicative of a desire to silence her than of a genuine belief that she was a Lollard (although there are indeed strong parallels between Kempe and Lollard women, the latter being accused of appropriating male roles in their religious practices, such as preaching and teaching).

Kempe often recounts incidents where she successfully defends herself against the challenges of hostile men:

> 'Ah, sir', said the clerics, 'here we know that she has a devil in her, for she speaks of the Gospel.' A great cleric quickly produced a book and quoted St Paul for his part against her, that no women should preach. She answering to this, said, 'I do not preach, sir; I do not go into any pulpit. I use only conversation and good words, and that I will do while I live.'[46]

> Then she, going back again to York, was received by many people, and by very worthy clerics, who rejoiced in our Lord, who had given her – uneducated as she was – the wit and wisdom to answer so many men . . . thanks be to God.[47]

It is interesting that, in the first quotation, Kempe's defence – 'I do not go into any pulpit. I use only conversation' – probably articulates one of the most threatening things about her. It was exactly by participating in spiritual activity *outside* the pulpit and in ordinary terms that Kempe was eroding the Church's control (as an old monk complains, 'I wish you were enclosed in a house of stone, so that no one should speak with you'). It is a credit to Kempe's powers of argument that she uses this fact to her own ends. The second quotation reveals a striking inconsistency: when she is accused, persecuted or hounded it is because she is a woman not conforming to the roles provided for her. However, when she *is* credited and recognised by 'worthy clerics', it is only as a vessel for God – God deserves praise, not Kempe. This is a clear illustration of the self-abnegation to which I have referred: Kempe does gain recognition, but only inasmuch as she allows God to speak through her.

We have seen, then, that speaking in the patriarchal realm of lay preaching is extremely problematic for Kempe. What, then, are we to make of the other languages she adopts, that of wails and cries, 'ghostly labours' and physical manifestations of Christ's suffering?[48] Is it possible to interpret this language as a subversion of the 'father tongue' of patriarchal discourse? Tempting as it may be to see these manifestations as a liberating, alternative 'female' discourse, it should be borne in mind that a condition of its existence is that the woman becomes a spectacle, and as such can be viewed, judged and named by men – as indeed has been the case with Margery Kempe – whether they have been clerics or literary critics.

Problems of language are central also in the case of Bertha Pappenheim. Dianne Hunter focuses on her 'functional disorganization of speech' in her instructive study on Pappenheim, and points out the 'liberating motive' behind what appear to be extremely distressing symptoms:

> Speaking coherent German meant integration into a cultural identity Bertha Pappenheim wanted to reject.[49]

Pappenheim's speech disorganisation manifests itself in a variety of ways: inability to speak whole sentences, use of infinitives or past participles of verbs only; complete inability to speak at all; making sentences from mixing four different languages, to the point of incomprehensibility; speaking nothing but English or French or Italian at different times; inventing words and phrases.

Pappenheim's speech disorganisation is not merely arbitrary: on close examination it is evident that it reveals important aspects of the struggles she was enduring. For instance, her use of only infinitives and participles deletes the person, the agent, from the verb (she recurringly utters the word 'tormenting'). This seems to be directly connected with her wish not to see herself or inability to see herself as an active subject, as illustrated by her anorexia and possibly by her hysteria itself. Similarly, it deletes agency from those around her, whom it is likely she feels unable to challenge or to implicate in her suffering. It is likely too that Pappenheim's confusion and refusal to speak her native German and her preference for other languages suggest, as Hunter argues, a resistance to what Pappenheim perceives as a fixed cultural identity, whilst her inventiveness shows that her keen intelligence is eager to replace this 'preordained' identity and language with new possibilities, new alternatives.

I have spoken of the mimetic nature of Kempe's mysticism and her strong physical identification with Christ and his suffering. I want to now consider the possibility that a similar mimesis is evident in Pappenheim's illness, in relation to her sick father.

When Pappenheim sees her father lying sick, she is witnessing the dethronement of a patriarch, albeit one of whom she is 'passionately fond'[50] (there is, in any case, some ambivalence about this assertion of Breuer's, as I will discuss later). Suddenly, her father is as power-less as she, indeed more so, as she takes on the role of a nurse. It is significant, then, that she develops a cough similar to his,[51] and in the very process of falling ill she imitates him.

It seems, then, that for both the hysteric and mystic, the witnessing of a 'crucifixion' or a dethronement from patriarchy produces a strong identification. But contained within the Passion is the promise of transcendence, through the Resurrection and Salvation: for Kempe the Saviour is Christ himself, while for Pappenheim he takes the form of Josef Breuer.

The nature of Pappenheim's hallucinations provides an insight into her struggles with her gendered identity. Breuer recalls a 'par-ticularly terrifying hallucination':

> While she was nursing her father she had seen him with a death's head. She and the people with her remembered that once, while she still appeared to be in good health, she had paid a visit to one of her relatives. She had opened the door and all at once fallen down unconscious. In order to get over the obstruction to our progress she visited the same place again and, on entering the room, again fell to the ground unconscious. During her sub-sequent evening hypnosis the obstacle was surmounted. As she came into the room, she had seen her pale face reflected in a mirror hanging opposite the door; but it was not herself that she saw but her father with a death's head.[52]

First, then, Pappenheim hallucinates her father with a death's head, then she sees her own image reflected as her father with a death's head. Let us consider this in relation to de Beauvoir's words:

> She is overwhelmed to see, man, man-God has assumed her role. She it is who is hanging on the tree, promised the splendour of the resurrection.[53]

It seems that Pappenheim has, unconsciously, seen herself in her sick father, and now in the mirror it is his image that she sees reflected, not her own. The role of the mirror in the acquisition of a gendered identity is central to the psychoanalytic theories of Jacques Lacan, and his essay on the 'mirror stage', which concerns the development of infants, is well known.[54] The mirror here seems no less relevant even though Pappenheim is twenty-one years old, for it seems that she is experiencing a prolonged adolescence in a rather suffocating environment and until this point may have resisted (to some extent) taking on the full identity of a 'woman', with all its implications. The turning point comes in the form of her taking on the role of nurse and carer – a strongly maternal, feminine role which involves relinquishing any fantasies of androgyny that she may have been able to maintain to that time. So when she sees her father with a death's head she is envisioning death encroaching on his power, his masculinity; when she looks in the mirror she sees her own hopes of androgyny, her own desire for expression of the masculine aspects of her personality, being stifled, dying through the adoption of a singularly feminine role, hence the powerful identification with her father.

It seems likely that although Pappenheim is 'passionately fond' of her father, she is also resentful of his power and the fact that it is his illness that has brought about her own identity crisis. She tries to repress these feelings, but they manifest themselves as symptoms (for instance, her cough, the 'tussis nervosa', happens for the first time when she is sitting at her father's bedside and hears dance music from a neighbouring house: she feels guilty for her 'sudden wish to be there').[55] In fact, according to Breuer, many of Pappenheim's symptoms occur as a result of her trying to repress some aspect of herself for the sake of those around her, including her squint when she tries to suppress her tears and a 'spasm of the glottis' and the loss of her speech when she suppresses remarks.

As I have mentioned, the Passion contains within it the promise of salvation, and the following excerpt from the case history of Anna O. reveals how such transformation works in the case of Pappenheim:

> Anna shared the duties of nursing him with her mother. She once woke up during the night in great anxiety about the patient, who was in a high fever; and she was under the strain of expecting the arrival of a surgeon from Vienna who was to operate. Her mother had gone away for a short time and Anna was sitting at the bedside with her right arm over the back of her chair. She fell into a waking dream and saw a black snake coming towards the sick man from the wall to bite him. (It is most likely that

there were in fact snakes in the field behind the house and that these had previously given the girl a fright; they would thus have provided the material for her hallucination.) She tried to keep the snake off, but it was as though she was paralysed. Her right arm, over the back of the chair, had gone to sleep and had become anaesthetic and paretic; and when she looked at it the fingers turned into little snakes with death's heads (the nails). (It seems probable that she had tried to use her paralysed right arm to drive off the snake and that its anaesthesia and paralysis had consequently become associated with the hallucination of the snake.) When the snake vanished, in her terror she tried to pray. But language failed her: she could find no tongue in which to speak, till at last she thought of some children's verses in English and then found herself able to think and pray in that language. The whistle of the train that was bringing the doctor whom she expected broke the spell.[56]

In this scenario, the absence of Pappenheim's mother is highly significant – she provided the role model for her daughter, and when she is removed from the scene it is her role that falls to Pappenheim alone. As I said before, it is the role of nurse that seems to push Pappenheim into a fixed gender role. The image of the black snake carries associations of phallic potency and threat; although a symbol representing male sexuality, it also seems to represent Pappenheim's sexuality, as well as her hidden aggression which is taboo and which she tries to suppress with such self-destructive results. She initially visualises this threat as coming from the wall, from an external source, something over which she has no control but feels she should be able to stop; subsequently, however, she perceives the threat as originating in her – it is her very own hand which turns into a mass of snakes. She can no longer pray because she has no voice, she has no identity – she is playing the role of a nurturing woman but perceives herself as the source of potent and threatening male sexuality and aggression. She takes refuge in children's verses in English, thus simultaneously rejecting adulthood and her own German language. The spell is broken for her only when the doctor arrives like a saviour, allowing her to relinquish her role and her responsibility.

In the incident discussed above, the doctor who arrives has come to tend to Pappenheim's father. By falling ill herself, she is granted the attentions of her own doctor and her own saviour – Dr Breuer.

As Dianne Hunter comments, Breuer provides an audience for Pappenheim's mental creations: he 'increased by one the attendance

of her "private theatre" '.[57] Hunter suggests that a mutual infatu-
ation develops between the two, which seems likely given the combination of Pappenheim's lively intelligence and 'physical attractions'[58]
and Breuer's charisma as a good-looking successful doctor, together
with the long hours they spend together talking through the most
minute and intimate details of her life. Significantly, Pappenheim's
other name for the talking cure is 'chimney sweeping', which,
according to Freud, is a metaphor for sexual intercourse. Hunter
describes the jealousies of Breuer's wife concerning the patient, and
Breuer's subsequent decision to end the treatment. Pappenheim
responds to this by staging a hysterical childbirth – suffering from
'abdominal cramps' which she explains with the words 'now Dr
Breuer's child is coming!'.[59] All of this indicates that ultimately
Pappenheim seeks transcendence and escape through very conventional means – the fantasy of a romantic hero whose love will
provide the basis for a new identity expressed in the form of an
imagined childbirth.

For Margery Kempe, the male victim and male hero exist in the
same person, Jesus Christ. In him, she finds a focus for her own
sufferings, and in her visions and encounters with Christ she also
finds a Saviour on whom she can displace all her earthly, familial
feelings. As indicated earlier Kempe projects her sexual desires
onto a fantasised spiritual union with Christ; similarly, all her other
problematic relationships become displaced onto his personhood:

> When you strive to please me, then you are a true daughter;
> when you weep and mourn for my pain and my Passion, then
> you are a true mother having compassion on her child; when you
> weep for other people's sin and adversities, then you are a true
> sister; and when you sorrow because you are kept so long from
> the bliss of heaven, then you are a true spouse and wife, for it
> is the wife's part to be with her husband and to have no true joy
> until she has his company.[60]

And yet, whilst Kempe's visions undoubtedly offer her much
strength and sustenance in a largely hostile world, they can be in
their own way just as terrifying and distressing as Pappenheim's.
Where Pappenheim sees black snakes, Kempe is tormented by the
sight of 'horrible and abominable visions'

> of seeing men's genitals, and other such abominations. She saw,
> as she really thought, various men of religion, priests and many
> others, both heathen and Christian, coming before her eyes so

that she could not avoid them or put them out of her sight, and showing her their naked genitals.

And with that the devil ordered her in her mind to choose which of them she would have first, and she must prostitute herself to them all. . . . Wherever she went or whatever she did, these accursed thoughts remained with her. When she would see the sacrament, say her prayers, or do any other good deed, such abomination was always put into her mind. She was shriven and did all that she could, but she found no release, until she was nearly in despair. It cannot be written what pain she felt, and what sorrow she was in.[61]

Kempe, then, is plagued by hallucinations or visions concerning a threatening male sexuality in much the same way as Pappenheim. Similarly, like Pappenheim, it seems that her own sexual desires are displaced and projected onto men and represented in the form of a phallus. It is the vision of Christ which enables Kempe to transcend the difficulties she expresses around her own sexuality by offering a realm in which they can take an acceptable form – the spiritual.

Kempe, too, experiences something of a rebirth through her Saviour, with her 'ghostly labours' at Calvary resembling an hysterical childbirth. Whilst this does not provide her with a 'new identity' in the way that Pappenheim's seems to promise, it is nonetheless an index of the extent to which Kempe *did* forge a new identity out of the role of wife and mother, and her remarkable courage in remaining firm in her life of pilgrimage and devotion in spite of the hostility and aggression around her, and her own 'inappropriateness' for such a life.

And what new identity does Pappenheim create for herself? Later in her life she becomes a renowned feminist and social worker, participating particularly in the German Jewish Women's Movement. In 1954 she was honoured by the Republic of West Germany as a 'Helper of Humanity'. Her activities as a feminist are strongly international – perhaps an indication of a positive aspect of her early problematic self-identification as German: she perceives bonds between women that reach across national boundaries. Ultimately, then, Pappenheim does achieve considerable powers of agency, although we need to read her history beyond Breuer's case study to understand this. In the case of Margery Kempe, her vigorous striving for, and success in achieving, a subject position which is a refusal of the victim role comes across strongly in her autobiography. Given this, it seems to me that the histories of these two women stand as testimonies to their courage, and to the possibility of negotiating forms of marginalisation in the struggle for subjectivity.

NOTES

1 Simone de Beauvoir, *The Second Sex*, Harmondsworth, Penguin Books, repr. 1976, p. 686.
2 Sigmund Freud and Josef Breuer, *Studies on Hysteria*, Harmondsworth, Penguin Books, 1974, p. 58.
3 Barry A. Windeatt (trans.) *The Book of Margery Kempe*, Harmondsworth, Penguin Books, 1985. All quotations in my essay are taken from this translation, which has now become the standard 'text' of Kempe's book. For the Middle English edition, see Sanford Brown Meech and Hope Emily Allen (eds) *The Book of Margery Kempe*, Early English Text Society, OS, 212, London, Oxford University Press, 1940.
4 For a useful recent summary of negative responses to Kempe's text, see Nancy F. Partner, 'Reading *The Book of Margery Kempe*', *Exemplaria*, 1991, vol. 3, no. 1, pp. 29–66; pp. 31–3, and pp. 62–3, and n. 55. As Sarah Beckwith observes in her article 'Problems of authority in late medieval English mysticism: language, agency, and authority in *The Book of Margery Kempe*', *Exemplaria*, 1992, vol. 4, no. 1, pp. 171–99, the accusations of Kempe's 'fraudulence' began with Hope Emily Allen in 1940; see p. 175, n. 11. For full documentation of these accusations, see Roberta Bux Bosse, 'Margery Kempe's tarnished reputation: a reassessment', *Fourteenth Century English Mystics Newsletter*, 1979, vol. 5, pp. 9–19. Yet, as Partner makes clear, the trend in recent scholarship of Kempe – especially, but not exclusively, in feminist scholarship – has been far less censorious than in the early responses following the discovery of the unique Butler-Bowden manuscript of Kempe's *Book* in 1934 and its publication in 1936; see Partner, op. cit., pp. 31–3. For a non-feminist defence of Kempe, see Susan Dickman, 'Margery Kempe and the English devotional tradition', in Marion Glasscoe (ed.) *The Medieval Mystical Tradition in England*, Exeter, University of Exeter Press, 1980, pp. 156–72.
5 Windeatt, op. cit., p. 189.
6 This is the diagnosis offered by Dr Anthony Ryle, quoted ibid., p. 301.
7 See, for example, David Aers, 'The making of Margery Kempe: individual and community', in David Aers, *Community, Gender and Individual Identity: English Writing 1360–1430*, London and New York, Routledge, 1988, p. 74; Sarah Beckwith, 'A very material mysticism: the medieval mysticism of Margery Kempe', in David Aers (ed.) *Medieval Literature: Criticism, History, Ideology*, Brighton, Harvester, 1986, p. 38; Partner, op. cit., pp. 62–3. Karma Lochrie's recent authoritative and scholarly study of medieval mysticism, *Margery Kempe and Translations of the Flesh*, Philadelphia, University of Pennsylvania Press, 1991, does not refer to Kempe's supposed 'hysteria', although she extensively documents a number of behaviours characteristic of late medieval mysticism which might earn the name of 'hysterical symptoms'. Lochrie deals at some length with 'mystical desire' but does not discuss this in the context

of recent Lacanian descriptions of the structure and trajectory of desire, and of the structure of hysterical desire in particular; see Jacques Lacan, *The Four Fundamental Concepts of Psychoanalysis*, ed. Jacques-Alain Miller, trans. Alan Sheridan, Harmondsworth, Penguin Books, 1986, pp. 13, 33, 38, 50. This may represent a desire on Lochrie's part not to participate in the pathologising of Kempe; see Lochrie's critique of Partner: Lochrie, op. cit., p. 235, n. 80. On Kempe as 'histrionic', see Beckwith, 'Problems', op. cit., p. 177.

8 Sheila Delany, 'Sexual economics, Chaucer's Wife of Bath and *The Book of Margery Kempe*, *Minnesota Review*, 1975, NS 5, pp. 104–15; reprinted in this volume, pp. 72–87.

9 Freud and Breuer, op. cit., pp. 73–102.

10 See, for example, Aers, op. cit.; Delany, op. cit.; and, to some extent, Partner, op. cit.

11 For a reading of Kempe's text as female autobiography, see Sidonie Smith, *A Poetics of Women's Autobiography: Marginality and the Fictions of Self-Representation*, Bloomington, Indiana, Indiana University Press, 1987, and Janel M. Mueller, 'Autobiography of a new "creatur": female spirituality, selfhood, and authorship in *The Book of Margery Kempe*', in Domna Stanton (ed.) *The Female Autograph*, Chicago, University of Chicago Press, 1984, pp. 57–69. For an important reassessment of Kempe's 'illiteracy', see Lochrie, op. cit., pp. 98–134.

12 See Dianne Hunter, 'Hysteria, psychoanalysis, and feminism: the case of Anna O.', *Feminist Studies*, 1983, vol. 9, no. 3, p. 465.

13 For an interesting discussion of the founding moment of psychoanalysis in terms of the problematic of writing history (albeit not a gender-conscious one, but nevertheless one which to some extent demystifies the account of Anna O.'s 'story' as authoritative (male) truth), see John Forrester, 'The true story of Anna O.', in John Forrester, *The Seductions of Psychoanalysis: Freud, Lacan and Derrida*, Cambridge, Cambridge University Press, 1990, pp. 17–29.

14 Windeatt, op. cit., p. 33.

15 ibid., p. 41.

16 Clarissa Atkinson, *Mystic and Pilgrim: The Book and World of Margery Kempe*, Ithaca, New York, Cornell University Press, 1983.

17 Partner invokes a similar argument: 'If, moved by some misapplied notion of sympathy with the past, we artificially take for granted what they unself-consciously assumed, we still cannot become authentically "medieval", and we also cannot interpret anything. We can only make new, analogous, "thicker" descriptions, forever placing historical events in the contexts they never, in any case, left. . . . [I]nterpretation requires that we deliberately take things out of context to see if they will fit the patterns of a new code and become freshly intelligible': Partner, op. cit., p. 54.

18 Hope Phyllis Weissman, 'Margery Kempe in Jerusalem: *Hysterica Compassio* in the late Middle Ages', in M. Carruthers and E. Kirk (eds) *Acts of Interpretation: The Text and its Contexts, 700–1600*, Norman, Oklahoma, Pilgrim Books, 1982, pp. 201–17; p. 206.

19 ibid., p. 206.

20 Partner discusses the problem of the use of psychoanalytic language,

and defends the construction of a psychohistory for Margery Kempe in the light of potential objections from historians: see Partner, op. cit., pp. 60–2.

21 Mary Flowers Braswell, 'Sin, the lady and the law: the English noblewoman in the late Middle Ages', *Medievalia et Humanistica*, 1986, vol. 14, p. 87.

22 Windeatt, op. cit., pp. 41–2.

23 ibid., p. 42.

24 ibid., p. 42.

25 Hunter, op. cit., p. 467.

26 Freud and Breuer, op. cit., p. 73.

27 ibid., p. 75.

28 Hunter, op. cit., p. 467.

29 For a fine recent feminist reinterpretation of anorexia nervosa as a site where the humanist assumptions of self-determination which underpin the project of much contemporary feminism (including post-structuralist feminist accounts of subjectivity) are both resisted and revealed, see Gillian Brown, 'Anorexia, humanism, and feminism', *Yale Journal of Criticism*, 1991, vol. 5, no. 1, pp. 189–215.

30 Windeatt, op. cit., p. 46.

31 Caroline Walker Bynum, 'Fast, feast, and flesh: the religious significance of food to medieval women', *Representations*, 1985, vol. 11, pp. 1–25. For an extended treatment of this subject, see Caroline Walker Bynum, *Holy Feast and Holy Fast: The Religious Significance of Food to Medieval Women*, Berkeley, University of California Press, 1987.

32 Bynum, 'Fast, feast, and flesh', op. cit., p. 2.

33 ibid., p. 3.

34 ibid., p. 10.

35 ibid., p. 10.

36 ibid., p. 10.

37 ibid., pp. 11–12.

38 Windeatt, op. cit., p. 46.

39 ibid., p. 59.

40 ibid., p. 60.

41 For an accessible introduction to the problematic of woman's position as a speaking subject within the realm of the Lacanian Symbolic, see Toril Moi, *Sexual/Textual Politics*, London, Methuen, 1985, pp. 11–12, 128–49, 156–71.

42 Beckwith, 'A very material mysticism', op. cit., p. 36.

43 For an explanation of the distinction between the mystical 'via negativa' and 'via positiva', see Clifton Wolters, *The Cloud of Unknowing, and Other Works*, Harmondsworth, Penguin Books, 1978, pp. 16–17. Negative and positive mysticism are frequently distinguished in accounts of medieval mysticism, although the phenomena may be named in different terms. Lochrie, for example, distinguishes between '[a]ffective spirituality, or positive mysticism' and 'Pseudo-Dionysian – or negative – mysticism': see Lochrie, op. cit., p. 31. Lochrie offers a useful account of these categories in terms of their differing perceptions of human cognition and the imagination, although her interpretation does not invoke gender as a critical tool; see pp. 27–37. On the historical gendering of

these distinctions, and the attendant danger of maintaining them as a gendered binary opposition for our understanding of the phenomenon of medieval *female* mysticism, see Beckwith, 'A very material mysticism', op. cit., pp. 38–41.

44 Beckwith, 'A very material mysticism', op. cit., p. 36.

45 Windeatt, op. cit., pp. 126–7.

46 ibid., p. 164.

47 ibid., p. 167.

48 See ibid., passim, and especially pp. 104–7. Partner suggests that we interpret her cries and seizures as a 'dramatic exaggeration' of orgasm, yet her argument, which claims that these episodes form part of a narrative structure of 'inordinate love and separation', is not especially subtle or compelling for feminist readers, although it does at least engage directly with issues of female sexuality; see Partner, op. cit., p. 56. Lochrie's book, on the other hand, deals at length, and with some subtlety, with many aspects of Kempe's specific *imitatio Christi*, but its analysis remains, disappointingly, somewhat utopian, and ungrounded in any critique of the metaphorical, which is precisely where Partner situates her feminist challenge to dominant constructions of medieval mystical experience. For example, Lochrie offers the following as a rereading of mystical utterance: 'Desire for God's presence in words or other visitations in the soul always produces suffering. Abundance arouses desire and suffering caused by the lack of the Other, and this in turn inspires the mystic's quest for fulfillment. Bernard of Clairvaux suggests that the suffering of desire is what makes a place for divine speech in the first place', Lochrie, op. cit., p. 84. For Partner's critique of 'metaphorical' readings of mysticism, see Partner, op. cit., pp. 33–8. On the problem of reading Kempe's 'voice' as authoritative, see Beckwith, 'Problems', op. cit., especially pp. 180–9 and 198–9. In her article Beckwith suggests that feminist interest in both Kempe's book and critical readings of it might be concerned (as both the book and its critics are) with problems of 'agency and its relation to authority': see Beckwith, 'Problems', op. cit., p. 198.

49 Hunter, op. cit., p. 468.

50 Freud and Breuer, op. cit., p. 75.

51 Hunter, op. cit., p. 467.

52 Freud and Breuer, op. cit., pp. 91–2.

53 de Beauvoir, op. cit., p. 686.

54 For readers unfamiliar with Lacanian theory, see Moi, op. cit., pp. 99–101, for a brief discussion of the mirror stage.

55 Freud and Breuer, op. cit., p. 95.

56 ibid., pp. 92–3.

57 Hunter, op. cit., p. 471.

58 ibid., p. 471.

59 ibid., p. 472.

60 Windeatt, op. cit., p. 67.

61 ibid., p. 184.

6 Body politics: engendering medieval cycle drama

Ruth Evans

FEMINIST INTERVENTIONS?

Theresa Coletti has remarked that one of the greatest pedagogical and critical obstacles to the advancement of a feminist approach to medieval cycle drama is 'the way that women do or do not figure in the texts'. Not only is the narrative offered by the cycles one 'largely dominated by males and male roles',[1] where with the exception of some individual pageants and the reconstructed N-Town *Mary Play*[2] women are generally peripheral to the action of the drama, but when they do figure there they are stereotypes of vice or virtue: the 'unruly woman', such as Noah's wife in the Wakefield, Chester and York cycles, or the ubiquitous Virgin Mary.[3] Recent work by Kathleen Ashley (1987) and Theresa Coletti (1990; 1993)[4] has done much to problematise these apparently fixed types. Coletti, for example, shows how the dramatic (con)texts significantly shift the meanings of these cultural stereotypes and evoke complex responses to them. In the case of Mary, the frequent comic mode of her presentation, such as in the semi-farcical episode of *Joseph's Trouble about Mary* included in all of the extant cycles, signals both celebration and anxiety. 'Mary' is a site where some of the more crucial and problematic areas of Christian dogma, like the miraculous paradox of the virgin birth, are played out in domestic and familial terms, registering 'the dis-ease and ambivalence that may result from embracing a notion so palpably difficult to follow'.[5]

Feminist criticism, however, embraces not only the question of the textual inscription of female gendered subjectivities. In the words of Jane Flax, 'To the extent that feminist discourse defines its problematic as "woman" it ... ironically privileges the man as unproblematic or exempted from determination by gender relations.'[6] Importantly, the work of recent feminist theorists has opened up the whole field of 'gender', insisting on the problematisation of the distinction between 'gender' and 'sex' upon which much early feminist work crucially depended,[7] and exploring the shifting borders between material bodies and a range of gendered identities, including non-heterosexual ones. Since men, and one Man in particular, are the central subjects on the medieval stage, a feminist critical practice can also intervene to problematise and historicise the inscription of male bodies and masculine gendered identities in the cycle drama. I therefore want first of all to re-examine the highly influential thesis, proposed by Mervyn James in 1983, that the Corpus Christi plays constitute a locus of meanings connected with the *social body* and the inscription of power in a late medieval urban context. James's thesis depends on an unproblematic, naturalised and universalised notion of 'body'. The powerful metaphor of 'body' that lies at the heart of both James's analysis and the eucharistic celebration which was the core of the Corpus Christi feast and the cycle drama needs to be engendered, so that the relationship among bodies, subjectivities and power in these discursive practices be made newly, and differently, visible.

SEXED BODIES

James's ground-breaking article, 'Ritual, drama and social body in the late medieval English town' (1983), is a study of the mythology of the late medieval urban Corpus Christi cult.[8] The significant practices associated with this cult were the Corpus Christi procession, in which the host was paraded through the streets, and the Corpus Christi play itself, made up of the various pageants presented by individual guilds.[9] James's argument, which is largely anthropological,[10] is that the Corpus Christi rituals provided a focus for the conceptualisation of the social order in terms of body, and that the primary function of the cult was social integration and the affirmation of an essential human bond underlying individual manifestations of difference. The Corpus Christi drama, with its vast public display of human and material resources, also 'made available a means by which visual and public recognition could be given to changes in relationships of superiority, dependence or co-operation which existed between occupations'.[11] However, as James says, the concept of society as a body 'in which differentiation was taken up into social wholeness' was 'in historical fact projected by societies which were deeply divided – riven by an intense competitiveness: by the struggle for honour and worship, status and precedence, power and wealth'.[12] Thus the Corpus Christi plays had an important mythical function in late medieval urban societies as a site where the deep divisions in occupational and social hierarchies could be occluded or effaced.

James's analysis has been rightly acknowledged as a significant critical intervention because it situates the early drama within a specific historical and ideological context, and reads that context as one marked by heterogeneity and conflict.[13] However, his argument does not accommodate all the possible areas of division and tension in late medieval urban societies, notably that of sexual difference. Furthermore, and this is of particular importance for a *feminist* reading of the dramatic texts, he does not view the plays as sites where meanings can be *contested*, perhaps with ambiguous results. In common with many semiotic anthropological approaches, he plays down the contradictory elements in his analysis, and suppresses questions of power: what it is, who its agents are, and how it is exercised.

What James's argument ignores is that all the metaphors of body which construct particular subjectivities or constituencies in the late Middle Ages, and all the analogies between one body and another which establish culturally specific relations of power, such as the body politic, the body of Christ, husband and wife as one body, the collective, renewable social body, or the body in carnivalesque iconography, were gender-specific. The frequent medieval analogies between the somatic self, the monarch and his subjects, and the husband–wife relation reinforce metonymically notions of spiritual and secular order, *natural* order (for what could be more 'natural' than a body?), and do so in explicitly gendered terms.[14] It is well known that the corporeal, for example, was frequently coded feminine in medieval culture, as one half of a set of binary oppositions – body/head, body/soul, Matter/Form – in which the feminine is associated with the bodily or material half, and the masculine with the cerebral or spiritual half.[15] Thus bodily metaphors are more complex than James's over-homogenised account of their deployment in the context of the Corpus Christi feast would suggest.[16]

Secondly, James's account ignores the specific political and economic threats posed by women's increasing participation in various socio-economic structures in the late medieval period. Such participation threatened the social order, and led to the progressive exclusion of women from the emerging concept of citizenship: this calls in question the notion of 'social wholeness' celebrated at Corpus Christi.[17] Martha Howell's important study of women's changing labour-status in northern European cities, *Women, Pro-duction and Patriarchy in Late Medieval Cities* (1986), looks at the mechanisms by which women's social, economic and political posi-tions were regulated in the late medieval period.[18] High labour-status was conferred on women working in family units of production, but 'the work which granted high labor-status was soon removed from the family production unit, leaving it a center of low-status work'.[19] Howell's analysis radically destabilises James's assumption of a 'cor-porate quality of urban life, permeating social life at every level'.[20] The corporate identity sought by the individual guilds during the moment of the Corpus Christi procession was not only achieved in contradistinction to that of the other (male) guilds, but was also enabled by their difference from women in the economic and social formation.

Finally, James represents the medieval urban body politic as a paradigm of egalitarian universal unity. Yet an alternative meaning is available, though not foregrounded, in his account, namely that this body politic was conceptualised as hierarchical, masculine, and only fully represented by the ruling classes. James quotes the words of a fifteenth-century judge who declared, 'The political body is made up of *men like us*. If the man's head is decapitated he himself is dead' (my italics).[21] This statement clearly understands the body politic as male and as exclusively embodied by the highest classes. It is tempting, though not inevitable, to see here a metaphor of castration, in which the violent depiction of dis-memberment haunts the image of body-as-wholeness, threatening always to return to disrupt its apparent unity. James's article does not offer sufficient evidence to pursue here the implications that the 'body politic' paradigm may be a potent site for the return of the repressed. However, the judge's metaphor may be more convincingly related to the fears of the upper bourgeoisie about social unrest, an ideological dimension which is possibly reinforced by James's references to the disorder which was also reported as a significant part of the Corpus Christi procession: 'lawsuits, riots and even bloodshed between gilds [*sic*] competing for the symbols of precedence and esteem which the procession conferred'.[22] James sees this conflict as an integral aspect of the urban 'honour culture', marked by aggressive competi-tiveness, but from a feminist perspective it is also possible to read the rivalry between groups of men in communities of honour, such as we find in the guild and trade organisations in late medieval towns and cities, as belonging to a pattern identified by Carolyn Dinshaw, namely that such rivalry is just an excuse, a 'pretext', for 'the consolidation of individual masculine identity with its eradication of threatening feminine difference'.[23] Such eradication is everywhere exemplified by the women excluded from the visible public domain celebrated at Corpus Christi. There is very little evidence to suggest that women played any effective *political* role in the craft guilds, or that they had any responsibility for the production of the plays.[24] My critique of James's thesis, then, suggests a cultural context in which the representations of bodies on the stage incarnate a far more complex set of differences than he initially mapped out.

What is also important is that such differences cannot be simply 'read off' from the plays. The discursive nature of the drama, namely the way it circulates knowledge in a particular discourse, allows for representation that exceeds the systems which attempt to organise that representation. It allows, for example, for female subjects who do not necessarily re-present cultural norms but who offer instead a range of behavioural options for women. Even if embodied on the stage by boys/men, female figures such as Mrs Noah or Mary Magdalene in the Digby play of *Mary Magdalene* have the potential to disrupt the discourses which construct women as either silent or sinful, and to suggest alternative historical understandings of female subjectivities.

READING THE MALE BODY

The York pageant of the *Crucifixion*,[25] a frequently anthologised and discussed piece, has as its focus a process of torture and physical marking which inscribes the (male) body of Christ with a set of social, sexually determinant meanings. The soldiers' attention to the concrete details of stretching and nailing Christ's tendons and sinews to fit the boreholes of the cross (e.g. 85–8; 98–104; 107–28; 133–48) insistently foregrounds the body of Christ and its corporeal intractability.[26] This emphasis on Christ's physical suffering is typical of late medieval dramatic and iconographic representations of the Passion, although the disturbing concentration on the processes of torture is peculiar to the York pageant.[27] The cultural narrative which the text dramatises is that central to medieval incarnational theology: the troping of the Incarnation as the spiritual Word made flesh. Christ as corporeal man em-bodies the Word of God. Yet Christ's body has, in late medieval culture, a corporeal specificity that is understood and defined in relation to women's. In my discussion of the pageant I will draw on the work of male theorists of the body, but

I will insist, following the work of the feminist philosopher Elizabeth Grosz, on understanding the body not in terms of a non-specified, neutral corporeality but as 'sexed, carnal, specific'.[28]

Caroline Walker Bynum's identification of the metaphor of 'Jesus as mother', and of the medieval Christ as having maternal and feminine attributes (the wound in his side signifying a lactating breast; his very fleshliness associating him with the female), has justifiably achieved a great deal of critical currency, although the 'meaning' of this femininity is seldom pursued.[29] Peter Travis's bold foray into the decoding of Christ's body in the cycle plays is very suggestive, although his work is limited in its understanding of sex/gender, particularly in its deployment of Bynum's analysis of Christ's 'double-gendered human nature', which Travis uses to identify those moments in the play when Christ is alternately 'masculine' and 'feminine'. For example, he reads the Passion scenes in a number of the cycles as a 'gang rape', in which Christ's weak, passive and 'feminine' nature is foregrounded, in contrast to his 'masculine' stance in the Harrowing of Hell episodes.[30]

What is unsatisfactory for feminists in this reading is that it stops short of analysis: it merely identifies *and reproduces* binary oppositions without questioning where, culturally or historically speaking, such oppositions come from, or whether the drama offers, in its discursive textuality, alternative cultural narratives to do with sex and gender. One of the difficulties of dealing with individual pageants rather than with a complete cycle is that it is hard to generalise about the representation of Christ, because the play disperses his attributes and roles across its component texts. Nevertheless, in the York *Crucifixion* pageant Christ cannot easily be read as occupying the 'feminine' pole in a binary structure, since his role is simultaneously passive (obedient to the soldiers) and active (taking the initiative):

> *III Miles* Haue done belyue boy, and make þe bounde,
> And bende þi bakke vnto þis tree.
> *IV Miles* Byhalde, hymselffe has ladde hym doune
> In lenghe and breede as he schulde bee.[31]

Moreover, to gloss 'feminised' as 'passive' and 'weak', as Travis does, assumes too readily that passivity and weakness were universally read as 'feminine' in the Middle Ages. As Felicity Riddy's essay in this volume makes clear, certain kinds of male passive and submissive behaviour, especially that which delights in an exaggerated suffering, can operate as markers of upper-class *masculinity*.

Clearly some other interpretative moves – other, that is, than allotting Christ an ahistorical 'masculine' or 'feminine' role – need to be employed here in order to break down the fixity of binary gender representations.

MAN IS TO WOMAN AS SOUL IS TO BODY?

The transcendence of difference promised by Christian theology, as witnessed in the words of St Paul to the Galatians – 'there is neither male nor female: for ye are all one in Christ Jesus' (Gal. 3:28) – can be understood at least partly as a retreat from the troubled territories of (sexual) difference. However, the body of Christ in the Corpus Christi play does *not* transcend the historical, social and cultural systems of difference within which it was positioned and from which it derived its meaning for a medieval audience. One such meaning, emphatically different from the words of St Paul in its insistence on *gendered* homologies, is located in the Augustinian dualism which associates spirit and soul with man, body and flesh with woman.[32] Such dualism served, of course, to bolster clerical celibacy and to reinforce clerical misogyny, yet was also capable of being reinterpreted in ways that altered the terms of the analogy. In the well-known words of Hildegard of Bingen in the twelfth century: 'Man . . . signifies the divinity of the Son of God and woman his humanity.'[33] Hildegard's words significantly recuperate despised feminine flesh as a desired and necessary aspect of the Incarnation.

Caroline Walker Bynum has challenged the prevalent academic view that medieval sex/gender divisions were *only* constructed by means of such dualistic analogies. This dualism, she argues, is not in fact upheld in texts: rather, the boundaries between the sexes in the period from 1200 to 1500 were 'extremely permeable' and biological sex itself was seen as labile.[34] Representations of Christ partake of this dual-sexed (and dual-gendered) identity:

> medieval writers and occasionally even artists represented God's body with both feminine and masculine characteristics. . . . Medieval thinkers and artists, however, saw not just the body of Christ but all bodies as both male and female.[35]

Bynum is not explicit, however, about the implications of her thesis for our reordering of the medieval (or modern) world. Although she provides the reader with a wealth of specific historical detail and her argument is invaluable for challenging late medieval analogic thought and the medieval construction of the corporeal (and hence women) as polluted and sinful, her analysis is nevertheless limited because it is unclear from her argument what possible disruptions to the social order a sexually ambiguous Christ could make, or how feminists today could reinterpret both the female body and the body of Christ in the Middle Ages in ways that challenge the fixity of gender-categories.

While it is true that the doctrine of the Incarnation troubled medieval theologians, and forced them to consider that flesh was somehow 'of God' and not a signifier of (female) inferiority, nevertheless we have to ask further, more sceptical, questions about why the Incarnation in its bodily aspects, and with its attendant 'feminising' of Christ, became so central for the period 1200–1500. One answer, as Bynum points out, is that the emphasis on Christ's humanity enabled the Church to counter the various Manichean heresies (such as Catharism) which claimed that all matter was evil, and which threatened the supremacy of orthodox Christianity.[36] We have to consider, then, whether the 'feminine' Christ, like the medieval medical knowledge which constructed female uro-genital physiology as the inverted counterpart of the male,[37] is not an example, in the words of Elizabeth Grosz, of 'male self-definitions requir[ing] and produc[ing] definitions of the female as their inverted or complementary counterpart'.[38] To rely on images and metaphors of the feminine and the female in this way was enabling for a masculine Church but highly problematic for women in the culture at large. To say this is to go some way towards recognising what kind of supports are used by various patriarchal structures at specific historical moments and thus to challenge their claims to 'naturalness'.

Although Christ in the York *Crucifixion* pageant does not have any maternal attributes, he does nevertheless show some supposedly 'feminine' qualities, namely his meekness and silence when subjected to the most horrific torture. This is difficult to illustrate in quotation, but it is clear in the staging, particularly in the two middle phases of the action in which he is fastened to the cross, and then raised on it. Christ only speaks twice: once, to proclaim his obedience to his father's word and to hope that the soldiers may be redeemed by his death (49–60); and the second time to announce, in the conventional but powerful lament from the cross, his pain, and to beg loving forgiveness for the soldiers (253–64).[39]

Yet these feminine attributes signify *differently* because they are embodied in the son of God; a son of God, moreover, who is a man. Christ's 'passivity' and subordinate position in this pageant are in fact understood as a *latent* power and authority; they derive from a long tradition (going back at least to the Anglo-Saxon poem *The Dream of the Rood*)[40] of Christ as Germanic warrior-hero, stoically enduring his fate and nobly dying for his people. Although Christ scarcely protests at the inhuman tortures to which he is subjected, his suffering empowers him, through God, to proffer forgiveness to his tormentors in a wholly authoritative way:

> *Jesus* My fadir, þat alle bales may bete,
>   Forgiffis þes men þat dois me pyne.
> What þei wirke wotte þai noght.
>
> (259–61)

The authority of this simple speech is achieved as a result of the contrast with the colloquial, rapidly alternating exchanges between the four soldiers, whose disparaging responses – 'he jangelis like a jay. . . . he patris like a py' (265–6) – are risible attempts to 'feminise' Christ, to reduce him to a chattering woman, the misogynist stereotype of the unstable woman of Proverbs, 'prepared to deceive souls; talkative and wandering, not bearing to be quiet, not able to abide still at home'.[41] Comparisons between chattering women and magpies are common in medieval misogynist narratives. One such example is enshrined in a proverb in the thirteenth-century French *conte* 'De la Femme et de la pye' ('Concerning the woman and the magpie'): 'With the chatter of a magpie one is led to the deceptiveness of a fox or a cat; with words a woman drives many a man crazy and masters him completely.'[42] Yet Christ's speech and performance throughout the pageant clearly belie such attempts by the agents of the law to feminise and control him.

Furthermore, Christ's magisterial words from the cross are based on the liturgy for Matins on Good Friday,[43] and thus position him as preacher to the laity:

> *Jesus* Al men þat walkis by waye or strete,
>   Takes tene ȝe schalle no trauayle tyne.
> Byholdes myn heede, myn handis, and my feete,
>   And fully feele nowe, or ȝe fyne,
> Yf any mournyng may be meete,
>   Or myscheue mesured vnto myne.
>
> (253–8)

Such a preaching role is one explicitly denied to women within the authority of the traditional Church.[44] I suggest that the figure of Christ in this pageant is at least as open to being read as a man as to being read as a woman.

THAT OBSCURE OBJECT OF DESIRE

Another way of interpreting the action of the York pageant is as a symbolic castration, an idea which Travis, interestingly enough, does not seem to have considered alongside his 'gang rape' reading, but which could equally be read as constructing a 'feminised' Christ. Such a reading, however, speaks more directly to masculine anxieties than to pleasurable (or fearful?) masculine fantasies of desire or power. And what of Christ as erotic object? Although he is not explicitly represented in this way in the York pageant, this is nevertheless a dominant late medieval 'knowledge'; several commentators have shown how particularly in the period 1200–1500 the body of Christ is the focus of complex desires, erotic and religious, for both men and women, and that he occupies a number of different subject-positions – father, lover, husband, mother – within various structures of desire and identification.[45] Christ as object of desire could be further problematised by decentring a heterosexual reading of the York pageant, and suggesting the homoerotic potential of this material, even though the whole issue of medieval homosexuality would need to be historicised, as is now beginning to happen.[46] It is striking that this pageant, unlike the corresponding pageants in the other cycles, completely lacks female figures. The fact that it is men who perform this act of ritualised punishment, on behalf of other men, and for a man whose only pleas are addressed to God the Father, suggests the creation of a fantasy of masculine anxiety, a fantasy in which the male body and male sexuality are regulated by men, and in which women's absence suggests the disturbing eradication of feminine difference.

Rape entails reading Christ as female; castration as *symbolically* female; sadomasochistic torture within a homoerotic frame constructs a yet more complex 'feminised' subject: yet each action speaks to very different desires and fears in the audience. When Travis argues for the audience's complicity in the on-stage 'rape' of Christ as 'voyeurs', this is to assume an undifferentiated masculine subject-position for everyone in the audience, medieval and modern; yet both men and women might respond, and might have responded, very differently to a staged 'rape'. I do not want to pursue these readings here, or to suggest that one have primacy over the others, for the issue about the 'right' reading is unresolvable, but rather I suggest that we attend to particular critical investments in specific readings, and insist on critics' awareness of their own sexualised constructions of the body of Christ. My own critical practice is not exempt from this.

But how else can we understand the physical pain in this pageant in terms of sexual difference? As Travis points out, the pain of Christ's torture was relatively impervious in the medieval period to 'exegetical [i.e. clerical] interpretation'.[47] He proposes a gender-neutral psychoanalytic/theological understanding: that the violently dismembered body of Christ, the image of the Lacanian *corps morcelé*, allows each member of the audience to re-experience the fantasy of their own disincorporation, and thus to open up the 'channels of grace' which lead to the Pauline ideal of 'unity of being'.[48] Travis's analysis thus provides a powerful new reading of the religious and community dynamic at work in this pageant, but it is nevertheless one which does not take into account the often-remarked-upon legal and political dimensions of the York play.

BODY-MARKING

The metaphor of corporeal inscription – of the body as a 'text', the central target and object of the workings of power, marked in specific ways, and capable of being read and interpreted – is elaborated in a number of recent theorists (Foucault, Deleuze, Irigaray, Lingis),[49] and is strikingly anticipated in the York *Crucifixion* pageant. The first three phases (preparation for torture; the torture; the raising and setting down of Christ on the cross) concentrate on the actions of the four soldiers as they literally engrave Christ's body with nails:

> *II Miles*   Here is a stubbe will stiffely stande,
> Thurgh bones and senous it schall be soght
>
> (102–3)

and alter his physical shape by stretching him with ropes:

> *I Miles*   Ther cordis haue evill encressed his paynes,
> Or he wer tille þe booryngis brought.
> *II Miles*   3aa, assoundir are bothe synnous and veynis
> On ilke a side, so haue we soughte.
>
> (145–8)

Furthermore, the pageant recognises, as the other pageants do not (Chester, for example, emphasises the divinity of Christ; Towneley the abstract nature of evil),[50] the *institutionalised* nature of such body-marking, and regards such branding as a material process to do with the active role of *social power*. The soldiers who torture Christ do so because this is the demand of Roman law: the first soldier remarks to the others at the very beginning that

> Ʒee wootte youreselffe als wele as I
> Howe lordis and leders of owre lawe
> Has geven dome þat þis doote schall dye.

(3–5)

And when it is all over, he remarks: 'Als Pilate demed is done and dight' (281). Christ's body in this pageant is directly subject to an economy of surveillance and control. In the words of Foucault, it is 'directly involved in a political field; power relations have an immediate hold upon it; they invest it, mark it, train it, torture it, force it to carry out tasks, to perform ceremonies, to emit signs'.[51] The audience of the York pageant watch the body of Christ tortured and visibly marked by the forces of state and legal control. 'The law functions', as Grosz remarks, 'because it is tattooed indelibly on the subject.'[52] But what if the subject's body is itself the law?

WITH MY BODY . . .

The medieval vernacular topos in which Christ's body is literally figured as a 'text' is the so-called 'Charter of Christ', in which the body of Christ, marked by the instruments of the Passion as if written upon with a pen, functions as a legal document granting heaven to humankind.[53] In this widespread literary-allegorical and iconographic tradition,

> the crucified Christ is represented as endowing man with heaven by granting him a charter. The texts of the allegory are written in pseudo-legal language, and each detail of document and materials is interpreted allegorically: the parchment is Christ's body, the pen the lance or the nails, the letters his wounds, the seal his wounded heart, and so on.[54]

A notable example is found in all the manuscripts of an early fifteenth-century treatise known as *Pore Caitiff*. I quote here from the version in MS Downside 26452:

> the chartre of this heritage, and the bulle of this euerlastyng pardon, is our Lord Ihesu Cryst, wretonn with al the might and vertu of God. The parchemyn of this heuenly chartre is neither of sheep, nor of calf, but it ys the body and the blessed skyn of

our Lord Ihesu, that lombe that neuere was spotted with wem of synne. . . . Herde neuere man fro the begynnyng of the world vnto now, neither shal hens to Domesday, that euere writer wrote vpon shepys skyn, or on calues, with so hard and hidous pennes, so bittre, so sore, and so depe, as wroten the cursed Iewes vpon the blessed body and suete skyn of our Lord Ihesu Cryst, with sharp nayles and sharp spere and sore prickyng thornes instede of here pennes.[55]

There are numerous other examples of this cultural topos in Middle English literature; one well-known allusion is found in the rule for anchoresses known as *Ancrene Wisse*,[56] and several other examples, including that found in the fourteenth-century meditations of the Monk of Farne, are quoted in the recent work of Karma Lochrie on mysticism and the female body.[57] The milieu of the Charter texts was, in the words of Andrew Breeze, 'almost completely English and popular',[58] the same context in which the Corpus Christi play was produced and consumed.

This bizarre imaging of Christ's body as written (legal) document is, I suggest, one of the social narratives which along with the eucharistic *Corpus Christi* and the harmonious body politic underwrites, in very specific ways, the actions and meanings of the York pageant. This narrative signifies Christ's powerful *spiritual* authority, but does so by fictionalising his body as a material object, a legal text, which functions with all the authority of the *temporal* body politic. In the York *Crucifixion* Christ explicitly signals the inscription of suffering on his body, and asks the audience to read that (authoritative) body:

Jesus Byholdes myn heede, myn handis, and my feete,
    And fully feele nowe, or ȝe fyne,
  Yf any mournyng may be meete,
    Or myscheue mesured vnto myne.

(255–8)

In her preliminary exploration of the use feminists might make of theorists of the body, Grosz asks: 'Do differently sexed bodies require different inscriptive tools to etch their different surfaces?'[59] In the period 1200–1500 the extreme somatic manifestations of *imitatio Christi* (stigmata, bodily effusions, tears, cryings) were overwhelmingly displayed by women mystics,[60] yet their patterns were produced very differently from those on the body of Christ. Christ's wounds are produced literally; the bodily insignia of female mystics are produced 'hysterically', so that each subject stands in a different relation to power and has different possibilities for negotiating that power. Although it is difficult to compare a cultural practice – *imitatio Christi* – and a social narrative – the Passion of Christ – I would argue that it is not so much that different tools are used on male and female bodies, although this is highly significant, but that those bodies lay claim to different regimes of 'reading', during a period when the literacy of men and women was sharply differentiated. The female mystic, according to Karma Lochrie, 'reads' the body of Christ, and displaces that reading on her body.[61] In one dominant clerical topos women are blank pages, virgin sheets ready to receive the imprint of the father.[62] The Charter of Christ fictionalisation might suggest a similar female subject-position for Christ, although Christ's physical resistance to his corporeal inscription, dramatised in the York pageant, suggests not so much blank page as recalcitrant surface. Yet while Lochrie's suggestion that the 'writing' on women's bodies is in fact a 'reading' is a fruitful one for decentring the opposition between writing and being written on, the Charter of Christ nevertheless suggests a powerful connection between the male body and actual writing, a writing which is in fact for the most part only able to be read by other men.

The audience, then, understands this metaphor of bodily inscription as producing specific sexed bodies: different regimes of marking construct male and female bodies differently within the culture. Biologically sexed bodies, then, and their respective capacities, are socially marked, coded into sexually distinct categories which carry specific socio-cultural meanings. This is a rather different thing from talking about the 'imposition' of a socially constructed gender. I don't assume an unproblematic, biologically sexed body with gender superimposed; rather, the biological body is itself discursively constructed in the way that it is inscribed with knowledges.[63] And that body in turn constructs the subject whose subjective experience is an effect of the knowledge offered by the discursive body. However, the body exceeds the systems of power which mark it, and is therefore capable of offering different knowledges about itself.

What we have not yet considered is how this pageant understands the function of the law, insofar as it brands bodies and constitutes subjects. Christ's body as legal charter to heaven *is* the law, and transcends temporal law. Christ in this pageant, while subject to torture and actively marked by the processes of the law, is also able to transcend that marking, and apparently remove himself altogether from the social systems of power which do the marking:

Jesus Almyghty God, my fadir free,
    Late þis materes be made in mynde:
þou badde þat I schulde buxome be
    For Adam plyght for to be pyned.
Here to dede I obblisshe me
    Fro þat synne for to saue mankynde.

                              (49–54)

As his torture is about to begin, Christ calls on the higher authority of God, who stands outside all temporal, social systems which mark the body. Christ must be obedient to his torturers 'for Adam plyght' (because Adam brought original sin into the world): this is the grand redemptive design of the Christian narrative, which requires punishment in the world but which also offers the audience the mystificatory knowledge that such punishment is in fact a working-out of the ultimate truth of the salvific promise of Christianity. The tortured (male) body is thus constituted, paradoxically, as an agent of justice.

This knowledge could operate in different ways for different members of the audience. Despite the paucity of information on public executions in the fourteenth and fifteenth centuries,[64] the physical marking of punishment on Christ's body belongs to the period identified by Foucault as that in which justice inscribed itself directly on the body; it was roughly at the end of the eighteenth century, in Europe and America at any rate, that 'the body as the major target of penal repression disappeared'.[65] The mystification of punishment offered by the York pageant might have allowed certain members of the audience to accept as 'natural' both the physical branding of the bodies of actual men and women and the fictionalisation of that process in the narratives of male and female saints, and to receive those textual bodies as Christ-like and transcendent without questioning the social meanings of the torture of male and female bodies.

A number of different regimes of power – that of the body of the Church, that of the social body of the urban trade guilds, that of the body politic of the king – coalesce in the representation of Christ in this pageant. The metaphor of Christ as self-authorising legal charter uncomfortably evokes the words of the increasingly tyrannical Richard II, who claimed, in the articles of deposition of 1399, that 'the laws were in his own mouth . . . they were in his own breast, and . . . he alone could change or establish the laws of this realm'.[66] Richard's words claim *body* – a male, regal body – as a source of temporal authority, just as in the Charter of Christ tradition Christ's body becomes a site of spiritual authority, powerfully underwritten by the metaphors of *temporal* power. In one sense, then, the text functions to confirm and legitimate the various operations of temporal power, especially in its most punitive aspects.

But if it confirmed them, it also disturbed them; the play cannot be read wholly within this confirmatory mode. Part of what disturbs lies in the text's total concentration on male figures, and the ritualised torture of a male body. Unusually, the York *Crucifixion* pageant completely lacks the topos of the sorrowing *mater dolorosa* beloved of the pietistic, devotional tradition; there are no women at all to make the horrific suffering of Christ in some measure acceptable to the audience. In the corresponding N-Town pageant, for example, the complaints of the two women, St Veronica's act of wiping Christ's face, Mary's laments and swooning, heighten the pathos and affective impact of the action, but also offer the audience positions from which to understand Christ's suffering in its social, as opposed to its transcendent, dimension. The audience is offered no such alternative positions in the York pageant. While this might appear to emphasise the transcendence of Christ's physical pain, it is also disturbing because suffering is 'unplaced'. No comforting dramatisations of appropriate responses to Christ's suffering are articulated within the text.[67]

This lack, I suggest, is precisely what *denaturalises* pain and suffering in the York pageant. The text refuses to call on female bodies to naturalise physical pain for the audience in socially and aesthetically acceptable ways. It does not use *female* figures of suffering and pathos to legitimate and ennoble, to place and define, *male* suffering. In this sense, it displays a resistance to temporal processes of law and branding, offering a view of torture which perhaps even indicates the limits of *male* bodies, such as the body of the king, to act with unquestioned authority. It is important to recognise here that, as Foucault has said, 'resistance is never in a position of exteriority in relation to power'.[68] My position on the resistance I locate in this pageant is not intended to be a 'romantic' one, where I identify something pitted over and against systems of repression; the systems of power-knowledge are as much productive as they are repressive. Thus points of resistance are integral to those systems, and provide evidence of the forms of power that operate in those systems.[69] This Corpus Christi pageant thus disseminates knowledge about politics and the law, but is also the site, as we have seen in my earlier discussion about the function of the pageants and the Corpus Christi procession itself in an urban, mercantile context, for offering new configurations of knowledge about the social order. My earlier suggestion that we modify James's original thesis about the function of the analogic metaphors of Corpus Christi by insisting on the sexed and gendered nature of those analogic bodies is borne out in relation to the York pageant: the body politic and the body of Christ do not support and underwrite each other in simple or continuous ways.

HISTORIES OF THE BODY?

In this paper I have used various metaphors of the body both as an enabling framework and as a specific focus, allowing me to move from text to con-text, and back again. There are problems in working with and between both levels: in negotiating the demands of seeing the entire cycle as a single unit, a 'play' (which was to a large extent its medieval conceptualisation), and of understanding the function of individual texts within that larger narrative structure. The Corpus Christi play as a practice was itself part of a wider context of medieval practices (along with other kinds of public and semi-public spectacles and entertainments, such as the Hocktide festival, the 'charivari' and Skimmington ride),[70] and was positioned within social and cultural myths which were inscribed in all aspects of the text and con-text. The specific meanings (dramatic, juridical, medical, social) of male and female sexed bodies are of interest to us today, but were also centrally important to medieval audiences as part of a totality of meanings to do with the corporeal.

In a late fifteenth-century Middle English document known as the Amesbury Rule the anonymous male author (a cleric) exhorts his female audience of two novice nuns to remember that

> oure master Cryste cambe ynto þys worllde nott only to redeme man by the meritys of hys passyon (wyche he myȝth ryȝth sone haue done yff hit hadde so pleasyd hym), but was heer also conuersant amongyst men contynually by the space of xxxiij yers and half one to the entent that hys good and virtuouse lyfe and conuersacion sholld be a sufficyent, directe and mek example for vs to order our leuyng therafter.

> [our master Christ came into this world not only to redeem man by the merits of his Passion (which he could have done right away if it had so pleased him), but also spent time here on earth in conversation with men for the duration of thirty-three and a half years with the aim that his good and virtuous life and conver-

sation should be a sufficient, direct and meek example for us thereafter to lead our lives by].[71]

In this text there is enacted a series of cultural displacements: the moment of the Passion is displaced by the space of a lifetime; the rapturously experienced somatic identifications of *imitatio Christi* by the sober imitation of a good life; desire for suffering by meek conversation.

The cultural and historical shifts which made this text possible in the later fifteenth century do not nevertheless mark a complete break with the late fourteenth- and early fifteenth-century focus on the devotional and co-suffering aspects of the Passion; there are continuities as well as discontinuities. However, these kinds of cultural shifts alter the topography of the body and its meanings, indicating the problematic character of the body's 'natural' status. Future attention could perhaps be directed at these diachronic aspects of the Corpus Christi play, investigating their relation to the body-writing metaphor, to the large numbers of women whose vocation was the imitation of the life of Christ, and to female representations in the play. The central signifier of the Passion would have received rather different emphases across the centuries of its performance as medieval English urban society registered changes in the meanings of suffering, pain and religious belief, each experienced differently in the lives of men and women, and carving out for them different regimes of subjectivity which altered their reception of the social meanings of the Corpus Christi play.

NOTES

I would like to acknowledge the valuable help of Lesley Johnson and Theresa Coletti in reading and commenting on early drafts of this essay.

1 Theresa Coletti, 'A feminist approach to the Corpus Christi cycles', in Richard Emmerson (ed.) *Approaches to Teaching Medieval English Drama*, New York, Modern Language Association of America, 1990, p. 79.

2 See Peter Meredith (ed.) *The Mary Play: From the N. town Manuscript*, London and New York, Longman, 1987.

3 In this essay I follow the terminology used in the journal *Medieval English Theatre*: 'cycle' refers to the large production made up of a number of smaller pageants which aimed to cover the span of Christian history from Creation to Doomsday (the only existing true cycle plays are those of York, Chester and Wakefield, but there are two pageants extant from the Coventry cycle, as well as documentary evidence of other urban centres which had cycles, such as Beverley, Newcastle upon

Tyne, Norwich, Lincoln, Dublin); 'pageant' refers to each short play within a cycle, each of which was the property of a particular guild (in contemporary records, confusingly, a 'pageant' can be either the short play or the waggon on which it was performed); 'play' refers to a collection of individual pageants, if those pageants are held to constitute an entire work (E.g. the York play, the N-Town *Mary Play*); N-Town (or sometimes N. town) is now the standard term of reference for the collection that has previously been known as both the *Hegge Plays* and the *Ludus Coventriae* (after Block's Early English Text Society edition: K. S. Block (ed.) *Ludus Coventriae or The Plaie called Corpus Christi*, Early English Text Society, Extra Series 120, London, New York and Toronto, Oxford University Press, 1922); see Gail McMurray Gibson, 'Bury St. Edmunds, Lydgate, and the *N-Town Cycle*', *Speculum*, 1981, vol. 56, no. 1, pp. 56–90, n. 3. The current scholarly consensus is that the N-Town collection is a fifteenth-century compilation made up from parts of longer plays on the life of Mary and the Passion, supplemented with earlier pageants: see Stephen Spector, 'Appendix 1: the composition and development of the N-Town Cycle', in Stephen Spector (ed.) *The N-Town Play*, vol. I: Introduction and Text, and vol. II: Commentary, Appendices and Glossary, Early English Text Society, Supplementary Series 11 and 12, Oxford, New York and Toronto, Oxford University Press, 1991, vol. II, pp. 537–43. Spector nevertheless keeps the usage 'N-Town cycle'. See also McMurray Gibson, op. cit., p. 85. Some scholars also maintain that the Towneley pageants are not a true cycle either, although this is not a generally accepted view: see David Mills, 'Towneley Play or Towneley Cycle?', *Leeds Studies in English*, 1986, vol. 17, pp. 95–104. The term 'Corpus Christi Play' is also used to refer to the cycle play because of its association with the feast of Corpus Christi. The standard editions of the plays are: Richard Beadle (ed.) *The York Plays*, London, Edward Arnold, 1982; Spector (ed.) *The N-Town Play*; R. M. Lumiansky and David Mills (eds) *The Chester Mystery Cycle*, vol. I: Text, Early English Text Society, Supplementary Series 3, London, New York, Toronto, Oxford University Press, 1974; George England and A. U. Pollard (eds) *The Towneley Plays*, Early English Text Society, Extra Series 71, London, Oxford University Press, 1897, repr. 1952; A. C. Cawley (ed.) *The Wakefield Pageants in the Towneley Cycle*, Manchester, Manchester University Press, 1958; Meredith (ed.), op. cit.; Norman Davis (ed.) *Non-Cycle Plays and Fragments*, Early English Text Society, Supplementary Series 1, London, New York, Toronto, Oxford University Press, 1970.

4 Kathleen M. Ashley, 'Medieval courtesy literature and dramatic mirrors of female conduct', in Nancy Armstrong and Leonard Tennenhouse (eds) *The Ideology of Conduct: Essays on Literature and the History of Sexuality*, New York and London, Methuen, 1987, pp. 25–38; Theresa Coletti, 'A feminist approach to the Corpus Christi cycles', in Emmerson, op. cit., pp. 78–89; Theresa Coletti, 'Purity and danger: the paradox of Mary's body and the engendering of the infancy narrative in the English mystery cycles', in Linda Lomperis and Sarah Stanbury (eds) *Feminist Approaches to the Body in Medieval Literature*, Philadelphia, University of Pennsylvania Press, 1993, pp. 65–95. See also Ruth Evans, 'Feminist

re-enactments: gender and the Towneley *Vxor Noe'*, in Juliette Dor (ed.) *A Wyf Ther Was: Essays in Honour of Paule Mertens-Fonck*, Liège, University of Liège Press, 1992, pp. 141–54.

5 Coletti, 'A feminist approach', op. cit., p. 88. Although only N-Town and York include the Joseph's Troubles episode in separate pageants, it appears in Coventry, Chester (briefly) and Towneley as well, where it balances the Annunciation pageant.

6 Jane Flax, 'Postmodernism and gender relations in feminist theory', in Linda J. Nicholson (ed.) *Feminism/Postmodernism*, New York and London, Routledge, 1990, pp. 39–62; p. 45.

7 See, for example, Judith Butler, *Gender Trouble: Feminism and the Subversion of Identity*, New York and London, Routledge, 1990, and Judith Butler, *Bodies That Matter: On the Discursive Limits of 'Sex'*, New York and London, Routledge, 1993. Butler's work has enabled the theorising of gender in relation to a number of other differences; Kathleen Biddick, for example, uses gender 'as a theory of borders that enables us to talk about the historical construction and maintenance of sexual boundaries, both intra- and intercorporeal, through powerful historical processes of repetition and containment.... Theories of gender ... need to be histories simultaneously of corporeal interiority and of exteriority: sex, flesh, body, race, nature, discourse and culture ... gender is a historically variable effect of maintaining unitary categories for the purposes of "naturalizing" sexual difference': Kathleen Biddick, 'Genders, bodies, borders: technologies of the visible', *Speculum*, 1993, vol. 68, pp. 389–418; p. 393.

8 Mervyn James, 'Ritual, drama and social body in the late medieval English town', *Past and Present*, 1983, vol. 98, pp. 3–29. The movable feast of Corpus Christi was inaugurated in 1264 and finally instituted in 1311 as an official marker of the doctrine of transsubstantiation; its dates fell within the period 21 May–24 June. For a history of the feast and its establishment, see Miri Rubin, *Corpus Christi: The Eucharist in Late Medieval Culture*, Cambridge, New York and Melbourne, Cambridge University Press, 1991, pp. 164–212 and p. 271. On the urban Corpus Christi rituals as occasions for the presentation of powerful myths to do with the body of Christ and the collective social body, with the corporeal and the spiritual, and with each as a metaphor of the other, see also Peter W. Travis, 'The semiotics of Christ's body in the English cycles', in Emmerson, op. cit., pp. 67–9; Rubin, op. cit., pp. 269–71; Sarah Beckwith, 'Ritual, church and theatre: medieval dramas of the sacramental body', in David Aers (ed.) *Culture and History 1350–1600: Essays on English Communities, Identities and Writing*, Hemel Hempstead, Harvester Wheatsheaf, 1992, pp. 65–89; Anthony Gash, 'Carnival against Lent: the ambivalence of medieval drama', in David Aers (ed.) *Medieval Literature: Criticism, History, Ideology*, Brighton, Harvester, 1986, pp. 74–98; p. 81.

9 On the various practices associated with the feast, see Rubin, op. cit., pp. 213–87.

10 James cites in particular Mary Douglas, *Natural Symbols: Explorations in Cosmology*, London, Barrie and Rockliff, The Cresset Press, 1970; Mary Douglas, *Purity and Danger: An Analysis of Concepts of Pollution*

and Taboo, London, Routledge & Kegan Paul, 1966. On anthropological approaches to medieval drama in general, see Kathleen M. Ashley, 'Cultural approaches to medieval drama', in Emmerson, op. cit., pp. 57–66. The question of the function of social rituals is problematic: carnival, with its status reversals and other inversions, has been subject to a number of conflicting interpretations: see Michael D. Bristol, 'The social function of festivity', in *Carnival and Theatre: Plebeian Culture and the Structure of Authority in Renaissance England*, New York and London, Routledge, 1989, pp. 26–39; and Natalie Zemon Davis, 'Women on top', in Natalie Zemon Davis, *Society and Culture in Early Modern France*, London, Duckworth, 1975, pp. 124–51. Davis, arguing about sexual inversion in particular, takes issue with the usual anthropological view, rehearsed also in James's article, that rites involving status reversal are ultimately sources of order and stability; she argues rather that 'the image of the disorderly woman did not *always* function to keep women in their place' but undermined norms by, for example, widening the behavioural options for women; see pp. 130–1. Davis is of course specifically discussing the early modern period, and her analysis may need to be applied with some caution to the Middle Ages. For an analysis of the drama in Bakhtinian terms, see Gash, op. cit., pp. 74–98. See also Harriet Hawkins, ' "Merrie England"?: contradictory interpretations of the Corpus Christi plays', *English*, 1981, vol. 30, pp. 189–200.

11 James, op. cit., p. 15. For a reconstruction of the early history of the Norwich play which links the pageants and the order of the Corpus Christi procession at Norwich to the economic rise and fall of the various guilds, see Joanna Dutka, 'Mystery Plays at Norwich: their formation and development', *Leeds Studies in English*, 1978, NS vol. 10, pp. 107–20.

12 James, op. cit., p. 8.

13 See David Aers, 'Rewriting the Middle Ages: some suggestions', *Journal of Medieval and Renaissance Studies*, 1988, vol. 18, no. 2, pp. 221–40; p. 227; Theresa Coletti, paper given at the Conference of the Modern Language Association of America, Washington, D.C., December 1989, pp. 3–4.

14 It is not that James is silent about gender: he talks, for example, about 'gild [*sic*] brothers' and the 'Corpus Christi fraternity' (p. 10), but he does not address the medieval analogy between the body politic and the somatic self in explicitly gendered terms. For an interesting discussion of the medieval use of rhetorical figures in which (exaggeratedly unworthy) women are paradoxically praised as a means of constructing the relationship between God and humanity, see Megan McLaughlin, 'Gender paradox and the Otherness of God', *Gender and History*, 1991, vol. 3, no. 2, pp. 147–59; McLaughlin's article provides valuable evidence of the use of the concept of gender in medieval theological writings to structure, legitimise and criticise various analogical relationships.

15 See McLaughlin, op. cit., p. 149; Caroline Walker Bynum, ' " . . . And woman his humanity": female imagery in the religious writing of the later Middle Ages', in Caroline Walker Bynum, *Fragmentation and Redemption: Essays on Gender and the Human Body in Medieval Religion*, New York, Zone Books, 1992, pp. 151–79; p. 151.

16 For a different call to rethink some of the fundamental premises of

James's theory, see Rubin, op. cit., p. 271: 'Mervyn James' seminal article places the social body at the centre; I believe the time has come for its decentring.' Rubin argues that the sheer variety of meanings available for 'body' in the Middle Ages makes unified and essential significations untenable: different social groupings related to the concept of 'body' very differently, and thus members of medieval audiences would have had very different responses to dramatic themes and subjects (p. 270). The evidence of medieval legal historians suggests that individuals in the late fourteenth and fifteenth centuries did not wholly see themselves as defined by incorporation in the body politic: see Susan Reynolds, 'The idea of the corporation in western Christendom before 1300', in J. A. Guy and H. G. Beale (eds) *Law and Social Change in British History. Papers presented to the Bristol Legal History Conference, 14–17 July 1981*, London, Royal Historical Society, and New Jersey, Humanities Press, 1984, pp. 27–33.

17 See Martha C. Howell, 'Citizenship and gender: women's political status in northern medieval cities', in Mary Erler and Maryanne Kowaleski (eds) *Women and Power in the Middle Ages*, Athens and London, University of Georgia Press, 1988, pp. 37–60. Howell, although she warns against reading the evidence from one town generally (p. 50), argues that changes in the political meaning of citizenship meant that it was redefined to make it directly and indirectly equivalent to access to rule; after the 1370s fewer women sought or were granted guild membership, and there was a correspondingly large fall in the proportion of women registering as citizens in the late fourteenth century in northern cities just when, in theory, citizenship was expanded to include *all* residents: see pp. 47–8. See also Judith M. Bennett's observations on women's exclusion from power in 'Public power and authority in the medieval English countryside', in Erler and Kowaleski, op. cit., pp. 18–36; p. 29.

18 Martha Howell, *Women, Production and Patriarchy in Late Medieval Cities*, Chicago and London, Chicago University Press, 1986.

19 ibid., p. 43.

20 James, op. cit., p. 19.

21 Quoted ibid., p. 11, n. 36.

22 ibid., p. 18. See also William Tydeman, *The Theatre in the Middle Ages*, Cambridge, New York and Melbourne, Cambridge University Press, 1978, p. 234.

23 See Carolyn Dinshaw, 'Quarrels, rivals and rape: Gower and Chaucer', in Dor, op. cit., pp. 112–22; p. 115. Dinshaw derives her argument from René Girard's analysis of the process of 'violent undifferentiation' which precedes the rivalry between men. It is tempting to see here also an example of Eve Sedgwick's 'homosocial bonds', a reworking of the 'erotic triangles' theorised by Freud and René Girard, although in order to perform the Sedgwickean trick of enabling male homosocial bonds the woman must be present, and in this case she is not: see Eve Kosofsky Sedgwick, 'Homosocial desire', in *Between Men: English Literature and Male Homosexual Desire*, New York, Columbia University Press, 1985, pp. 1–5; and ch. 1, 'Gender asymmetry and erotic triangles', pp. 21–7; on medieval honour cultures, see Mervyn James, *English Politics and the*

Concept of Honor, Past and Present, Supplement 3, Oxford, Oxford University Press, 1978.

24 For an account of women's roles in guilds, see Maryanne Kowaleski and Judith M. Bennett, 'Crafts, gilds and women in the Middle Ages: fifty years after Marian K. Dale', in Judith M. Bennett, Elizabeth A. Clark, Jean F. O'Barr, B. Anne Vilen and Sarah Westphal-Wihl (eds) *Sisters and Workers in the Middle Ages*, Chicago and London, University of Chicago Press, 1989, pp. 11–38. They argue that in most English towns women did *not* organise into guilds; they were taught to have strong identities as members of families but weak identities as workers. Evidence that women did or did not produce the plays is virtually non-existent, but this does not necessarily argue that they were not involved; for a summary of the evidence that women did not act in the plays, see Meg Twycross, ' "Transvestism" in the mystery plays', *Medieval English Theatre*, 1983, vol. 5, no. 2, pp. 123–80, especially pp. 124–34. See also Richard Rastall, 'Female roles in all-male casts', *Medieval English Theatre*, 1985, vol. 7, no. 1, pp. 25–51, and Lynette R. Muir, 'Women on the medieval stage: the evidence from France', *Medieval English Theatre*, 1985, vol. 7, no. 2, pp. 107–19.

25 Beadle, op. cit., pp. 315–23, 'XXXV The Pinners: *The Crucifixion*'.

26 The stretching of Christ's limbs to fit the cross is found in each of the extant English cycles and in the N-Town play. The drilling of holes in the cross to the wrong size was part of the late medieval devotional tradition, and is a detail found also in the Chester *Passion* pageant: see V. A. Kolve, *The Play Called Corpus Christi*, Stanford, Stanford University Press, 1966, p. 188; p. 190; see also the reference by Margery Kempe in Sanford Brown Meech and Hope Emily Allen (eds) with prefatory note by Hope Emily Allen, *The Book of Margery Kempe*, Early English Text Society, OS 212, London, Oxford University Press, 1940, p. 192; 'Than sey sche wyth hyr gostly eye how þe Jewys festenyd ropis on þe oþer hand, for þe senwys & veynys wer so schrynkyn wyth peyne þat it myth not come to þe hole þat þei had morkyn þerfor, & drowyn þeron to makyn it mete wyth þe hole.' On the emphasis on Christ's suffering in late medieval piety, see Douglas Gray, *Themes and Images in the Medieval English Religious Lyric*, London and Boston, Routledge & Kegan Paul, 1972, p. 125.

27 Cf. Ashley, 'Cultural approaches', op. cit., p. 66; 'The Passion sequences of the four cycles . . . dramatize the ordeal of Christ in significantly distinctive ways. Chester's emphasis on his divine power minimises his human vulnerability, while Towneley's interest in larger-than-life evil characters is quite different from York's complex portrayal of political and legal institutions.'

28 Elizabeth Grosz, 'Inscriptions and body-maps: representations and the corporeal', in Terry Threadgold and Anne Cranny-Francis (eds) *Feminine/Masculine and Representation*, Sydney, Wellington, London and Winchester, Mass., Allen & Unwin, 1990, pp. 62–74; p. 71.

29 Bynum's best-known work in this area is represented by her critique of the work of the Renaissance art historian Leo Steinberg, in her essay, 'The body of Christ in the later Middle Ages: a reply to Leo Steinberg', in Bynum, *Fragmentation*, op. cit., pp. 79–117, and by her book, *Jesus as*

Mother: Studies in the Spirituality of the High Middle Ages, Berkeley, University of California Press, 1982. See also Jennifer Ash, 'The discursive construction of Christ's body in the later Middle Ages: resistance and autonomy', in Threadgold and Cranny-Francis, op. cit., pp. 75–105. Ash refers briefly to Corpus Christi and the cycle plays in a context that suggests possibilities for a semiotic reading of the gendered valences of Christ's body in the drama: see p. 81.

30 Travis, op. cit., p. 71.

31 Beadle, op. cit., pp. 315–23, 'XXXV The Pinners: *The Crucifixion*', lines 73–6; all references to this pageant henceforth are to the line numbers of this edition, and will subsequently appear in the text.

32 See Bynum, ' "... And woman his humanity" ': '*Male* and *female* were contrasted and asymmetrically valued as intellect/body, active/passive, rational/irrational, reason/emotion, self-control/lust, judgment/mercy and order/disorder' (p. 151); McLaughlin, 'Gender paradox', p. 149. Such dualistic thinking was by no means universal, nor did it necessarily give rise to a monolithic politics of the body; as Caroline Walker Bynum's work demonstrates, medieval thinkers often produced and conceptualised the body heterogeneously, even when drawing on soul/body, inner/outer distinctions: see also Jocelyn Wogan-Browne's detailed reading of concepts of the body in medieval anchoritic treatises: Jocelyn Price, ' "Inner" and "Outer": conceptualising the body in *Ancrene Wisse* and Ælred's *De institutione inclusarum*', in Gregory Kratzman and James Simpson (eds) *Medieval English Religious and Ethical Literature: Essays in Honour of G. H. Russell*, Cambridge, D. S. Brewer, 1986, pp. 192–208.

33 Hildegard of Bingen, *Liber Divinorum Operum*, bk 1, ch. 4, para. 100, J. P. Migne (ed.) *Patrologiae Cursus Competus: Series Latina*, Paris, 1844–64, vol. 197, col. 885, quoted in Bynum, *Fragmentation*, pp. 171–2. On the significance of Hildegard's binary opposition for an understanding of the various medieval theological representations of the humanity of Christ, see Bynum, *Fragmentation*, op. cit., pp. 98 and 171–2.

34 Caroline Walker Bynum, 'The female body and religious practice in the later Middle Ages', in Bynum, *Fragmentation*, op. cit., pp. 181–238; p. 220.

35 Bynum, 'The body of Christ in the later Middle Ages', in Bynum, *Fragmentation*, op. cit., p. 108.

36 See Bynum, *Fragmentation*, op. cit., p. 195; see also McLaughlin, 'Gender paradox', for an interesting discussion of early fifth-century theological debates over the humanity of Christ, in particular Rufinus's use of gender-paradoxes to counter Origen's extreme scorn 'for the "fleshiness" of earthly bodies' (pp. 149–50).

37 Thus, for example, Galen, in the following paraphrase by Thomas Laqueur: 'Women ... are inverted, and hence less perfect, men. They have exactly the same organs but in exactly the wrong places': Thomas Laqueur, *Making Sex: Body and Gender from the Greeks to Freud*, Cambridge, Mass. and London, Harvard University Press, 1990, p. 26. Laqueur's impressive scholarly and theoretically informed analysis of the medieval 'one-sex' model of the body offers stimulating new interpretations of the body which enable a retheorising of historical relationships between sex and gender. For some examples of the Middle English

gynaecological texts attributed to 'Trotula', and some commentary on their particular constructions of female physiology, see Alexandra Barratt (ed.) *Women's Writing in Middle English*, Harlow and New York, Longman, 1992, pp. 27–39.

38 Grosz, op. cit., p. 74.

39 Christ's silence is traditional; it is a feature of all the extant plays of the Passion sequence, and is usually read as an index of his infinite patience: see Christine Richardson and Jackie Johnston, *Medieval Drama*, Basingstoke and London, Macmillan, 1991, p. 68.

40 See Michael Swanton (ed.) *The Dream of the Rood*, Manchester and New York, Manchester University Press and Barnes and Noble, 1970, and Michael Swanton, *English Literature Before Chaucer*, Harlow, Longman, 1987, p. 98.

41 Prov. 7:10–11, quoted in the modern English version in Robert P. Miller (ed.) *Chaucer: Sources and Backgrounds*, New York, Oxford University Press, 1977, p. 404.

42 See R. Howard Bloch, *Medieval Misogyny and the Invention of Western Romantic Love*, Chicago and London, Chicago University Press, 1991, p. 21.

43 Based on Lam. 1:12, used in the Sarum Office for Good Friday, Matins, in primo Nocturno, lectio i: 'O vos omnes qui transitis per viam attendite et videte si est dolor sicut dolor meus': see Marion Glasscoe, 'Time of passion: latent relationships between liturgy and meditation in two Middle English mystics', in Helen Phillips (ed.) *Langland, the Mystics, and the Medieval English Religious Tradition*, Cambridge, D. S. Brewer, 1990, pp. 141–60; pp. 149–50.

44 This prohibition derives ultimately from St Paul (1 Cor. 14.34–35): 'Let women keep silence in the churches: for it is not permitted them to speak, but to be subject, as also the law saith. But if they would learn anything, let them ask their husbands at home', and see also Paul's words to Timothy (1 Tim. 2.11–12): 'But I suffer not a woman to teach, nor to use authority over the man: but to be in silence': see Carolyn Dinshaw, *Chaucer's Sexual Poetics*, Madison, University of Wisconsin Press, 1989, p. 19, for further discussion of male clerical anxiety about women speaking, and see also Julia Long (this volume, p. 101). Medieval theology held that women were incapable of the priesthood because of their carnal pollution: 'the inferior female body . . . [was] prohibited from representing God': Bynum, 'The female body', op. cit., pp. 215–18.

45 Ash discusses how the body of Christ in a range of Middle English texts (such as Rolle's *Meditations on the Passion, The Book of Margery Kempe* and the anonymous *Wohunge of Ure Lauerd*) is not only the object of worship but also the object of desire: 'The bleeding wounds are privileged, invested with meaning which is not only salvific but also erotic': Ash, 'Discursive construction', p. 82. In his controversial essay in *Seminar XX, Encore,* 'God and the *Jouissance* of the woman', Jacques Lacan attempts to theorise female sexuality in terms of a *jouissance* beyond the phallus, and finds support for this idea in female mystics' erotic desire for Christ/God: see Juliet Mitchell and Jacqueline Rose (eds) *Feminine Sexuality: Jacques Lacan and the école freudienne*, trans. Jacqueline Rose, Basingstoke and London, Macmillan, 1982, pp. 137–48,

esp. pp. 146–7. For a very different perspective on medieval desire for, and identification with, Christ, see David Herlihy, 'The making of the medieval family: symmetry, structure and sentiment', *Journal of Family History*, 1983, vol. 8, no. 2, pp. 116–30.

46 A debate about medieval sexualities, and about the extent to which 'sexuality' is an exclusively modern cultural construct, has been opened up in a recent issue of *Medieval Feminist Newsletter*, with contributions from E. Ann Matter, Simon Gaunt, Carolyn Dinshaw, Sylvia Huot, Susan Schibanoff and Mary Anne Campbell: see 'Forum: gay and lesbian concerns in medieval studies', *MFN*, 1992, vol. 13, pp. 1–15.

47 Travis, op. cit., p. 72.

48 ibid., p. 72. On the Lacanian *corps morcelé*, see Jacques Lacan, 'The mirror stage as formative of the function of the I as revealed in psycho-analytic experience', in Jacques Lacan, *Ecrits: A Selection*, trans. Alan Sheridan, London, Tavistock Publications, 1977, pp. 1–7, esp. pp. 4–5: 'The *mirror stage* is a drama whose internal thrust is precipitated from insufficiency to anticipation – and which manufactures for the subject . . . the succession of phantasies that extends from a fragmented body-image to a form of its totality that I shall call orthopaedic – and, lastly, to the assumption of the armour of an alienating identity. . . . This moment when the mirror-stage comes to an end inaugurates . . . the dialectic that will henceforth link the *I* to socially elaborated situations.'

49 See Grosz, op. cit., esp. p. 63, and pp. 68–71. See also Elaine Scarry, *The Body in Pain: The Making and Unmaking of the World*, New York, Oxford University Press, 1985.

50 See above, n. 27.

51 Michel Foucault, *Discipline and Punish: The Birth of the Prison*, trans. Alan Sheridan, Harmondsworth, Penguin Books, 1977, pp. 25–6. For a convincing feminist appropriation of Foucault's work, see Chris Weedon, *Feminist Practice and Poststructuralist Theory*, Oxford and New York, Blackwell, 1987. Foucault's analysis of power needs to be emphatically differentiated from that in which a single institution is seen as the repressive force; rather, such analysis requires that one attend to histori-cally specific forms of power, often dispersed across several institutions and with no single, all-encompassing 'cause'. For an interesting non-Foucauldian analysis of the N-Town cycle in terms of the repressive mechanisms of the late medieval legal system, see Lynn Squires, 'Law and disorder in *Ludus Coventriae*', in Clifford Davidson *et al.* (eds) *The Drama of the Middle Ages: Comparative and Critical Essays*, New York, A. M. S. Press, 1982, pp. 272–85: 'the trial and punishment of Christ is carried out specifically within the jurisdiction and following the proce-dures of the fifteenth-century court of common law. In other words, Englishmen watched themselves try, condemn, and crucify Christ. . . . Not only did Christ die *for* them but also *because* of them – as a victim of their own courts of law': p. 273.

52 Grosz, op. cit., p. 67.

53 See M. C. Spalding, *The Middle English Charters of Christ*, Bryn Mawr College Monographs, Bryn Mawr, Pa., Bryn Mawr Library, 1914; Rose-mary Woolf, *The English Mystery Plays*, London, Routledge & Kegan Paul, 1972, pp. 210–14; Gray, op. cit., pp. 129–30, 269–70, and plate 5;

Andrew Breeze, 'The Charter of Christ in medieval English, Welsh and Irish', *Celtica*, 1987, vol. 19, pp. 111–20. See also F. J. Furnivall (ed.) *The Minor Poems of the Vernon MS*, vol. 2, Early English Text Society, OS 117, London, Oxford University Press, 1902, pp. 637–57.

54 Breeze, op. cit., p. 111.

55 MS Downside 26452, f. 141v. I am grateful to Nicholas Watson of the University of Western Ontario for this reference, and for allowing me access to his transcription. The editing of the text is my own.

56 Geoffrey Shepherd (ed.) *Ancrene Wisse: Parts Six and Seven*, Manchester and New York, Manchester University Press and Barnes and Noble, 1972, p. 21: 'On ende he com him seoluen & brohte þe godspel as leattres iopenet & wrat wið his ahne blod saluz to his leofmon.'

57 Karma Lochrie, *Margery Kempe and Translations of the Flesh*, Philadelphia, University of Pennsylvania Press, 1991, pp. 167–73.

58 Breeze, op. cit., p. 111. Closely related to the Charter tradition is a literary type known as Christ's Last Will and Testament: the Testaments do not use the metaphor of Christ's body as a written document, but they nevertheless, in their use of legal language, associate Christ with a powerful, authoritative mode of *writing*, as opposed to orality. A good example of such a Testament is found in Deguileville's *Le Pèlerinage de la vie humaine*; see Avril Henry (ed.) *The Pilgrymage of the Lyfe of the Manhode*, Early English Text Society, OS 228, Oxford and New York, Oxford University Press, 1985, vol. 1, Introduction and Text, ll. 1340–1412. I am grateful to Catherine Bore, of the University of East Anglia, for this reference. Another literary and iconographical topos found widely in English vernacular religious and devotional texts of the fourteenth and fifteenth centuries and relevant to the representation of Christ in the York pageant is that of 'the picture of Christ crucified', in which the body of the crucified Christ is, according to Vincent Gillespie, 'repeatedly described as a book which can be perused by those who have acquired the grammar and syntax of this branch of meditation': see Vincent Gillespie, 'Strange images of death: the Passion in later medieval English devotional and mystical writing', *Analecta Cartusiana*, 1987, vol. 117, no. 3, pp. 111–59; p. 111. Gillespie cites Rolle's use of the metaphor: 'Now, swete Jhesu, graunt me to rede upon þy boke, and somwhate to undrestond þe swetnes of þat writynge, and to have likynge in studious abydynge of þat redynge': H. E. Allen (ed.), *English Writings of Richard Rolle*, Oxford, Oxford University Press, 1931, p. 36. On the question of which social groups were able to participate in this devotional and meditative mode of 'reading' the 'grammar' of Christ's body, see Vincent Gillespie, '*Lukynge in haly bukes: Lectio* in some late medieval spiritual miscellanies', *Analecta Cartusiana*, 1984, vol. 106, no. 2, pp. 1–27: 'Nuns, anchoresses and recluses had always been assumed to possess a less fully developed capacity for independent reading and meditation' (p. 4). I am grateful to Nicholas Watson of the University of Western Ontario, for the references to the articles by Gillespie.

59 Grosz, op. cit., p. 70.

60 Bynum, *Fragmentation*, pp. 186–8.

61 Lochrie, op. cit., p. 168.

62 On the medieval gendering of writing as masculine and writing surfaces

as feminine, and on medieval literary activity as a set of gendered processes, see Dinshaw, op. cit., pp. 9–27, esp. p. 17 and n. 36. See also Eugene Vance's comments about 'the link between carnal desire and reading' and 'Paul's equation of carnal circumcision with the *textuality* of the Law itself and with the *letter* of that text of stone': Eugene Vance, *Mervelous Signals: Poetics and Sign Theory in the Middle Ages*, Lincoln and London, University of Nebraska Press, 1986, pp. 8–9.

63 See Grosz, op. cit., p. 66 for further problematising of the material body, see Butler, *Gender Trouble* and Butler, *Bodies that Matter*.

64 See Pieter Spierenburg, *The Spectacle of Suffering: Executions and the Evolution of Repression: From a Preindustrial Metropolis to the European Experience*, Cambridge, New York and Melbourne, Cambridge University Press, 1984, p. 44: 'Too little evidence is available to say with certainty that staging played a lesser part in medieval executions. There is hardly any detailed account of the practice of punishment in the fourteenth and fifteenth centuries.' See also Barbara Hanawalt, 'Violent death in fourteenth- and early fifteenth-century England', *Comparative Studies in Society and History*, 1976, vol. 18, pp. 297–320.

65 Foucault, op. cit., p. 8. For a valuable critique of the Eurocentric assumptions underpinning Foucault's chronological progression from 'torture' to 'punishment' to 'discipline', see Page DuBois, *Torture and Truth*, New York and London, Routledge, 1991, pp. 153–4.

66 Quoted in David Wallace, ' "Whan she translated was": a Chaucerian critique of the Petrarchan Academy', in Lee Patterson (ed.) *Literary Practice and Social Change in Britain, 1380–1530*, Berkeley, Los Angeles and Oxford, University of California Press, 1990, pp. 156–215; p. 208.

67 On the mystical and affective devotional tradition of meditation on the Passion, see Glasscoe, 'Time of passion', pp. 141–60.

68 Foucault, op. cit., p. 209.

69 For the formulation of this point I am very much indebted to Emily Martin, 'Body narratives, body boundaries', in Lawrence Grossberg, Cary Nelson, Paula Treichler (eds) with Linda Baughman and assistance from John Macgregor Wise, *Cultural Studies*, New York and London, Routledge, 1992, pp. 409–23.

70 On the Skimmington ride, see Lisa Jardine, *Still Harping on Daughters: Women and Drama in the Age of Shakespeare*, Brighton, Harvester, 1983, pp. 116–17.

71 The unique copy of the whole text appears in Oxford, Bodley MS. Add. A.42 (Bodleian Summary Catalogue, S.C. 30149), ff. 1r–30r (Jolliffe 0.35). According to the Bodleian *Summary Catalogue*, it was copied in the early sixteenth century, although in the opinion of Nicholas Watson the text is almost certainly fifteenth century. The text has not yet appeared in published form.

7 Lady Holy Church and Meed the Maid: re-envisioning female personifications in *Piers Plowman*

Colette Murphy

I

The very canonical security of some texts seems to preclude any re-examination of how we read them. *Piers Plowman*, a work which occupies an important place in courses on medieval English literature, seems not to have been the subject of any feminist readings. But then the fair field of Langland studies has not attracted the kinds of critical discussions and theoretical contests which have been played out in the field of Chaucer criticism.[1] As David Aers has pointed out, the dominant trend in twentieth-century readings of *Piers Plowman* has been to see the poem (or rather poems) as the vehicle of religious orthodoxy, and as the production of a politically conservative writer.[2] This is not a reading which would necessarily coincide with that of its earliest audiences: evidence of the early reception of *Piers Plowman* would suggest, as Aers has shown, that its representation of issues concerning ecclesiastical and political power was reclaimed as dissident and/or orthodox depending on the context in which it was being read. And, as part of his efforts to open up the modern reception of Langland's work, Aers himself has argued, both in theory and in practice, for critical approaches to the poem which take more account of the cultural conditions in which it was produced and received (and, by implication, continues to be received). As he notes:

> The generation of meaning and individual experience cannot be understood apart from the social relations of a specific community, its organisation of power manifest in the prevailing arrangements of class, gender, political rule, religion, armed force, and not infrequently race. So any reading that hopes to have relevance to a particular text must include an attempt to relocate

it in the web of discourses and social practices within which it was made and which determined its horizons.[3]

It is high time for issues of sexual politics and gender representation to be incorporated into the field of Langland criticism, and the essay which follows constitutes a first foray into reading *Piers Plowman* from a feminist perspective. I will discuss the ways in which the male dreamer imagines/images two female figures who loom over his first vision, Lady Holy Church and Meed the Maid, and examine some of the languages (or discourses) of femininity used in their representation. In particular I will tease out some of the implications of the gender/class alignments used in the dramatic representation of these two figures.[4] This choice of focus does not imply that feminists reading Langland's work should confine their discussion to its female protagonists alone (the 'for gender read women' approach). Rather, this line of inquiry simply seems to offer a useful and obvious way of opening up the discussion of the engendering processes (the formation of masculine and feminine identities) which permeate the dreamer's visions and ways of knowing (and necessarily those of his readers, past and present too).

Texts which use personifications are of particular interest for feminist readers precisely because they reveal how notions of masculinity and femininity permeate the conceptualising process. One way of defining personification would be to see it as 'the translation whereby things absent, abstract, inanimate, are made human and present'.[5] In narratives which make sustained use of processes of personification the meaning of 'abstract' nouns is often investigated through their embodiment in systems of socialised relations. The process of personification is one which necessarily makes connections between the belief systems of a society and its social practices, and in fact frequently uses the former to illuminate the latter. As Lavinia Griffiths has observed:

> personification allegories set up equations which allow for a bridging of temporal textual and ontological gaps. They see abstract intellectual systems – cosmology, ethics, logic, history – in terms of human relations.[6]

But that act of 'seeing' is not neutral: it is affected by the ways in which human relations are perceived to be organised, in social theory and practice, in the writer's own time and culture (and by the text's readers too). Thus although personifications are certainly 'linguistic phenomena' whose 'nature is governed by linguistic

factors like gender', as Lavinia Griffiths points out, they are also
social, historical and cultural phenomena, and there is a gender
'agenda', in a broader sense, in personification allegories (not only
in narrative poems such as *Piers Plowman*, but also in works of
drama) which has attracted little attention from critics of medieval
English literature to date.[7]

General studies of the uses of personification and/or allegory
which include some discussion of the gender politics of such modes
of representation are difficult to find. Marina Warner's historical
survey of the use of female forms to embody abstract ideals and
concepts, *Monuments and Maidens: The Allegory of the Female
Form*, offers a useful backdrop to my particular line of discussion
here.[8] In Warner's view, there is a discrepancy between the apparent
usefulness of the female form in the symbolic realm and the limitations on the roles women can actually perform in the material
world which deserves further discussion. She observes that '[o]ften
the recognition of a difference between the symbolic order,
inhabited by ideal, allegorical figures and the actual order, of judges,
statesmen, soldiers, philosophers, inventors, depends on the unlikeli-
hood of women practising the concepts they represent'.[9] Although
Warner's discussion does not probe very deeply into the reasons
why this should be so, she does draw attention to the complexity of
the issue. As she observes, many abstract nouns of virtue, knowledge, spirituality are feminine in gender in Greek and Latin and in
the languages which derive/borrow from them, but 'the relations of
linguistic gender and society are extremely hard to describe and the
interaction is certainly not straightforward'.[10] The question of what
determines the gender of an 'embodied' abstract concept in the
works of writers past and present is not answered in Warner's
study, but her analysis does avoid setting up simplistic causative
models.

In contrast, Helen Cooper takes a more grammatically determin-
istic line in her discussion 'Gender and personification in *Piers
Plowman*', an essay which sketches out some of the precedents for
the personifying traditions with which Langland is working.[11] For
Cooper it is *because* 'most abstract nouns, in Latin and in the
Romance languages, are of a feminine gender' that 'when a writer
imagines them, gives them mental form, the personification is inevitably feminine', which in turn 'invites further attributes of female-
ness'.[12] Cooper's argument is that Langland is liberated from these
grammatical constraints on personifying ideals and abstract concepts
because 'in the last century before Langland wrote, English had lost

the last traces of its Germanic gender structure'. However, she observes that 'given the freedom to choose what sexual form his personifications will take, over and over again it is the male of the species that [Langland] chooses'.[13] Ultimately, Cooper suggests that Langland's preponderance of masculine personifications reflects a wider cultural constraint, that of the 'patriarchal structure of dominance of his time', but if cultural constraints can operate on the process of personification in *Piers Plowman*, why should they not do so with or without the presence of grammatical factors too?[14] Grammatical gender, as Lavinia Griffiths points out, 'does not always determine the sex of the personification', and, of course, personifications themselves can slip and shift between male and female forms within texts as well as between texts.[15] The 'grammatical' model of explaining why some abstract nouns are envisioned in female rather than male bodies is not 'sufficient' in itself: it seems to me that any examination of texts which use personifications must take into account the multiple and contradictory resonances of notions of masculinity and femininity in circulation in the society in which the test was produced and is received.

The whole issue of how and why abstract ideas and concepts are embodied in one form rather than another is a very complex and challenging one about which there is a good deal more to be said, in theory and in practice. As I have indicated, my focus here will be specific, rather than general, and will concentrate on the representation of the two major female personifications in *Piers Plowman*. I am not going to suggest (against Helen Cooper's line of argument) that we can discern a radical policy on gender at work in the dream-vision sequence of *Piers Plowman*, but rather that certain tensions in contemporary attitudes towards women's positions in society and the perceived value of the feminine form can be traced in the protagonists and processes of the Dreamer's visions. The co-ordination of selected female forms/bodies with registers of social rank and status produce some interesting female personae whose role and significance cannot be accommodated within any simple binary opposition of 'good' and 'bad' categories. I will argue that in the Dreamer's encounter with Lady Holy Church we can trace certain tensions in the masculine perception of an idealised body of the Church in female form;[16] in the story of the marital fortunes of the more mobile figure of Meed the Maid we can see how the reward-dynamic of contemporary society is apprehended by the Dreamer. Meed seems to embody at various stages both the dynamic of a reward-based society and its most common currency:

material gifts and money. That she embodies an antithetical social order to that of Lady Holy Church and/or represents a lower social class are interpretations which depend on whose 'version' of Meed is being represented at any particular time in the Dreamer's vision. Her changing form (from, for example, illegitimate rich maid to legitimate 'muliere' to common whore) is an index of the contested definition of her proper name.[17] In the story of the changing marital prospects of this very much man-made object of desire, no less than in the story of Lady Holy Church, we can see something of the operations of the traffic in reward in the Dreamer's society and something, too, of his society's 'traffic in women'.[18]

II

In the opening sequence of *Piers Plowman* we are presented with a Dreamer who falls asleep to the murmuring sounds of a brook and who enters a dreamscape strikingly different from the conditions of his waking life. The Dreamer, in his waking life, appears to be of indeterminate social status. He wanders on the Malvern Hills with no precise object in mind, and his identity is made more obscure by the clothes he wears in preparation for his 'adventure':

> In a somer seson, whan softe was the sonne,
> I shoop me into shroudes as I a sheep were,
> In habite as an heremite unholy of werkes,
> Went wide in this world wondres to here.

> (I, 1–4)

Is the Dreamer a sheep or a shepherd? How can he be 'unholy of werkes' and do hermit's work in any case?[19]

The Dreamer in waking seems to have opted out of society only to be confronted with that society when he begins to dream. But the ambiguity which is attached to this figure in his waking world may seem to disappear when he is inside his vision. There, at least, he seems to be empowered as an observer of society and can evaluate the groups in the fair field of folk according to his value system (ploughmen at the top and pardoners at the bottom). He can change his dreaming scenario too: when the Dreamer is angered by the constant money-changing in the field and frustrated by the disguises which money can buy (Prologue, 75), he closes down the field and, through a series of puns on the word 'cardinal' (which allows a brief glimpse at the sources of papal power – Prologue, 100–111), switches the context from one depicting medieval mercantilism at work to one which shows how society is organised feudally, with the king, knighthood and the clergy in control. Yet just at the point when he promises to decipher his vision and its parameters, his role as dream guide and reader is displaced by the appearance of an authoritative figure, a Lady from Truth's castle:

What this mountaigne bymeneth and the merke dale
And the feld ful of folk, I shal yow faire shewe.
A lovely lady of leere in lynnen yclothed
Cam doun from [the] castel and called me faire,
And seide, 'Sone, slepestow? Sestow this peple –
How bisie they ben aboute the maze?
The mooste partie of this peple that passeth on this erthe,
Have thei worship in this world, thei wilne no bettre;
Of oother hevene than here holde thei no tale.'
I was afered of hire face, theigh she faire weere,
And seide, 'Mercy, Madame, what [may] this [be] to mene?'

(I, 1–11)

This authoritative figure seems to have the potential to play the conventional role of enlightener and dream guide to the Dreamer, though her effect in practice is to draw the Dreamer's attention to all that he should, but does not, know.

There are, of course, many literary precedents for the use of a female figure as a dream guide. In other visionary texts, from the medieval and classical period, the female guide figure may function as the arbiter of the themes of a work; she may operate as a judge in the debates which arise; she may embody the male protagonist's aspirations and desires.[20] When the figure of the authoritative Lady appears in the opening lines of Passus 1 all of these potential structural and thematic functions are invoked in her wake. There are, too, longstanding traditions in Christian culture of representing the figure of the Church in female form. By the fourteenth century, as Marina Warner has shown in her study of the iconography of the female form, the realisation of the figure of the Church as the Bride of Christ and as Mother Church had considerable currency in the imagistic repertoire of Western Christianity:

According to theology ... every member of the Church, of Ecclesia, partook of her essence in the here and now, was incorporated into her body, the mystical body of the eternally renewed Christ, and re-lived his re-capitulated redemption, through the ritual of the Mass and sacrament of the Eucharist. Through each year's liturgical re-enactment every believer experienced the cycle of his life, and so ingested the wisdom of God, itself alive in the world through his foundation, the Holy Church.[21]

Furthermore, as a figure who seems to embody the wisdom of God the Lady appears to provide the answers to the Dreamer's desire to find meaning in his dream-landscape.[22] The Dreamer's idealistic search for truth appears to have been given legitimate expression in his encounter with Lady Holy Church, as she makes possible a level of interpretation in the text where eternal values can be discussed. Her discourse, at once clerical and metaphorical, strikes such a different note from what has gone before that she may appear to offer the alternative to the material and quotidien contradictions inherent in society. In imagining the Church in personified form, the Dreamer seems to be registering the need to communicate with the most important guide available to him as a Christian. In imagining the Church in the form of a female personification, he seems to be registering his desire to communicate with a figure of the Church who is apart from the male-dominated body of the Church as it manifests itself to him in actual social practice in his waking world (which he has represented in such a critical light in the Prologue). But in the Dreamer's difficult encounter with this visionary female guide, we may trace a lesson in the problems of a masculine projection of ideals in an idealised female form.

It is significant that the Dreamer does not initially recognise the Lady in personal terms. The authority of the 'lovely lady of leere in lynnen yclothed' (I, 3) is signalled by her social orientation as an inhabitant of the fixed and stable castle, and it is with an overwhelming sense of her 'otherness' (in class and gender terms) that the Dreamer begins his dialogue ('I was afered of hire face, theigh she faire weere' I, 10). However, it seems that Lady Holy Church's power as an effective visionary guide for the Dreamer begins to be undermined as soon as he finds out her name and begs for her grace (I, 71–9). At this point, Lady Holy Church appeals to the Dreamer's earlier acquaintance with her:

'Holi Chirche I am,' quod she, 'thow oughtest me to knowe.
I underfeng thee first and the feith taughte.
Thow broughtest me borwes my biddyng to fulfille,
And to loven me leelly the while thi lif dureth.'

                                                            (I, 75–8)

Here the female personification of the Church begins to be mobilised in this depiction of the Baptismal relationship between the Church and its members in terms of a relationship between a mother and her son (a point already anticipated in Lady Holy Church's first address to the Dreamer as 'sone' – I, 5). Here, in effect, Lady Holy Church asks why the Dreamer has not recognised her, since she has an important place in his society, and draws attention to the spiritual and sacramental relationship with the Church (which has not been accounted for in the representation of ecclesiastical practices in the Prologue). Already, then, we may observe a discrepancy between the perception the Dreamer has of Lady Holy Church in an idealised female form excluded, it seems, from his everyday life and the Lady's view of herself, which insists on her spiritual reality and her social immanence.

What is almost comic about the Dreamer's response, at this point, is his stubborn refusal to see this Lady as having a social base: he chooses to discuss his personal salvation ('How may I save my soul that seint art holden?' – I, 84) as if his relationship with the Church were an entirely private affair. His guide, however, does not allow this visionary journey to become simply a personal quest. In her constant recapitulation of the idea that truth is the best treasure, she links this analogy with the feudal model of social organisation and thus explains, in gradational terms, how earth's hierarchies should be connected to their spiritual counterparts (I, 95–136).[23] The Lady insists that social morality is central to the search for salvation. One of the powerful functions of this Lady Holy Church, then, is to insist on the link between the individual and society, on the link between the activities of the 'fair field of folk' and those of the individual, on the link between social politics and personal politics.

Although Lady Holy Church avoids answering the Dreamer's question about salvation in the way he expects, she does, in fact, answer him. If a person wishes to save their soul, it is not dreaming that will help. Time and time again Lady Holy Church tells the Dreamer he must act (I, 13, 89, 147). Lady Holy Church emphasises that the Dreamer's vision is socially determined yet fictional; as is her representation within it. The 'real' Church is not female, nor perfected, any more than 'real' Christians are likely to find their salvation by merely dreaming. Even when Lady Holy Church does insist on the primacy of personal choice, the Dreamer seems not to understand her. He asks:

> Ac the moneie of this mold that men so faste holdeth –
> Telleth me to whom that tresour appendeth.

(I, 44–5)

Repeating Christ's words 'Give to Caesar what is Caesar's and to God what is God's' (Matthew 22:21), Lady Holy Church suggests that the use of money is primarily a personal decision. The Dreamer, however, uses this answer as a pretext for deferring his choice on the grounds that his guide figure has not yet given him all the answers to his problems in ways he can understand.

The depiction of Holy Church in female form serves, then, a number of functions, but the tensions between them limit her usefulness as a guide figure. The 'otherness' of her aristocratic female form (in comparison with the Dreamer's male and marginal social identity) may suggest that she should represent an ideal (and idealised) form of the authority of the Church which is separate from the compromised male-hegemonic form which the Dreamer knows from his waking world. Yet, as I have pointed out, the words of Lady Holy Church continually direct the Dreamer's attention back to the manifested presence of the Church in his society (and as she does so, she undermines her power to represent the perfected Church in his eyes). But the 'otherness' of Lady Holy Church (the Dreamer recognises the ladylike beauty of her face, but fears it) may also signal the Dreamer's alienation from the body of the Church, and perhaps its mystifying effect on him. He cannot learn from her precisely because she does not connect up with his experience and thus the usefulness of this imagined, idealised, female guide seems to be circumscribed.[24]

By the time we get to the Dreamer's comment:

> Yet I have no kynde knowynge, ye mote kenne me bettre
> By what crafte in my cors it comseth ...

(I, 139–40)

it is clear that the Dreamer is finding it hard to understand the words of his guide: he needs to learn in a more practical experiential way, in terms more direct than the clerical and metaphorical language of Lady Church appears to allow. This estrangement from his dream guide is made explicit at the beginning of Passus II with the Dreamer's request that Lady Holy Church should 'Kenne me by som craft to knowe the false' (II, 4): the Dreamer appears to insist that he should learn through his experience – of which she is now a part rather than an alternative. Now the image of the idealised female figure, through whom the Dreamer had hoped to encounter perfected Truth, is set against another stereotyped image of femininity, that of Meed the Maid. Previously the Dreamer had asked his dream guide 'Telleth me to whom [the moneie of this mold] appendeth' (I, 44–5): now his question about ownership is rephrased in terms of ownership of a woman as he wonders of the woman 'wonderliche yclothed' whom he sees on his left side 'what she was and whos wif she weere' (II, 18). The answer, such as it is, comes in the form of a dramatised narrative sequence which explores who possesses and who has a right to possess Meed the Maid.[25]

III

In Passus I, the Dreamer idealises the female figure in an attempt to escape his social responsibilities and replace them with a species of individual fantasy, and is thwarted in his efforts. In Passus II, in contrast, he witnesses how other men in his society elevate another female figure. Both Lady Holy Church and Meed represent projections of male desire, although the desire for Meed seems to be more immediately recognisable by the Dreamer. When he sees Meed, he too is ravished by her appearance:

I loked on my left half as the Lady me taughte,
And was war of a womman wonderliche yclothed –
Purfiled with pelure, the pureste on erthe,
Ycorouned with a coroune, the Kyng hath noon bettre,
Fetisliche hire fyngres were fretted with gold wyr,
And thereon rede rubies as rede as any glede,
And diamaundes of derrest pris and double manere saphires,
Orientals and ewages envenymes to destroye.
Hire robe was ful riche, of reed scarlet engreyned,
With ribanes of reed gold and of riche stones.
Hire array me ravysshed, swich richesse saugh I nevere.

(II, 8–16)

In this arrangement of women, on the right and the left, Lady Holy Church and Meed the Maid, it seems as though the Dreamer is drawing on a cultural cliché, a version of the Mary/Eve opposition, to express and explore other kinds of antithetical values, spiritual and secular.[26] One kind of polarised binary opposition in circulation in his culture (the splitting of womankind into two opposed figures) provides him with a way into exploring other kinds of oppositions: the dichotomy between the operations of the heavenly economy of redemption and an earthly economy involving material reward appears to be aligned to the split between Lady Holy Church's world of guaranteed truth (alienating and mystifying though its language has proved to the Dreamer) and the context in which her rival Meed is ensconced. Yet the apprehension of a clear-cut division between these two women begins to break down as soon as more details about Meed are provided. Although in the eyes of some readers of the poem, Meed may seem to be fixed as 'a curious fusion of the Whore of Babylon and Richesse of the *Roman de la Rose*, Saint John's oriental vision of evil reclothed in courtly medieval splendour' (a view which might be encouraged by Lady Holy Church's description of her), Meed's role in the narrative has more complex resonances which undermine any simplistic oppositional distinctions between herself and Lady Holy Church and make the reading of these two figures a more demanding experience.[27] As I have suggested, there are already some equivocal aspects to Lady Holy Church's role in the vision, as guide figure, agent of answers and purveyor of mystification to the Dreamer. That she is the figure who invokes her apparent 'counter-image', Meed the Maid, could be read as a signal that she herself is bound up in the production of such a figure. Indeed the more Lady Holy Church says about Meed, the more her own idealisation is undermined; the relationship between these two figures is expressive of much more than a straightforward 'true/false' opposition.

At the beginning of her account of Meed in Passus II, Lady Holy Church stresses the difference between her status and that of Meed in lineal, feudal terms, and as she does so her own stance as a representative of, and spokesperson for, the feudal order becomes more apparent. She, Lady Holy Church, has a 'lemman' called Leautee, whereas Meed is a 'mayde', an unclaimed woman who lurks in the system as a threat to the truth of husbands (35–9).[28] Lady Holy Church contrasts her own legitimacy and superior social status, as a descendant of Truth, as a Lady from the Tower of Truth, with the illegitimacy of Meed's status, as a bastard (24) who 'naturally' takes after her father 'False' (27):[29]

'That is Mede the mayde,' quod she, 'hath noyed me ful ofte,
And ylakked my lemman that Leautee is hoten ...
In the Popes paleis she is as pryvee as myselve,
But sothnesse wolde noght so – for she is a bastard ...
I oughte ben hyere than [heo] – I kam of a bettre.

(II, 20–8)

The good tutor of the previous Passus now begins to express herself much more emotively as the situation becomes one of rivalry between two women and their respective marital fortunes: the attractions of breeding are pitted against other kinds of social capital. Meed seems, from Lady Holy Church's account of her, to represent simultaneously a destabilising dynamic (seductive materialism) which may disrupt the reproduction of feudal society and the hierarchical ordering of the Church (she circulates freely in the Pope's court) and the product of this destabilising dynamic: a female bastard-heir who excites the attention and attraction of many men and whose eligibility excites the anger, and to a certain extent the jealousy, of her 'better-bred' female rival. But when Lady Holy Church invokes her own legitimate feudal superiority over Meed as a means of distinguishing her moral supremacy over this 'other' woman, the implications of her argument rebound on her in ways which may draw our attention to the potential contradictions and limitations involved in representing the Church in the form of an aristocratic lady.

In describing her position as validated by her father, her lover, her potential husband, Lady Holy Church reveals that her authority in society is delegated and administered by men. It is clear that aristocratic ladies are not exempt from this patriarchal society's 'traffic in women'. According to her, God, her father, so loves her that he:

> ... hath yeven me Mercy to marie with myselve,
> And what man be merciful and leely me love
> Shal be my lord and I his leef in heighe heven;

> (II, 31–3)

Previously we have been invited to blame Meed for her bastardy, over which, after all, she has no control, condemn her for her lack of social status, and see her as a potential rival for Lady Holy Church's 'lemman' Leautee. Now we are being asked to accept the prospect of her apparent superior, Lady Holy Church, having another designated partner, 'Mercy', and of her being married off, in heaven at least, to anyone who shows mercy. Heaven's hierarchy does not seem to require the monogamous faithfulness whose absence on earth has constituted one of the main criticisms which Lady Holy Church has levelled at her rival. Although what is being signalled by Lady Holy Church's metaphor has a certain spiritual logic, the signifiers in the construct allow all kinds of ambiguities to develop so that the truth of her revelation itself begins to appear unstable.

The operations of the traffic in women are more starkly portrayed in the narrative sequences which chart Meed's marital career. If men are shown to be the 'natural' power-brokers in a feudal model of society, so are they too in a market-economy model. Meed appears to be the object of many men's desire (II, 55–62). Insofar as she is understood to represent material power, she appears to offer to men the chance to use her for their own social advancement to gain power which may be denied them by their lack of 'birth rights': thus she seems to be particularly attractive to the bourgeoisie, to merchants and, more ominously, to lawyers. In contrast to the 'treasure' which Lady Holy Church offers, ideally as a gift, which brings with it few earthly claims to precedence, Meed seems to represent a preferable kind of treasure which makes her highly eligible. In the marital arrangements of Meed we are shown the operations of the 'market' model in arranging familial and social relationships (a model which attracts further critical comments from the Dreamer at later stages in the poem):[30]

> ... Mede is ymaried more for hire goodes
> Than for any vertue or fairnesse or any free kynde.
> Falsnesse is fayn of hire for he woot hire riche;
>
> (II, 76–8)

The marriage charter which Simony and Civil Law read (II, 72–107) formally encodes the moral, economic and social breakdown which ensues from this match.

The use of a female figure to embody seductive materiality, which is just one way of understanding the function of Meed the Maid, is not Langland's innovation. As John A. Yunck has shown, some of the material dramatised in the marriage of Meed episode belongs to a longstanding tradition of 'venality satire' in which there are precedents for the personification of the concept of reward or, on some occasions, money itself, in female form (though male bodies are frequently used too).[31] Presumably, one of the attractions for (male/clerical) writers of the use of a female personification for 'reward' or 'money' is that it allows some of the clichés from the anti-feminist repertoire of representation to be recycled at the same time. The female sex is the sex particularly associated with the weaknesses of the flesh, and desires potentially stimulated by the female body are often projected back onto the female figure so that she is endowed with the ability to seduce and tempt: these are the kinds of anti-feminist clichés which can be taken up and used in venality satire, and they are, to some extent, made visible in the representation of Meed.[32] Male desire and its object (material and sexual) are embodied in a female personification who may, at the same time, actively 'seduce' the men around her. The affective/seductive quality of Meed is signalled by the Dreamer's response to her and amplified in the response of other men in her ambit. Thus, at a later stage in the narrative, we are shown Meed apparently 'affecting' the echelons of the civic administration:

> Ac Mede the mayde the mair h[eo] bisought[e]
> Of alle swiche selleris [i.e. the 'regatrie' – the retail trade]
>   silver to take,
> Or presents withouten pens – as pieces of silver,
> Rynges or oother richesse the regratiers to mayntene.
> 'For my love,' quod that lady, 'love hem echone,
> And suffre hem to selle somdel ayeins reson.'

> (III, 87–92)

The dynamic of Meed's social circulation is later re-presented by Conscience as one of prostitution: he exploits the conjunction of projected material/sexual desire she embodies and accuses her of selling her body to all and encouraging other women to do likewise (III, 120–69).[33]

Yet Meed the Maid is not depicted consistently through this sequence as if she were self-determined, a broker of herself. For much of the time she seems to be as much a victim of the desires of the men who surround her and subject her to their misuse and their reading (unlike Lady Holy Church, Meed is not an active interlocutor in the opening frames of her story). Nor is it clear that she should be understood simply as embodying material reward, or read as if she represented simply a much-desired female bastard heir. She (and by implication, what she represents) has lawful, legitimate potential. The semantic range of Meed is opened up by Theology's intervention (II, 115–41): Meed, he proposes, is born of 'amendes' and thus has a legitimacy, and therefore rights by virtue of her birth, which would be undermined by her marriage to 'Fals'. Now the matter of Meed's marriage becomes a matter which has to be decided by the King and his council at Westminster. This depiction of Meed as a noun embodied in female form makes at least two kinds of judgements on her necessary. On the one hand Meed, as an ambiguously positioned female subject, has to be judged by the King as head of civil justice. He has to decide what should be the place of 'reward' in social structures. We, on the other hand, as readers of the poem conscious of the gender 'agenda' of this story, are given an opportunity to follow another narrative line which unravels here and to observe how much the social position of women depends on their definition by men and what social structures can do to women when they seek a share of social power.

As Meed's possible range of semantic significance is broadened by Theology's intervention, so too is her social mobility: as she nears the King's court, the centre of social power, she becomes all things to all men. Her courteous reception from the King affirms both her powers of attraction and her potential respectability, and she seems to be treated as if she were a royal ward.[34] Even as a legitimate 'muliere' her choice of partner appears to be no more free than when she was regarded simply as an attractive commodity in the marriage market: now her choice of partner is to be guided by the King, who ultimately proposes to endorse her respectable status by marrying her to one of his chief knights, Conscience.[35] The meaning of Meed's 'proper' name becomes the central issue in the debate over the propriety of this match.

In the sequence in which Conscience argues against his proposed marriage to Meed (again on the grounds of disparagement of rank), the common ground between anti-venal and anti-feminist satire becomes clear: in both, the circulation of the female body as a currency between men of all social ranks can be used to figure debased values and social order. In the eyes of Conscience, Meed is 'tikel of hire tail, talewis of tonge/As commune as the cartwey to [knaves and to alle]' (III, 131–2). Meed is the very anti-type of the 'good woman': she is a prostitute. Conscience's tactics, as he develops his argument (III, 101–353), are to try to fix Meed's meaning and then to construct rules which would reduce her sphere of legitimate operation and power.

Conscience refuses to marry Meed because, he argues, personal relations should be based on truth and not contracted for the purposes of financial gain (III, 122–6). Following this, however, Conscience cuts down the possible semantic range of Meed, which Theology had earlier opened up, by working through a series of social milieux in which Meed has no rightful place. Meed, he argues, is not 'pay', so she has no place in legitimate 'mesurable hire', where labour is exchanged for wages: 'reward' has no place in legal circles, where the law must be seen to operate fairly and justice must be balanced. In this way, as Conscience defines Meed's inappropriate use in public life, her status diminishes and she becomes easier to eliminate, and to dismiss.

From Meed's point of view, once the option of marriage closes down, her operations elsewhere become less tenable. She does, however, attempt to mount a case for herself on the grounds of her social usefulness. Against Conscience's claim that she is potentially an anarchic force in society, Meed maintains that the feudal model of society has actually depended for its smooth running upon 'rewards' and cites examples from the recent past to support her claims (III, 186–227).[36] Here, though, she accepts the terms of her self-definition (social usefulness in the feudal system) which Conscience has laid out. Later, as her social mobility becomes severely circumscribed through Conscience's systematic efforts to remove from her any legitimate place of social power, Meed makes one final bid for a more powerful definition of her role by attempting to imitate Conscience's debating technique. Admitting she knows no Latin, she nevertheless cites a Biblical text in order to gain Scriptural authority for the legitimacy of her use: 'Honorem adquiret qui dat munera' (III, 335a) – 'he that maketh presents shall purchase victory and honour' (Proverbs 22:9). This tactic elicits the misogynist response:

> 'I leve wel, lady,' quod Conscience, 'that thi Latyne be
> trewe.
> Ac thow art lik a lady that radde a lesson ones,
> Was "omnia probate", and that plesed hire herte –
> For that lyne was no lenger at the leves ende.
> Hadde she loked that other half and the leef torned,
> She sholde have founden fele wordes folwynge therafter:
> "Quod bonum est tenete" – Truthe that text made.
> And so [mys]ferde ye, madame – ye kouthe na moore fynde
> Tho ye loked on Sapience, sittynge in youre studie.
> Ac yow failed a konnynge clerk that kouthe the leef han
> torned.
> And if ye seche Sapience eft, fynde shul ye that folweth,
> A ful teneful text to hem that taketh mede:
> And that is "Animam autem aufert accipientium . . ." '
>
> (III, 337–50)

As Conscience's reply makes clear, no matter how aristocratic the female interpreter is, she is dependent upon a 'konnynge' clerk to ensure she turns over the correct page in her Bible. Not only are the ladies dependent upon clerks for their education, but, as Conscience's clerical procedures have shown, the feudal model of society depends on the arguments of clerks for its theoretical validity. There is a debate in progress here over the social place of reward, but in the process by which it is represented we may trace another story about State/clerical textual politics. The feudal State relies on the Church for clarification of its ideology: the male-dominated Church's monopoly on education can be seen to be a key factor in keeping traditional patriarchal structures in place in this society.

The argument between Conscience and Meed at this point seems to be a battle between a lady and a clerk in which the lady's ignorance is used against her in order to prevent her from occupying any position of interpretative power in the events of the narrative. This opposition also suggests that the world of royal justice established by Conscience and Reason does not allow for women's participation because they, like the Commune, where Meed still continues to operate, are too uneducated to be able to have any significant stake in the operations of the law.

The debate between Conscience and Meed is not argued through to a conclusion, but is played out to a conclusion on another level of the action through the processes of the suit against Wrong (whose crimes involve those of rape), in which Meed intervenes to offer compensation to the plaintiff, Peace, for the losses he has suffered (IV, 47–181). Now the formulation of the narrative is made to weigh against Meed, in favour of Conscience's account of her corrupting influence on the process of the law. In the terms offered by the narrative, Meed's intervention in the lawsuit on the side of Wrong, in order to ameliorate his punishment, can only *be* wrong. Conscience's argument appears to be clinched as Meed is now publicly perceived as a stigmatised figure: 'the mooste commune of that court called hire an hore' (IV, 166). Meed, however, does not disappear from the Dreamer's visions from this point, but 'meed' no longer appears in female form and is given only a nominal, rather than a personified, status in subsequent references.

IV

In the opening section of this essay I drew attention to Marina Warner's observation about the discrepancy between the uses of the female form in the symbolic realm, where abstract concepts such as 'Justice' and 'Wisdom' may be embodied as women, and the actual order 'of judges, statesmen, soldiers...', in which women are unlikely to practise that which the female form is otherwise used to represent.[37] Now, having traced some of the complex ramifications of the collision between two female personifications in the early Passus of *Piers Plowman*, and the range of male/female encounters which take place around them, I would like to qualify the way in which that opposition between the 'symbolic' and the 'actual' order works, at least in any application to Langland's text. The implication of my discussion of the interaction between the Dreamer and Lady Holy Church is that it is this discrepancy which limits the usefulness of this female dream guide for the Dreamer. The Church, in its idealised abstract form, is engendered in a female body, but that is inadequate for the Dreamer: he needs to know in ways which relate to his experience.

But then that point leads on to a larger one: the notion of separable orders of the 'symbolic' and 'actual' is not an adequate conceptual tool in any case with which to read *Piers Plowman*. The Dreamer, in his visions, does not have access to a pure symbolic order: his visions, his conceptualising abilities, are socially based and culture bound. The female forms he imagines are figured as social beings, with particular class-based interests (which in this case appear to be in competition), not actually as females in the abstract (something which is virtually impossible to figure in isolation anyway). The languages of femininity, of feudalism, of mercantilism (to name just three of the discourses in combination here) are in dialogue in the figures of Lady Holy Church and Meed the Maid, just as these figures are engaged, to a greater or lesser extent, in dialogues with the male figures who are around them, whose own access to social, material, spiritual capital is a variable (and in these stakes the Dreamer seems a poor man all round).

Gender, as Toril Moi observes, is 'a peculiarly combinatory social category' which cannot be articulated in isolation, but is one which 'influences and infiltrates every other social category'.[38] That much is clear from examining even a small section of *Piers Plowman* in which the complexity of Langland's modes of representation (which involve so many categories of social and spiritual experience in simultaneous interaction) is evident. But because female and male bodies are not of equivalent value either in Langland's culture or in our own, there is still something to be gained from asking crude and bold questions about the particular significance of personification of an abstract concept in one kind of body rather than another (or in one set of bodies). The use of a female personification in the Meed sequence, for example, is not the only option available to Langland. There are precedents for the use of a male body to figure material value (as in the case of the 'Sir Penny' poems) in other medieval texts; just as there are precedents for using marriage as a way of representing other kinds of social alliances (including an example of the male being the disputed partner).[39] But as the Meed sequences show, the use of a female figure (or more accurately figures) to personify changing notions of value is especially resonant because it can be linked up with pejorative notions about the changeable nature of women in general which were in circulation in Langland's culture. Moreover, the analogies which can be traced between society's trafficking in the currency of value (between men for the most part), which fixates the Dreamer, and his society's trafficking in the ownership (prospective and retrospective) of women provide much narrative potential. Much more remains to be said about the congruencies between the representation of the circulation of female bodies and of money currencies in medieval texts. But then much more remains to be said generally, by new generations of Langland's readers, about how best to work out what difference gender difference makes in the production and reception processes of this demanding and challenging text.

NOTES

1 For an overview of the critical history of *Piers Plowman* see Anne Middleton, 'The critical heritage', in John Alford (ed.) *A Companion to Piers Plowman*, Berkeley and Los Angeles, University of California Press, 1988, pp. 1–25 and the 'Guide to further study' Middleton provides on p. 25.

2 See David Aers, 'Reading *Piers Plowman*: literature, history, criticism', *Literature and History*, 1990, NS, vol. 1, pp. 4–23 and his general comments on the reception of *Piers Plowman* in *Community, Gender, and Individual Identity*, London, Routledge, 1988. Other studies of the reception of Langland's work in the late fourteenth to sixteenth centuries include John Burrow, 'The audience of Piers Plowman', *Anglia*, 1957, vol. 75, pp. 373–84; Anne Middleton, 'The audience and public of *Piers Plowman*', in David Lawton (ed.) *Middle English Alliterative Poetry and its Background*, Cambridge, D. S. Brewer, 1982, pp. 101–23; Anne Hudson, 'Epilogue: the legacy of *Piers Plowman*', in Alford, op. cit., pp. 251–66. In the discussion which follows I shall be concentrating on the so-called B-text version of *Piers Plowman* because that is the version most frequently studied, and all my quotations unless otherwise indicated will be taken from A. V. C. Schmidt (ed.) *William Langland: The Vision of Piers Plowman. A Complete Edition of the B-Text*, London, Dent, 1978. For an overview of the relations between the A, B and C versions of Langland's work see John Alford, 'The design of the poem' in Alford, op. cit., pp. 29–64, especially pp. 29–32. I shall draw attention

to some of the differences between the B and C versions of the poem at appropriate points in my discussion.

3 Aers, *Community, Gender, and Individual Identity,* op. cit., p. 4. The issue of gender identity is taken up by David Aers in relation to the *Book of Margery Kempe, Troilus and Criseyde* and *Sir Gawain and the Green Knight* in his study, but not in relation to *Piers Plowman.*

4 As will be clear from these remarks, the kind of critical practice that I aspire to might be labelled 'materialist feminist'. For further discussion of this kind of practice and its theoretical basis see Judith Newton and Deborah Rosenfelt, 'Toward a materialist-feminist criticism', in *Feminist Criticism and Social Change,* New York and London, Methuen, 1985, pp. x–xxxix. Newton and Rosenfelt stress the importance of not discussing 'women' as if they constituted a single and homogeneous social formation: 'women, like men, appear divided from each other, enmeshed not in a simple polarity with males but in a complex and contradictory web of relationships and loyalties' (p. xxvi).

5 Lavinia Griffiths, *Personification in Piers Plowman,* Cambridge, D. S. Brewer, 1985, p. 1. Griffiths discusses various kinds of definitions of personification on pp. 3–5 and, for the purposes of her study, settles on the definition of personification as 'the grammatical transformation of a noun or other part of speech into a proper name' (p. 5) as her preferred approach. Griffiths' study is stimulating in many respects, but the framework of analysis could profitably be expanded to include gender and class issues (as I propose to do here on a small scale): hence, though she discusses the representation of Lady Holy Church and Meed at some length (pp. 17–40), her discussion does not cover all the resonances of this sequence. The issue of gender appears fleetingly in Griffiths's study as a 'linguistic factor' (p. 5).

6 ibid., p. 105.

7 ibid., pp. 4–5. Helen Cooper discusses issues of gender and personification primarily in linguistic terms in 'Gender and personification in *Piers Plowman', Yearbook of Langland Studies,* 1991, vol. 5, pp. 31–48. For further comments on the limitations of discussing 'gender' as if it were only a linguistic factor, see Deborah Cameron, *Feminism and Linguistic Theory,* London, Macmillan, 1987. For a brief discussion of the implications of the choice of male and female forms for the personifications dramatised in the medieval English morality plays see Charlotte Spivak, 'Masculine and feminine in English morality drama', *Fifteenth-Century Studies,* 1988, vol. 13, pp. 137–44: more work remains to be done on the co-expression of gender, class, race identities here. See Felicity Riddy's comments in this volume on the representation of the 'distancing' aspects of the Rose's response to the Lover in the *Roman de la Rose* in the figure of a male peasant (p. 59). Christine de Pisan uses traditions of representing abstract virtues in female form in the service of building a defence for women in her *Livre de la Cité des Dames* (which Susan Schibanoff discusses in her essay on pp. 221–245 of this volume).

8 *Monuments and Maidens: The Allegory of the Female Form,* London, Weidenfeld & Nicolson, 1985.

9 ibid., p. xx.

10 ibid., p. 69.

11 See n. 7 above.

12 Cooper, op. cit., pp. 31–2.

13 ibid., p. 33.

14 ibid., p. 49. Helen Cooper has little to say about this in any detail.

15 *Personification in Piers Plowman*, n. 6, p. 7 and references therein.

16 The projection of an ideal in an idealised (which means, in effect, a genteel) female form recurs only in a smaller-scale descriptive sequence in Passus IX when Wit describes Anima (the soul) as a lady who lives in a castle, protected by a feudal entourage, under the lordship of Kynde (IX, 1–59). The technique of using male/female, lord/lady analogies to represent spiritual relationships is, of course, extremely common in medieval culture, though the fact that the female Anima lives within a castle of the flesh (which must necessarily include bodies of both sexes) complicates any simple opposition between male and female. However, Will does not meet Anima in this idealised female form: in Passus XV he encounters a 'composite' male figure who encompasses the feminine Anima.

17 Although modern critics tend to refer to Meed as 'Lady Meed', that is not an accurate representation of the naming of this figure in Langland's text. As Gerald Morgan remarks, 'Langland uses a number of titles [for the figure of Meed], carefully discriminated in their distribution among the dreamer and the characters in the fiction, and also their use at different states of the fiction', 'The status and meaning of Meed in the first vision of *Piers Plowman*', *Neophilologus*, 1988, vol. 72, pp. 449–63 (p. 449). He goes on to note that 'the only reference to Meed as a lady in Passus II is as a result of editorial emendation', n. 2, p. 462. For the meaning of *mulier(e)*, see the *Middle English Dictionary*, (b) 'legitimate, born in wedlock'.

18 I draw the phrase 'traffic in women', and its significance, from Gayle Rubin, 'The traffic in women: notes on the "political economy" of sex' in Rayna R. Reiter (ed.) *Toward an Anthropology of Women*, New York and London, Monthly Review Press, 1975, pp. 157–210. As Rubin notes, 'the "Exchange of Women" is a shorthand for expressing that the social relationships of a kinship system specify that men have certain rights in their female kin, and that women do not have the same rights either to themselves or to their male kin' (p. 177). For a discussion of the 'trafficking in women' in *Sir Gawain and the Green Knight*, see Sheila Fisher, 'Token men and token women in *Sir Gawain and the Green Knight*', in Sheila Fisher and Janet Halley (eds) *Seeking the Woman in Later Medieval and Renaissance Writings*, Knoxville, University of Tennessee Press, 1989, pp. 71–105.

19 For further discussion of the enigmatic self-presentation of the Dreamer see A. D. Mills, 'The role of the Dreamer in Piers Plowman', in S. S. Hussey (ed.) *Piers Plowman: Critical Approaches*, London, Methuen, 1969, pp. 180–212.

20 For further discussion of the use of the dream-guide device, see Paul Piehler, *The Visionary Landscape: A Study in Medieval Allegory*, London, Edward Arnold, 1971 and Barbara Nolan, *The Gothic Visionary Perspective*, Princeton, Princeton University Press, 1977, especially

pp. 214–15. Precedents for the use of a female visionary guide include
the figure of 'Grace-Dieu' in the mid-fourteenth-century *Pèlerinage de
l'âme* by Guillaume de Deguileville, which is most conveniently accessible in John Lydgate's fifteenth-century translation, F. J. Furnivall (ed.)
The Pilgrimage of the Life of Man, Early English Text Society, ES 77,
83, 92, London, Oxford University Press, 1899–1904; Dame Natura in
Alan of Lille's *De Planctu Naturae*, James Sheridan (trans.) *Alan of
Lille: The Plaint of Nature*, Toronto, Pontifical Institute of Mediaeval
Studies, 1980; Lady Philosophy in Boethius' *De Consolatione Philoso-
phiae* (although Boethius' visionary experience does not take the form
of a dream vision), V. E. Watts (trans.) *Boethius: The Consolation of
Philosophy*, Harmondsworth, Penguin, 1969.

21 Warner, op. cit., pp. 199–200; for the Church as Bride of Christ, see
Marina Warner, *Alone of All her Sex*, London, Weidenfeld & Nicolson,
1976, pp. 123–5.

22 For the tradition of representing the wisdom of God in female form,
see Warner, *Monuments and Maidens*, op. cit., pp. 177–209.

23 The analogy which Lady Holy Church establishes here may be seen in
a more amplified form in Stephen of Tournai's description of the hierarchies of the Church and State and the interconnection between them:
'In the same city and under the same king there are two peoples, and
corresponding to the two peoples two ways of life, corresponding to the
two ways of life two authorities, corresponding to the two authorities two
orders of jurisdiction. The City is the Church and the King is Christ.
The two peoples are the two orders in the Church, the clergy and the
laity. The two ways of life are the spiritual and the carnal (or secular),
the two authorities are the priesthood and the kingship, the two jurisdic-
tions are the divine and human laws (canon and civil law). Give to each
its due and all things will agree.' Quoted by Christopher Dawson, *Medieval Religion*, London, Sheed & Ward, 1934, p. 27.

24 Mary Carruthers discusses the Dreamer's problematic encounter with
Lady Holy Church as a possible sign of the failure of orthodox Christian
rhetoric to communicate effectively with lay people in *The Search for
St Truth*, Evanston, North Western University Press, 1973 (especially ch.
2). Lavinia Griffiths also discusses the way in which Lady Holy Church's
speech is 'terribly simple and yet obscure' in *Personification in Piers
Plowman*, op. cit., pp. 21–2.

25 Many critics have discussed the meaning of the figure of Meed; see, for
example, Morgan, op. cit. Despite his recognition, in a general way, that
the status and meaning of Meed shift according to the larger context in
which she is placed, and to whom she is attached, Morgan still follows
the trend of many modern critics in seeking to 'fix' the essential status
of Meed from the beginning of his discussion. In his view, Lady Holy
Church's introduction to Meed 'enables us to be certain from the beginning of the falseness of Meed' (p. 450). Although I have offered some
readings of Meed's significance already, I would argue that it is important
to allow more space to recognise the complex and shifting semantic
resonances of her persona before (and indeed despite) Conscience's
attempts to 'fix' her definition in pejorative terms. A. G. Mitchell argued
against the tide of criticism of the Meed sequence of the text in his call

for readings which allow the resonances of this figure to develop 'through the whole movement of the narrative', 'Lady Meed and the art of *Piers Plowman*', in Robert Blanch (ed.) *Style and Symbolism in Piers Plowman*, Knoxville, University of Tennessee Press, 1969, pp. 174–93 (p. 193). Anna Baldwin's discussion of Meed as a figure of the corrupt (male) lord illuminates some of the resonances of the figure of Meed, but overlooks others, notably her possible bastardy, and the repercussions of her female form: see *The Theme of Government in Piers Plowman*, pp. 24–31. C. David Benson reads Meed as a *figura* of Christ in 'The function of Lady Meed in *Piers Plowman*', *English Studies*, 1980, vol. 61, pp. 193–205. Bernard F. Huppé attempts to solve the problem of Meed's identity by reading her exclusively as a figure for Alice Perrers, the mistress of Edward III in '*Piers Plowman* and the Norman Wars', *PMLA*, 1939, vol. 54, pp. 37–64.

26 'The governing paradigm [of the ideology of the fourteenth- and fifteenth-century Church] continued to be the ancient antithesis between carnal Eve, whose lust for sex and knowledge resulted in her subjugation to wedlock and childbearing, and the Virgin Mary, whose perfect purity released her soul and body from earthly bonds', Hope Phyllis Weissman, 'Margery Kempe in Jerusalem: *Hysterica compassio* in the Late Middle Ages', in M. Carruthers and E. Kirk (eds) *Acts of Interpretation: The Text and its Contexts 700–1600*, Norman, Oklahoma, Pilgrim Books, 1982, pp. 201–17 (p. 203). See also Marina Warner's comments on the dichotomy between the Virgin Mary and Mary Magdalene, *Alone of All her Sex*, op. cit., p. 225. This antithesis is something of a commonplace in modern studies of medieval culture, although its status (along with other kinds of binary oppositions such as the body/soul divide etc.) has been questioned recently by Caroline Bynum Walker, who argues that modern scholars have perhaps oversimplified the system of analogous, binary categories of which it forms a part. See Caroline Bynum Walker, 'The female body and religious practice in the Later Middle Ages', in Michel Feher *et al.* (eds) *Fragments for a History of the Human Body: Part One*, New York, Zone Books, 1989, pp. 161–219, especially p. 162.

27 John A. Yunck, *The Lineage of Lady Meed*, Notre Dame, University of Notre Dame Press, 1963, p. 289.

28 'Lemman' does not seem to carry the same pejorative value here for Langland's readers as it seems to do for Chaucer's audience in the *Manciple's Tale* (203–21), where it is described by the narrator as belonging to the register of 'knavysh speche'.

29 The lineage of Meed varies in three versions of *Piers Plowman*. As Yunck notes, 'in the B-text the figure of Meed is identified as the daughter of False who is to be married to False Fikel Tongue; in the A-text she is the daughter of Wrong and in the C-text she is the daughter of Favel', Yunck, op. cit., p. 6. In the C-text, Theology names 'Amendes' as Meed's mother.

30 In Passus IX (108–18), for example, Wit outlines a consensual theory of marriage, invoked elsewhere in *Piers Plowman*. In this model, the role of the wife is to act as helpmate to her husband and his legitimate object of procreative sexual desire. It is worth noting that though Wit stresses that wedlock should be founded on mutual love, he still repre-

sents its sexual function in a way which renders the female as the sexual object for the male: 'Whiles thow art yong, and thi wepene kene,/Wreke thee with wyvyng, if thow wolt ben excused' (182–3). Wit explicitly criticises the market model of marital relations in lines 160–78. The analogy of a 'covetous marriage' is invoked by the Dreamer to describe the Friars' desire to appropriate his body and goods in Passus XI (71–2) and, at a later stage of the narrative, Patience praises maidens who decide to forfeit material comfort and take a poor marital match for reasons of love alone as truly 'love-worthy' women (XIV, 266–72). The discrepancies between theories and practices of marriage arrangements are, of course, the subject of the *Wife of Bath's Prologue and Tale*: for further comments on the practices of the marriage market see the essays by Sheila Delany and Mary Carruthers in this volume. For the official teaching of the Church on the sacrament of marriage see Michael Sheehan, 'Choice of Marriage Partner in the Middle Ages: Development and Mode of Application of a Theory of Marriage', *Studies in Medieval and Renaissance History*, 1975, vol. 1, pp. 3–33.

31 See Yunck, op. cit. It is clear from his discussion that the female personifications of figures such as 'Munera' and 'Pecunia' offer precedents for the female embodiment of Meed, though Yunck's study does not focus on the issue of sexual difference in charting the lineage of Meed, who, in any case, cannot be understood as simply representing 'money'. Male personifications of coinage/money (in the form of 'Dan Denier' – whose Middle English equivalent might be 'Sir Penny') were also used in medieval French satirical literary traditions; the way in which material corruption is represented in these satirical texts necessarily differs according to whether male or female personifications are used. See also John A. Yunck, 'Medieval French money satire', *Modern Language Quarterly*, 1960, vol. 21, pp. 73–82. 'Meed', too, is found in male form in some later poems in Middle English, as Anna Baldwin points out in her discussion of Meed in *The Theme of Government in Piers Plowman*, Cambridge, D. S. Brewer, 1981, p. 25. Further analysis of the variable relationship between the engendering of the personification and the narrative sequences they enact would be useful.

32 Yunck comments on potential overlap between the representational strategies of anti-feminist and anti-venal satire in *The Lineage of Lady Meed*, op. cit., p. 187, but does not develop this point at any length.

33 The representation of Meed in female form has paradoxical implications for the roles women may play in commercial society as it is described in Langland's work. On one hand, she offers an example of how material power might enable women to 'affect an effect' on the power-broking ranks of society, although Meed is still subject to a male economy of desire; on the other hand, since no other women are represented as desiring her (through this double sex/money dynamic), women are effectively disenfranchised from their role in commercial society as it is represented through Mede's history; their only option, as Conscience describes it (III, 123–6), is to follow Mede's example, literally, and to sell their bodies.

34 Anna Baldwin discusses Meed's presentation as a ward of court in *The Theme of Government in Piers Plowman*, op. cit., pp. 33–4.

35 It should be noted that arrangements for the marriage of male wards, as well as female wards, could be constrained by the desires of their guardians. The constraint frequently took the form of a financial penalty if the match did not meet the wishes of the lord, as S. Walker points out in 'Free consent and marriage of feudal wards in medieval England', *Journal of Medieval History*, 1982, vol. 8, pp. 124–34.

36 The interpretation of this sequence is difficult: for further commentary and explication see Mitchell, op. cit., and James Simpson, *Piers Plowman: An Introduction to the B-Text*, Harlow, Longman, 1990, pp. 43–9.

37 Warner, *Monuments and Maidens*, op. cit., p. xx.

38 Toril Moi, 'Appropriating Bourdieu: feminist theory and Pierre Bourdieu's sociology of culture', *New Literary History*, 1991, vol. 22, pp. 1017–49, p. 1035.

39 For more details of the gender variables of Meed and 'Sir Penny' see n. 31 above. Roberta Cornelius draws attention to some interesting parallels and contrasts between the sequences involving the marriage of Meed and those concerning the problematic marriage of 'Fauvel' (a male personification of deceit) in the early fourteenth-century *Roman de Fauvel* (and notes Langland's distinctive use of the word 'Favel', which seems to be derived from this text): see '*Piers Plowman* and the *Roman de Fauvel*', *PMLA*, 1932, vol. 47, pp. 363–7. For other examples of the use of marriage paradigms to express, allegorically, other kinds of social relations (corrupting relations for the most part) in exemplary stories used in sermons, see G. R. Owst, *Literature and Pulpit in Medieval England*, Oxford, Blackwell, 1966, pp. 93–7.

8 The Virgin's Tale

Jocelyn Wogan-Browne

In medieval accounts of occupational categories (such as those of the estates handbooks drawn on by Chaucer in the General Prologue to the *Canterbury Tales* and by Langland in *Piers Plowman*), women are seldom mentioned at all.[1] When they are, there are two careers they can have: the biologically active one of wife or the professionally chaste one of nun. (This categorisation of course ignores many of the skills and occupations actually practised by medieval women, but is nonetheless powerful in forming attitudes to women.)[2] Virginity is thus a potentially crucial entry-qualification for all the occupations officially available to women: for marriage women are required, ideally, to have and lose it; for the religious life they are required, ideally, to have and maintain it. 'Marien maydenes or maken hem nonnes' (*Piers Plowman*, VII, 29); Wife of Bath or Prioress: in these categorisations of women, the virgin's opposite is as much the housewife as the whore.

There is a large medieval literature of virginity, consisting mainly of prescriptive treatises and letters and the exemplary biographies of virgin martyr hagiography. This chapter will be concerned with some of the many virgin's tales written for medieval women and with the one Chaucer in a sense did not write. A sense of the relations between Chaucer and his virginity material is less a part of the canon of modern study of medieval literature than is a sense of Chaucer's relations with romance. This needs redress both as it concerns Chaucer and with regard to the literature prescribing and imagining chaste female lives, the more so as the hagiographic representation of virginity is one of the principal European narrative representations of women. In this vast genre, extending throughout the middle ages and beyond, the *passio* of the tortured and dismembered virgin is the dominant representation of female sanctity: it is told and retold alongside newer models of exemplary biography.

Modern hagiographic scholarship has sometimes approached this genre with an intellectual 'neutrality' or 'objectivity' (amounting to a 'tacit acceptance of patriarchal power politics'[3]) which either dismisses these narratives as sensational and popular or allows the represented stripping and torture of virgin martyrs to be described as the 'disrobing of the [misanthropic] maiden'.[4] Such accounts need replacing (and have recently begun to be replaced) by attention to the issues of female desire and subject status in the narratives of virginity and in the lives of their medieval audiences.

Although there are some important male virgins (Christ, St John, Perceval and Galahad, for instance) and although celibacy is an issue in male medieval monasticism, virginity was primarily gender-marked as female and most virginity texts were produced by men for women.[5] Lacking full institutionalised access to clerisy, women did not usually write about their own virginity, and a major vehicle for virginity theory and modes of life was the letter or treatise of guidance and instruction written by a male cleric for women under his pastoral care. Works of this kind from the early church fathers were reused and adapted throughout the middle ages. In North-western Europe there was an efflorescence of virginity literature in the eleventh to early thirteenth centuries in treatises and letters by such writers as Hildebert of Lavardin, Peter of Blois, Ivo of Chartres, Osbert of Clare, Anselm and Aelred and in the vernacular writings derived from them.[6] This intensified interest in virginity, as I shall argue, needs to be seen alongside contemporary high medieval constructions of women as romance heroines, and its implications are not restricted to the technically intact.

The early church fathers emphasise virginity as a way for women to shed their cultural gender and become more like men: 'while a woman serves for birth and children, she is different from man as body is from soul. But when she wants to serve Christ more than the world, then she shall cease to be woman and shall be called man.'[7] In the high middle ages, although the idea of the virgin as a *vir-ago*, a woman acting like a man, survives, virginity is (re-) sexualised and feminised: virginity writers are less inclined to congratulate women on becoming like men in their choice of virginity, and place more emphasis on virginity as the choice of the bride who has opted for the best groom of all.[8] So virginity is rewritten as marriage, just as marriage can be rewritten (and according to some high medieval exemplary biographies, practised) as chastity.[9]

Most medieval treatises, like their patristic precedents, give exhortation and instruction as well as practical recommendations, and much of this writing insists that technical intactness is unimportant compared with spiritual disposition. Virginity is a disciplined and demanding mode of life in which a moment's pride – even pride in one's virginity – can plunge the practitioner down in a recapitulated Fall and render technical intactness meaningless. The treatises are eloquent on virginity's value as humanity's best image of the *vita angelica* lost to it in the Fall and on virginity as a counter to the alienation inevitably felt by humanity in this world. Virginity is powerfully theorised as the original, natural and best human condition, since (as St Jerome argues) wedlock, being post-lapsarian, 'only follows guilt'.[10] It is necessary here to be clear that in orthodox Christian thought the ideal of virginity as a superior state does not entail seeing sexuality *per se* as the cause of the Fall, which is the outcome of pride and disobedience. Sexuality is a powerful appetite with the potential of blurring and distorting human concentration on God, but is part of God's created universe. It is not that marriage is bad and virginity good, but that marital sexuality is legitimate, a permitted concession, and virginity is better. All the major writers on virginity insist that marriage is not wrong, merely third best to chastity and virginity.[11] Virginity is the counsel of perfection: it can only be chosen by rational informed souls, freely willing a meaningful choice of this demanding spiritual career. When the Wife of Bath insists that virginity is not commanded but *counselled* by St Paul (1 Cor. 7.25), her claim is perfectly orthodox.[12] Not surprisingly, in argument, marriage can slip from being less than virginity to being virginity's opposite and seen as entirely negative, but such a position is not *entailed* by orthodox thought.

Since marriage is not wrong, and virginity is an inner state to be constantly maintained and negotiated, a humble married woman can, in theory, rank as highly in spiritual terms as a technically intact virgin. The spiritual aspirations and life-styles of virginity are not exclusive to the technically intact but apply to the chastity undertaken by a range of women (consecrated nuns, lay and religious recluses and vowesses) and to the behavioural ideals offered to married women and widows. In a conceptually uncomfortable manner for an apparently unambiguous state, virginity is gradable and negotiable. One might compare here the way in which the impossible virgin fecundity of Christ's mother is in part mediated to 'fallen' (i.e. biologically active) medieval women (i.e. mothers) by the figure of the Magdalene. A repentant harlot restored through penitence to spiritual virginity, the Magdalene, in the development of her cult and the kinds of miracles ascribed her, is as importantly associated with maternal care and responsibility as she is with transgressive sexuality.[13] In an analogous way, though virginity remains the highest entry level, chaste widows, or wives whose husbands have agreed to their taking a vow of celibacy, can become honorary virgins and brides of Christ.[14] Technical intactness can be written in and out as needed: it is (to use a distinction made in Middle English) a condition of 'maydenhede', but not always a prerequisite for spiritual 'virginite'.[15]

Virginity nonetheless remains defined in some contexts via oppositions in which, for women, technical intactness matters very much. For male virginity, anatomical marking is not considered necessary or possible, but for female virginity, the presence of a hymen can be the *sine qua non*, so much so that recipes for the manufacture of hymens are found in medieval medical collections:

> This remedy will be needed by any girl who has been induced to open her legs and lose her virginity by the follies of passion, secret love, and promises. . . . When it is time for her to marry . . . let her take ground sugar and the white of an egg and mix them in rainwater in which alum, fleabane, and the dry wood of a vine have been boiled down with other similar herbs . . . or let her mix rainwater with well-ground fresh oak bark . . . but best of all is this deception: the day before her marriage let her put a leech very cautiously on the labia, taking care lest it slip in by mistake; then she should allow blood to trickle out and form a crust on the orifice; the flux of blood will tighten the passage.[16]

The question of how far and by whom such recipes were used is a complex one, but the construction of virginity as physically certifiable is present not only in medieval medical discourse, but in some social practices and some doctrinal discussions. The mystery plays' representation of the midwives' 'trial by finger' *à propos* the Virgin Mary's post-partum integrity, for instance, dramatises a practice which Augustine had discussed as an impropriety in his *City of God*.[17] For a woman wanting to become a consecrated religious, the equivalent demand for hymenal sealing is to be found in the claustration and strict enclosure prescribed with much more intensity for women religious than for their male colleagues.[18] The biographer of St Gilbert of Sempringham, twelfth-century founder of an order for women, says of the first seven women enclosed as professional virgins under the saint's care that they were allowed a single window (for servant girls to pass necessary food etc. through) and that there was also a door, but it was never unlocked except by his command, and it was not for the women to go out through, but for him to go in to them when necessary. He himself was the keeper of this door and its key. For wherever he went . . . like an ardent and jealous lover he carried with him the key to that door as the seal of their purity.[19]

Key, seal, lock, purity: St Gilbert's key-carrying functions here in the spiritual domain as the symbolic (and material) equivalent of eggwhite.

Veiled and sealed in this way, both virginity and the female body are contained. The bride of Christ is not consigned to the domain of an earthly husband's household, but she is enclosed in her cell, anchorhold, or convent, her virginity in the custody of a spiritual director rather than given to an earthly spouse. There is thus, in the cultural construction of female occupation, a moment in which for all women the display and disposal of 'maydenhede' is pivotal: the 'authenticated' virgin (or honorary virgin) passes briefly through 'public' space as a bride before being consigned to secular or religious enclosure. This nuptial passage from paternal to marital or ecclesiastical custody focuses a great many concerns: matters of lineage, affiliation and belief attend questions of legitimate and illicit marriage and sexuality. It is not surprising that this moment is so culturally freighted, especially given the high middle ages' increased attention to the sacrament of marriage in matters both of doctrine and social history, and the development of nuptial metaphor as a major trope of scriptural exegesis and devotional writing.[20]

It is also not surprising if the question 'what does the virginity literature so often written *for* women have to offer *to* women?' is a complicated one. Virginity literature has at least the potential of offering an account of chaste lives from something like a female subject position, for it must address the interior life and not just the presence of a hymen in its female audience. On the other hand a life contained in the cell of an anchorhold or a convent does not necessarily represent more than a relative female autonomy and volitional freedom. Yet virginity literature is at least a potential source for the critique of secular romantic constructions of female selves, though it also partly replicates them. Secular romance glosses marriage as an acceptable and desirable career for women.[21] In the representations of virginity literature, women are the brides of Christ in parallel to the secular romance heroine's position as the object of male desire and the prize of male exertion. But the parallel is not quite exact. The representation of Christ's desire for mortal women inevitably has a figurative dimension, and the romance of the virgin often has slippages less readily available in secular romance, spaces and freedoms for women as subjects and not only objects. The literature of virginity reiterates but also clarifies and to an extent exposes the strategies of romance.

The most important group of virginity texts in English before Chaucer is from the period in which St Gilbert's foundations for women flourished and the period when 'medieval sexual doctrine ... [takes] its classic form'.[22] The Katherine Group of treatises and biographies, textually associated with the famous Middle English *Guide for Anchoresses, (Ancrene Wisse)*, and the 'Wooing Group' of prayers and meditations, was written and/or collected together for three well-born anchoressses in the early thirteenth century.[23] The texts in the group were quickly adapted for (in some cases also already envisage) wider audiences: a larger female community, young women who might choose consecrated virginity rather than marriage, widows and wives, and lay people without Latin.[24]

Replacing marriage and the household with church and cell as the site of female ambitions and sense of self, the Katherine Group texts expose aspects of socio-economic destiny usually kept well veiled from the medieval romance heroine. The *Letter on Virginity for the Encouragement of Virgins*, for instance, warns women that 'supported by a man, you will suffer cruelly for his sake and the world's, since neither can be relied on', and claims that the woman who marries becomes 'a serf to man and his slave ... gives herself up to drudgery, [to] managing house and servants'.[25] For

> hwet ȝef Ich easki ... hu þet wif stondeð, þe ihereð hwen ha kimeð in hire bearn schreamen, sið þe cat et te fliche ant ed te hude þe hund, hire cake bearnen o þe stan ant hire kelf suken, þe crohe eornen i þe fur – *ant* te cheorl chideð?
>
> (34/6–9)

what if I should ask ... what kind of position the wife is in who, when she comes in, hears her child screaming, sees the cat at the flitch and the dog at the hide, her loaf burning on the hearth and her calf sucking, the pot boiling over into the fire – *and* her husband is complaining?[26]

There are also graphic accounts of violence and sexual harassment within marriage (28/1–18) and of the pains of pregnancy (30/27–32/ 13). Maternity is often placed beyond narrative closure for the romance heroine, but its difficulties and sorrows are detailed here (32/18–34/5). The socio-economics of marriage are unmasked along with its tribulations: if in marriage, the *Letter* asks, even the wealthiest queens and countesses are 'licking honey off thorns' (6/32), what is it like for poor women – 'like almost all gentlewomen living at present who do not have the wherewithall to buy themselves a bridegroom of their own rank, and give themselves up to the service of a man of lower rank, with all that they own. Alas, Lord Jesus, what a dishonourable bargain!' (8/2–5)?

Contrasted with these miseries are the tranquillity and personal autonomy of the consecrated virgin, who, as the bride of the impeccable groom Christ, is calm and secure. Though many medieval consecrated virgins inhabited a cell, the *Letter*'s chief metaphor for the virgin's position is that she is in a tower (2/27–9 *et passim*). This is a symbol at once of spiritual elevation and of high social class, and locates the virgin close to God and to the king of the [heavenly] court.[27] In the superior and elegant enclosure of her chastity, moreover, the virgin no more forfeits the drama of a continuing emotional history and romantic career than does the courtly lady in her tower. The devil's arrows of lechery attack the virgin's tower as vividly as the weapons of siege warfare provide secular erotic imagery (12/31ff.), and the virgin must defend herself, since the only way out from the tower is downwards, to marriage or worse. In the tower of virginity, not only are the embarrassing and sometimes squalid cares of the wife and mother avoided, but superior spiritual rewards (here literalised as aristocratic marks of favour and rank) are gained. In the court of heaven, virgins will have the highest position, a song of their own, the prettiest garlands, and a distinctive and exclusive crown, the *aureola*. The virgin is thus an elegant, eternal débutante, neither troubled by the harassments of the housewife's life, nor made socially or biologically unattractive as the price for her (relative) freedom. She has a handsome bridegroom and a spiritual progeny of virtues without the pain, immodesty and humiliation of childbirth (36/7–19). Heroine of a divine romance, intact, unencumbered and at once child-like and queenly, the virgin lives in a tower, wears a crown and does no housework.

The literature of the tower-cell offers women a paradoxical version of autonomy and self-fashioning at once empowering and disabling. Legitimated by a spiritual patriarchy and institutionalised in an ecclesiastical one, the virgin's freedom perhaps amounts to no more than the contribution (kin permitting) of dowry to a convent rather than a family. The *Letter* both makes visible and remasks women's socio-economic inferiority, briefly revealing the housewife's low status in order to kindle female aspirations to romance heroinism in figurative, spiritual ways. Though it warns women against being traded in marriage's debasement of personal worth, the *Letter* nonetheless offers them a spiritual bridegroom. In unmasking the commodification of women in marriage, virginity literature exposes romance courtliness as a gloss to the exchange of women but reappropriates romance for its own purposes.

Yet the model virgin self at least offers some kind of alternative. Against the *Letter*'s account of women's household lives as ones of economic subservience, liability to treatment as a chattel irrespective of initial social class, self-effacement in the maintenance of households for the service of others and continual distraction from any continuous self with its own volition and priorities, the alternative of solitude is attractive. Moreover professional religious solitude for medieval women of the twelfth and thirteenth centuries connotes a life unappended to an earthly man rather than a life without any human companionship. The figure of the consecrated virgin, nun or recluse implies a network of socio-economic support (from noble patrons, from town or village communities, from ecclesiastics), as well as a life in the miniature community of the anchorhold or the more extended community of the convent.[28] Not many of the varied forms of life in a 'cell of one's own' in the high middle ages were designed specifically with the needs of women in mind, but the 'solitude' (or, better, 'unappendedness') offered by professional chastity in ecclesiastical and para-ecclesiastical female communities was actively chosen by women in increasing numbers in the twelfth and thirteenth centuries.[29] Indeed, in the most austere version of the solitary life, anchoritic enclosure, female recluses outnumber male by 3 to 1 in England during this period, and the gentry or nobility status of many such women suggests this was hardly a choice of last resort.[30] Some medieval women seem thus to have felt, as well as been told, that enclosure offered an attractive form of autonomy-within-limits.

As well as the *Letter*'s reconstruction of the romance heroine's position in the tower of virginity, the Katherine Group provides a narrative romance of the life of the virgin. Just as the isolation of modern housebound women can be partly relieved and partly confirmed by the narrative structures and thematic concerns of the soap opera, so too in virginity literature the solitude of the high medieval cell is peopled with the figurative family structures of spiritual patriarchy, which it is the business of the virgin's life to encounter.[31] The

Group's saints' lives of Juliana, Margaret and Katherine (hereafter SJ, SM, SK) are all lives of legendary or semi-legendary virgin martyrs, an enduring hagiographic type, but one of special prominence in Britain in this period.[32] The Katherine Group lives share their themes and narrative morphology to some extent with other virgin lives, but seem to have been collected together and written into the same stylistic koinē as a deliberate exploitation of the possibilities of repetitive formulaic reading.[33] Here hagiography's characteristic intertextuality is heightened in a miniature female legendary, which, despite differences of production methods and scale, offers narrative structures and a particular reading experience not unlike those of the formulaic romances currently mass-marketed to women.[34] The legendary's calendared procession of readings systematically varies and renews the life of the saints through the liturgical year: the Katherine Group lives systematically repeat with variations the romance of the virgin's life.

It is thus possible without gross distortion to give a collective summary of all three. Such a Virgin's Tale would be: the heroine is young, beautiful, rich and noble. Her father is part of the Roman pagan establishment, or if he is absent, his narrative function is encoded in the pagan suitor and/or judge eventually encountered by the virgin. The virgin's mother is frequently absent from the virgin's life.[35] The virgin's counsels are thus her own and she is secretly a Christian. The virgin's faith and the disposition of her sexual and reproductive powers are simultaneously put at issue in the moment of her becoming visible to this patriarchy, either when she is seen and desired by a tyrant or when her father seeks to marry her off to a bridegroom undesired by her. When the virgin refuses marriage and/or seduction and conversion back to the pagan law of her father, she is argued with and punished by her father/judge and/or suitor/prosecutor. She is delivered over to some kind of public process in which she is threatened, incarcerated, publicly stripped, flogged, lacerated, burned or boiled, and dismembered in some way. When she is sent into a dungeon to consider her position, the conflict is amplified by heavenly and hellish manifestations in her cell. Brought out from her dungeon, the virgin continues to be spectacularly punished by tortures of increasing ferocity. Her conduct during all this remains impeccable, her ability to reason unimpaired. To the frustration of her tyrant, her bearing and her arguments frequently convert his attendant soldiery or populace, whom he then has to martyr as well. Attempts to execute or punish the virgin with extra refinements of torture technology consistently fail, either because no impression is made on her, or because there is divine intervention or both. The tortures return upon their organisers (cauldrons of boiling oil spill out on spectators, razor-edged wheels are shattered by angels and kill their operators etc.). When the virgin's persistence has outlasted all the tyrant's resources and he can no longer stand the sight of her, she is sent off to the standard form of upper-class formal execution and is beheaded. While her tyrant loses his credibility, his followers and his wits, the virgin proceeds, with attendant doves and angelic hosts, to the court of heaven, to be welcomed into the bower of the greatest and most handsome of bridegrooms and into top rank at the heavenly court.

How far is this literature *for* women? There are obviously many problems with these lives. As in the *Letter on Virginity*, the patriarchy condemned as literal and pagan is replaced by a spiritual Father and Son and the virgin articulates her loyalty to them rather than directly arguing her own autonomy. Moreover, even if the heroine is seen to reject unwanted suitors, her destiny remains that of some kind of marriage, her 'choice' only that of demonstrating loyalty to one or other kind of male figure and being appended to him as a reward. And though the virgin may desire and choose her preferred bridegroom, Christ, she is shown stripped, whipped, beaten and dismembered for maintaining her choice. In addition, these processes involve a spectacular 'theatre of punishment' for the display of female bodies. One of the *Letter*'s direst threats to the virgin is of herself as theatrical spectacle: if she fails in her fight with lechery, angels will weep in the heavenly upper circle while vulgar groundling devils caper in triumph, clapping their hands and jeering ('kenchinde', 14/26) at her fall into social shame and embarrassment. Yet in the Katherine Group's exemplary biographies the heroine is, precisely, delivered over to public stripping and torture, though here it is Christian spectators who 'kenchen', and those on the devil's side who are dismayed (SK 104/734). Displaying this spectacle, Christian clerical narrators and authors are poised between voyeurism and witness and are not themselves free of the ambivalences informing the actions of the pagan torturers. They can be seen as engaged in a writerly dismemberment which distributes the virgin's speech as the voice of God rather than the virgin's own, and the body as the virgin's language, hence mirroring 'pagan' patriarchy's vengeful dissection. When a father in these lives beats his daughter, he is a pagan attacking a saint. But he is also a father behaving within the norms of Christian patriarchal control and punishment of daughters. When the narrator describes the dismembering of the virgin, he is a witness, testifying to the saint's spiritual heroinism. But he also replicates the anatomising and consuming gaze of narrators and courtly lovers in lyric and romance: in exhibiting the heroine, he mirrors the 'paganity' from which saints' lives officially distinguish themselves.

The contradictions between veiled enclosure and spectacular exposure are officially mediated by the spiritual nature of the spectacle, whose true significance occurs on the virgin and God's level, uncomprehended by the literalist pagan torturers. A saint's body is supposedly discardable: only the pagan or the literal-minded would fail to concur with the saint's privileging of the spiritual significance of what is done to her body – the tearing away of an outer husk to expose inner meaning. Yet the virgin's body cannot be simply abstracted in this way: it is a body with a distinctive morphology, addressed in particular ways in the *passio* narrative, and we cannot here neglect, for the sake of a putative 'objectivity', the politics of representation.[36] On the other hand, to assume that readers of saints' lives have always adopted and must continue to adopt masculinist readings in which such narratives are only either symbolic rapes or reconfinements of women to the body seems a counsel of despair (and one that assumes only passivity on the part of medieval female readers).[37] Rather than accounting in such totalising ways for the tortures of the Katherine Group lives, a case can be made for their handling of torture as a narrative sub-code of some richness and useful indeterminacy of meaning. We need to look more closely at these bodies for a nuanced account of what is at stake in medieval Christian culture's simultaneous enclosure and exhibition of medieval female virginity.

That these lives stylise their violence is immediately evident. The sword of Roman law rather than the fire of medieval heresy-procedures is the convention of closure for the virgin's *passio*, and her preceding tortures are not paralleled in medieval inquisition until the reintroduction of juridical torture in the mid-thirteenth century.[38] Hagiographic torture may subsume echoes of historical and social practices into its own literary structures of meaning, but the narrative meanings of torture are not exhausted in the mimesis of social practice. As a narrative sub-code, torture is, among other things, a dramatic dialogue between God and the devil, where the pagan inquisitors' technologically inventive provision of new and more agonising tortures is countered by appropriate miracles manifested in the saint. God's ability to shape natural laws is always more fecund than human ingenuity, and his martyrs' deaths demonstrate God's effortlessly greater command of signifying capacity.[39] The question of who can make torture mean what is thus already encoded as a field of semiotic and ideological conflict in the *passio*.

Though the lives are concerned to show the display and maintenance of virginity, no hagiographic tyrant is seen raping or directly attempting to rape a virgin martyr. It may therefore be tempting to assume that because rape is alluded to, but not shown, it is the 'real' subject of these narratives, and to see the lives' accounts of bodily dismemberment and assaults on the will as covert rape fantasies. Yet such an argument ignores the pre-existing imbrication of virginity and faith and the conceptual lability of literal intactness in medieval virginity theory: the virgin's body is always already symbolic. In all three Katherine Group lives, the heroines' refusal of marriage or concubinage entails revealing their Christian loyalty to a spiritual bridegroom, so that sexual socialisation and submission to paganism parallel and underwrite each other in literal and spiritual interplay. Just as enforced betrothal to a pagan figures attempted ravishing of the virgin's will to faith, so marriage – sexual involvement with literal men – becomes positioned as potentially pagan preferment of fathers and suitors over God and Christ. Though it will be reinscribed for a spiritual patriarchy, power of disposal over the virgin's body on the part of earthly members of the patriarchy is at least proposed as illegitimate here. This does not mean that readings of such narratives as rape fantasies are impossible, but it does mean that neither the narratives nor their readers can be fully accounted for in these terms.

The Katherine Group's handling of torture links the three lives as closely as possible. The narrative morphology of female virgin martyr torture is already well articulated in the Latin sources of the Katherine Group, and is further stylised and aligned in the vernacular texts, with SK and SJ borrowing from each other's wheel, and all three lives using common lexis.[40] Thus, diagrammatically,

SJ	beating	molten brass	prison (disguised demon)	wheel	fire	beheading
SM	beating	awls	prison (dragon and demon)	tapers	cauldron	beheading
SK	detention	beating (disputatio)	prison (converts' visit)	(breasts) (converts' torture)		beheading

There is variation here (Juliana has three beatings before incarceration, Katherine's tortures are distributed in the sub-plot as well as to the saint herself etc.), but there is also a shared narrative morphology, in which the thematics of torture are more than usually legible, both generically and in the individual text. Juliana, who has the most apparently courtly suitor and the false authority of her father to deal with, resists a demon posing as an angel in her dungeon and remains whole in her fire (at once a heretic to her pagan judges and an unblemished saintly sign in the fiery furnace of Christian virginity).[41] Margaret, on the other hand, defies transparently aggressive attempts to consume her by her tyrant Olibrius, her hellish dragon and a boiling cauldron.[42] She also resists the pagan marking of her body with awls and tapers while continuing to signify God's inscription in his creation: heightened visualisation of the natural world in her prayers' gorgeous psalmody is the complement to her desire to encounter her enemy in visible manifestation in her dungeon.[43] Katherine, unlike Juliana, is not dismembered by her wheel, even in order to be miraculously reconstituted, for it never touches her: faced with it, she retains (as befits the patron saint of female learning) her clarity of mind and steadiness of purpose, and an angel duly shatters it (SK 104/726–30).

In each life the heroine is stripped 'steort-naket' (SK 80/564; SJ 15/156; SM 52/7), before her body is further outlined by being made to 'liðer' – 'foam, lather' – in its own blood (SK 80/566–7; SJ 15/157; SM 52/10). In keeping with the thematics of visualisation in her life, it is perhaps unsurprising that Margaret's body is doubly outlined, by fire as well as initial stripping and bloodying: the spectators see the romance heroine's attributes ('softe siden', SM 74/22) punitively violated and watch Margaret's 'snow-white skin' blackening and blistering, her 'beautiful body' crackling in the flame (SM 74/19–21). This formulaic stripping and beating outlines the virgin's body as the locus of argument in a manner different from the represented torture of male saints, in which tortures are addressed to a more fully articulated body (heads, hands, feet etc.) as part of juridical argument and contest.[44] In the female virgin lives, the whole body is outlined and addressed in a way that maps virginity and ideological purity in terms of each other.[45] Just as the power and integrity of secular kings is mapped onto the body of the queen, so the boundaries of Christian polity are policed on the bodies of virgins: represented bodily integrity serves an exclusionary definition of Christian community asserted against the 'pagan'.[46] The figure of the pagan in this way encodes contemporary anxieties about heresy and, very pointedly in the Katherine Group as in *Ancrene Wisse*, contemporary anti-Semitism. The female audiences of these texts are encouraged to define themselves against 'the envious Jews', especially in calibrating the refinement and ardour of their feeling for Christ.[47]

The Katherine Group saints are all represented as reappropriating metonymic equations of women's bodies and territory. They remain unsacked citadels, and have spiritual castles and lands of their own. Juliana's castle, built 'on true ground', fears no 'fall to wind or weather' (SJ 65/711–12); Margaret has 'the brightest chamber' prepared, in heaven (SM 80/14); Katherine eloquently describes her heavenly citadel 'inwið [i] [the] heorte', surrounded by a precious wall, shining and fair, of gemstones (SK 86/602–90/629), and offers her convert, the Empress '[in exchange] for a little earthly territory, the heavenly kingdom, and for a man of clay, he who is lord of life' (SK 112/785–7). These moves may legitimate wider political exclusionary purposes, but also, if read specifically as female exemplary biography, propose at least the contained autonomy of a spiritual domain for women. Rape is less the desire of such narratives than is a more complicated and reciprocal investigation, for both male and female, of social and cultural boundaries to identity.[48]

The virgins' torturers are, moreover, clearly victims of their own desire. The hectic masculinity, the bullying, bashing, beating, burning and technological ingenuity by which they express their will, rebounds on them, and they end up mad, self-lacerating, stripped of their power, emotionally bruised to pieces, or even dead and dismembered. For all their ambitions of scopic and literal possession, their gaze makes no impression on the heroine or her body even when extended by clawing hooks, lathering whips and knife-studded wheels. Like some modern theories of perception, medieval visual theory sees the lover's desirous gaze as actively affected by what it falls on: there could hardly be a clearer case than these lives of 'the female body as the quintessential and deeply problematic object of sight' or of its capacity both to mirror and disavow the 'imaginary coherence of the male subject'.[49] The heroine's steady reception of the tyrant's gaze and effortless negation of its power makes his world incoherent, and his ability to gaze rationally, wholly and commandingly becomes dishevelled and fractured on the body of the virgin. Juliana's gaze back at her demon devastates him in a comic piece of street theatre. He pursues her, jeering, to her execution, but dodges 'as for a schoten arewe' when she looks back at him, and throws himself into hell ('in the [deepest of all] ditches for a devil of a way', SJ 65/701, 705). (With the tonal and stylistic richness characteristic of these lives, this scene is immediately succeeded by Juliana's eloquent final address to the crowd, a speech of plangent high seriousness, SJ 65/709–67/731.)

Like the heroines of some modern (including some modern feminist) slice and dice movies, the virgin martyr is a Final Girl, a survivor.[50] But she contends powerfully for semiotic control not only at the end of the narrative but throughout. A privileged reader of Christian signs and manifestations, the heroine always has Christ available to her as a measure of the self-thwarting literalness of her tyrant. She understands a wider range of meanings than the pagan tyrant: in a comic reworking of a long-standing hagiographic trope, for instance, Juliana's father simply cannot comprehend her assertion that she is already betrothed, as, to his knowledge, he has never even met her groom (SJ 13/135–39).[51] When they are sent off into dungeons, enclosed and starved in the hope of changing their minds, virgin martyrs converse with the macrocosmic forces of heaven and hell involved in their *passio*, responding appropriately to demons and angels, and sometimes to Christ himself. Enclosed 'inside', they are in contact with more reality, not less. The virgins' larger vision and rationality are registered in their greater verbal prowess: their speeches exhibit deft syntactic control, and a capacity both for lucid, fervent and rational eloquence, and bluntly effective rebuke.[52] The narrative action underwrites their perspective. Deflatingly presented in a comedy of frustration and literal-mindedness, the tyrant cannot see what his subordinates and populace can: that to gaze on the heroine is to confront a transforming source of power (further testified to by the mass conversions of torturers, spectators and executioners in hagiographic lives).

As well as rhetorically reappropriating their bodies as territory they own or rule, the virgins rescript the meaning of their tortures. Margaret redirects her boiling cauldron into a baptismal bath (SM 76/4–13), and, as the tapers blacken and blister her 'snawhwit' skin, spiritualises these tongues of fire into a personal female Pentecost, more eloquent and more searing than ever in her love for God (SM 74/23–24). In the sub-plot of St Katherine's *passio*, the saint's autonomy, learning, defeat of fifty philosophers and unswerving discrimination of false idols and spiritual concubinage are countered by savagely explicit violence to her gender rather than her own person: the Empress converted by Katherine has her breasts pierced with iron nails and ripped out 'by the . . . roots' (SK 110/776). This is undeniably an ambivalent model of encouragement to learning for women, yet it is part of a thematics of virgin fecundity in the life. At her decapitation, Katherine herself bleeds milk, thus reasserting a spiritual capacity for nurture and productivity which survives the attack of the Emperor.[53] Women readers of Margaret seem to have appropriated her legend from a virgin–dragon confrontation into an aid in childbirth; the saint's prayers that where her life is heard, held, touched etc., children can be born whole and mothers survive the birth are a late addition to her Latin lives, and may come from audience demand.[54]

Such rescriptings, whether by represented virgins or historical female readers, may not constitute a locus for the ' "impossible place" ' of female desire around which feminist criticism and semiotic practice might hope to 'reconstruct vision'.[55] Considered as the represented speech of women, for example, the lives' nuptial language of desire as expressed in the saints' prayers is, arguably, a ventriloquised script for, rather than an articulation of, female desire. But the lives do at least open up the possibility of resistant readings, which in particular contexts may constitute relative empowerment or recuperation. Like the *Letter on Virginity*, the lives in many ways have useful information for the virgin heroine. They show her how tough she will have to be if she wants to become a career virgin. Her parents will try to marry her off, they will beat her if she says no, and her suitors may look like courtly lovers when wooing her, but have no serious interest in her volition and selfhood. If the *Letter* positions the virgin as spiritual débutante, the lives equip her to distinguish legitimate and improper suitors by splitting the hero, 'sign of the patriarchy, enemy and lover' into pagan suitor/tyrant and Christ-bridegroom.[56] In reinscribing rejected pagan alliance as marriage to Christ, the lives not only replicate appendage to a man as the virgin's destiny, but allow an unusually explicit and empowered critique of male desire and the violation of female volition.

A great deal of comic exposure of male desire accordingly goes on: the beasts of the arena met by early Christians re-emerge in the bestialising desire felt by pagan suitors for virgin heroines. St Margaret's Olibrius wants to consume her, his gaze as prehensile as the dragon's tongue: 'Seize her at once', he commands his soldiers on sight of Margaret (SM 46/24). St Katherine's Emperor Maxentius is a married man and wrathful potentate who becomes in his desire for the saint a 'rabid wolf' (SK 96/678). The most courtly wooer, Juliana's patrician young suitor Eleusius, eventually degenerates into a 'bristled boar', foaming and grinding his teeth at the saint (SJ 61/670). His love-malady symptoms (SJ 5/33–8; 17/195–19/204) are seen to become indexes of violence, not refinements of feeling, and his 'courtly' wounds of love are externalised into assaults on Juliana's body. The saints' lives subvert gradational hierarchies of desire such as we find in the three suitor eagles of *The Parlement of Foules* or Palamon and Arcite in the *Knight's Tale*. From the view-point of a virgin (such as Emily or the lady eagle or the martyr heroines), the entire violent and intense struggle to distinguish more and less worthy courtly lovers offers only distinctions without difference if one is to be married off willy-nilly in any case. When Juliana's Eleusius goes on a quest to impress Juliana, his achievement of higher rank is exposed as the fruit of nepotism rather than valour (SJ 7/61–63). In Katherine's life, the pagan Emperor's offer to make the saint a worshipped queen and to construct a golden statue of her reveals the 'elevation' of women in the figure of the romance heroine as a literally idolatrous putting of women on a pedestal (SK 76/536–78/543).

Saints' lives, then, potentially constitute an important critique of courtly love for their female readers, and in contrast to, for instance, the Loathly Lady tales of medieval romance, they achieve this not by splitting the heroine, but by dividing the hero.[57] Moreover, unlike Emily or the lady eagle of Chaucer's *Parlement*, virgin heroines can both gaze and answer back and are shown as much cleverer than their tormenters. These are points of potential significance in a culture on the whole counselling women to silence and obedience. In a society which frequently countermanded its own canon law precept that both partners should freely consent in marriage and which constrained female choice for the sake of territorially and lineally advantageous matches, the lives offer an important model of resistance. As divine comedies, these texts, with their heroines' supernaturally underwritten insistence that when women say no, no is what they mean, can offer serious encouragement to female readers.[58]

We can position Chaucer here as a decent rewriter and redirector of such material. His positioning of virginity discourses in the *Wife of Bath's Prologue* considers those discourses from an unprecedented 'female' position, explicitly confronting the misogyny with which virginity's arguments against marriage are often continuous.[59] Chaucer's own decoding of the violence of desire is done with contextualised subtlety and complexity in the metaphoric sub-strand of pursuit, impressment and consumption with which Pandarus and Troilus approach Criseyde, after she opposes hagiographic texts ('holy seyntes lyves') to their romance script for her (*Tr. & Cr.*, bk.

II, 118).[60] In *The Legend of Good Women*, Chaucer borrows none of the spiritual legitimation of the hagiographic legendary. His account of the serial production of good women as dead women offers repeated secular martyrdoms, emphasising the problems of a patriarchy and a masculinity that needs to produce itself, so to speak, over female bodies.[61] In addition to his generic realignments, Chaucer's choices in points of detail for his virgin martyrs suggest a discomfort with some of the conventions of saints' lives: his hagiographic tales develop the politics of maidenhood and birth, but leave stripping and whipping aside.

In *The Canterbury Tales*, his only hagiographic virgin martyr is presented in the *Second Nun's Tale* as a married virgin who with relative decorousness is suffocated in her own house. When she is fetched by her tyrant Almachius, 'that he myghte hire see' (*CT* VIII G, 422), Cecilia's status as a gently-born Roman woman remains effective, and the narrative records her arguments rather than outlining her body. Almachius does not lust and rant but says that he will suffer Cecilia's 'wrong' to him 'as a philosophre' (489–90). The saint is sent home to be stifled; she is not shown being stripped.[62] When the bath fails to kill her, Cecilia's body is torn open by bungled decapitation, but the execution is still within the enclosure of Cecilia's own house. From this territory she continues to speak for three days, pursuing her words and work of conversion before turning her house into a church and dying. Chaucer thematises virgin sainthood as fruitfulness and busyness in the Prologue to the legend (98, 116): chastity is here activity, not the fixed object of a salacious gaze, still less a blank absence awaiting inscription, impressment and dissection. Cecilia's lucid analysis of her judge's comments as 'lewed' and full of 'nycetee' (430, 494–7) and the Nun's Prologue's creation of an ardent and dignified Marian piety sustain the association of virginity and aristocracy characteristic of the virgin martyr heroine.[63]

In the *Physician's Tale* Chaucer's classical martyred virgin is again decorously murdered inside, beheaded at home by her father. Removing explicit Christian–pagan apologetics, Chaucer compresses virgin martyr hagiography's elucidation of patriarchal constructions of women to its 'degré zéro'. Virginia is a model virgin, an exemplary book for other maidens to read (107–10), living within the enclosure of her own decorum and virtue: 'shamefast she was in maydens shamefastnesse' (55). Going out to the temple with her mother, she is seen by corrupt officialdom, and the lecherous judge Apius plots with a man of low rank, the 'cherl' (140) Claudius, to obtain her.

Virginia is proclaimed not Virginius' daughter but a servant, a 'thral' (183) belonging to Claudius. Rather than hand Virginia over, Virginius goes home and kills her. There is no extended debate, no public and spectacular manifestation of the virgin as God's sign, no production of converts, or progress to a heavenly bridegroom. After requesting a small space for 'complaint' (followed by the eloquent silences of her two swoons, 245, 253), Virginia is beheaded. Her father takes and displays her 'mayden hede' (the *virgin* head severed from the *mayden*'s body) to the corrupt judge Apius who has desired it.[64] At this sight, public plebian feeling rallies to outrage over the violated virgin, Apius commits suicide, and Virginius' noble 'pitee' (272) can come into action. His position is reconfirmed against Apius' and Claudius' as he secures for the plotting churl a mercy unavailable to his daughter.

In the *Physician's Tale*, the hagiographic convention of outlining and lacerating the bodies of virgins as the site of ideological argument undergoes a grimly literalising *reductio ad absurdum*. Saintly martyrs are first visible to their tyrants in the nuptial or pseudo-nuptial moment in which the disposal of their sexuality and their beliefs is at issue. Chaucer here shows us 'mayden hede' literally held up and displayed to a patriarchy that desires and murders it while disposing of its daughters in the maintenance of class groups and beliefs.[65] Patriarchy's dealings with its virgin daughters are thus economically and shockingly compressed into 'deeth or shame' (214). Why should children be brought up at all for this – 'is ther no grace, is ther no remedye' (236)? In this stripped-down narrative, the killing of Virginia, as Jill Mann has argued, renovates the daughter's capacity for Christ-likeness, but also, in the conspicuous absence of a spiritual rationale for the action, sharply raises the problem of how the virgin martyr's suffering can be licensed.[66] Chaucer's murdered virgin is not stripped and tortured, but the motives and legitimating genres for the sacrifice of patriarchy's virgin daughters are exposed and reconsidered.

Chaucer positions Virginia's martyrdom within a nuanced awareness of the political and the social. A great deal of the narrative elaboration of the *Physician's Tale* is devoted to problematising upper-class patriarchy and its production of children in the reproduction of kin-groups, family interests and continued ruling power. Who creates and who brings up Virginia? The *Tale*'s initial descriptions of Virginia's growth and upbringing pose these questions (5–116). They posit Virginia as a creation of Nature's art as well as of her parents and, in their complex interplay between nature and culture, problematise the rule of the fathers and its setting of women as wardens over each other's chastity (72–92). The Physician's version of the 'life of angels' (*vita angelica*, see above, p. 167), is sundered from the Edenic myth of pre-lapsarian wholeness and eventual resurrection: for him virginity is either to be contained in a liminal pre-sexuality or must grow into a (bestial) sexuality. In this account of an aborted virgin death, it is no accident that the false judge rules 'she nys his doghter nat' (187), and Virginia is reassigned: 'the cherl [Claudius] shal have his thral' (202). When their tyrants demand their identity, the virgin martyrs' response frequently plays class and belief off against one another: they declare themselves the daughters of kings and noblemen but handmaids and thralls to Christ.[67] But if the hagiographic virgin's high birth becomes a metaphor of grace, high birth in the *Physician's Tale* is just high birth, sustained by ungodly means. In the *Tale*'s final taking-apart of class relations and the justice of patriarchal institutions, the self-destruction of the tyrant judges and fathers of saints' lives is alluded to, but rewritten as a mechanism for sustaining class prerogatives.[68]

Chaucer's use of virginity material thus takes up the burden of patriarchy's self-construction and explores and exposes it in his radicalising and oblique repositioning of genres and themes. Yet though Chaucer is both uneasy and exploratory here in a profoundly intelligent and creative way, it is arguable that the more hectically stylised romance of the virgin *passio* is in the end as eloquent, at least for women's lives. As has been argued of some recent low-budget rape-revenge movies, the lives keep the dismembered body of a woman at their centre, they legitimate and explore fantasy (which, so often the substance of prescribed and chosen female reading, is as important as high culture's more respectable 'imagination'), and they are highly but richly stylised and sustain a plurality of readings, including recuperative readings by women.[69] Chaucer, as Carolyn Dinshaw and others have argued, is deeply interested in exploring beyond 'reading like a man' by feminising the reader or by privileging female figures as readers to an unusual degree, and saints' lives are associated with women by him with regard to the representation of both female roles and female speech.[70] Yet in improving the romance and fantasy of this genre, he also makes over the culture and texts of female sub-culture. Chaucer's conscious and nuanced explorations of the socio-political implications of the guarding of female chastity in the end perhaps speak not so much for women as for the anxieties of men. The less canonical texts of female virgin lives may yet have more to say to us in representing medieval women. Here I have only pointed to some aspects of these texts and issues: not only the writing, but the reading of exemplary biographies and prescriptive treatises can be a complex and active process, and there is a great deal more to be learned about women's reading in the middle ages.

Female readers still pay unacceptably high prices and make unnecessarily hard career choices: it is worth mapping out the extent to which their alternatives have been represented as only those of wife-and-mother or professional virgin. The centuries-long representation of women in the virgin martyr passion needs to be taken into full, and fully historicised, account in the politics of gender and representation.[71] It is also worth deciding on what terms we can live with the innumerable narratives of European culture that have told many more readers than Chaucer's Dorigen (V [F], 1364–456) that women should prefer violence and death to the devaluation of losing their chastity.

NOTES

1 I am grateful to the Universities of Adelaide, Sydney, Cardiff, York and Liège and the Australian National University for opportunities to try out this chapter and related material as first written in 1989 and as revised in 1990–1. My thanks also to the editors of this volume for patient and stimulating editing.

2 On estates texts, see Ruth Mohl, *The Three Estates in Medieval and Renaissance Literature*, New York, Columbia University Press, 1933, republished Ungar, 1962, pp. 20–1 (on the absence of women); pp. 20–71 (where, in spite of the word 'Continental' in the chapter heading, many texts relevant to insular culture are discussed); pp. 97–139 (for English estates texts from the fourteenth to the sixteenth centuries).

3 Toril Moi, 'Feminist literary criticism', in Ann Jefferson and David Robey (eds) *Modern Literary Theory: A Comparative Introduction*, 2nd edn, London, Batsford, 1986, p. 206.

4 T. J. Heffernan, *Sacred Biography: Saints and their Biographies in the Middle Ages*, Oxford, Oxford University Press, 1989, ch. 6, 'Images of female militancy', *passim*. Arlyn Diamond, 'Engendering criticism', *Thought*, 1989, vol. 64, pp. 298–309, provides in her valuable analysis of courtly love scholarship a model which could usefully be extended to hagiographic scholarship.

5 On medieval virginity treatises and their audiences see Matthaus Bernard, *Speculum Virginum: Geistigkeit und Seelenleben der Frau im Hochmittelalter*, Cologne, Bohlau, 1955; Bella Millett (ed.) *Hali Meiðhad*, Early English Text Society, OS 284, London, Oxford University Press, 1982, p. xxiv. On virginity in the patristic era, see Jo-Ann MacNamara, *A New Song: Celibate Women in the First Three Christian Centuries*, Binghamton, New York, Harrington Park Press, 1985; on early

attitudes to the body, see Peter Brown, *The Body and Society: Men, Women and Sexual Renunciation in Early Christianity*, New York and London, Columbia University Press, 1988.

6 For later medieval English translations see P. S. Joliffe, *A Checklist of the Writings of Spiritual Guidance in Middle English*, Toronto, Pontifical Institute of Mediaeval Studies, 1976, Section O, and Robert R. Raymo, 'Works of religious and philosophical instruction', in Albert E. Hartung (gen. ed.) *A Manual of the Writings in Middle English 1050–1500*, Connecticut Academy of Arts and Sciences, Hamden, Connecticut, Archon Books, 1967–, vol. 7, 1986, pp. 2467–577; for earlier Latin writers on virginity see Millett, 1982, op. cit., pp. xxiv–xxvi, and Barbara Newman, 'Flaws in the Golden Bowl: gender and spiritual formation in the twelfth century', *Traditio*, 1989–90, vol. 45, pp. 111–46.

7 Ambrose, *Commentary on Ephesians*, II, *PL* 26.533.

8 See John Bugge, *Virginitas: An Essay in the History of a Medieval Ideal*, The Hague, Martinus Nijhoff, 1975, ch. 4. Bugge's arguments for gnostic elements in high medieval texts need to be treated with caution: see the review by J. Leclercq, *Medium Ævum*, 1977, vol. 46, pp. 129–31 and Millett, 1982, op. cit., pp. xxvi–xxvii.

9 On chaste marriage see Dyan Elliott, *Spiritual Marriage: Sexual Abstinence in Medieval Wedlock*, Princeton, New Jersey, Princeton University Press, 1993.

10 Letter XXII (to Eustochium), in F. A. Wright (ed. and tr.) *Select Letters of St Jerome*, London, W. Heinemann, 1933, p. 94.

11 The three-fold gradational hierarchy of the estates of the flesh (marriage good, chastity better, virginity best) is based on Matthew's parable of the sower (Matt. 13.23): see Millett, 1982, op. cit., pp. xxxviii–xxxix.

12 L. D. Benson *et al.* (eds) *The Riverside Chaucer*, 3rd edn, Oxford, Oxford University Press, 1988, *Canterbury Tales*, III [D], esp. ll. 66–112. Future references will be to this edition, cited by line number in the text.

13 On the Virgin Mary see Hilda Graef, *Mary: A History of Doctrine and Devotion*, vol. 1, London and New York, Sheed & Ward, 1963. For a general study of Mary Magdalene see Susan Haskins, *Mary Magdalene: Myth and Metaphor*, London, HarperCollins, 1993. The fundamental study is Victor Saxer, *La Culte de Sainte Marie Madeleine en occident des origines à la fin du moyen age*, Auxerre and Paris, 1959. For lives associating the Magdalene with fertility and the nurture of children see Theodor Graesse (ed.) *Jacobi a Voragine, Legenda Aurea*, 2nd edn, Leipzig, 1850, repr. Osnabrück, Zeller, 1969, pp. 407–17, and the vernacular lives listed in Wogan-Browne, ' "Clerc u lai, muïne u dame": women and Anglo-Norman hagiography', in Carol Meale (ed.) *Women and Literature in Britain 1150–1500*, Cambridge, Cambridge University Press, 1993, p. 77, n. 4, and in Charlotte d'Evelyn, 'Saints legends', in Hartung, op. cit., vol. 2, 1970, pp. 610–11.

14 Clarissa Atkinson, ' "Precious balsam in a fragile glass": the ideology of virginity in the later Middle Ages', *Journal of Family History*, 1983, vol. 8, pp. 131–43.

15 In Middle English, 'maidenhede' as technical intactness is distinguished from 'virginite' as spiritual condition: Hans Kurath and Sherman M.

Kuhn, *Middle English Dictionary*, Ann Arbor, University of Michigan Press, 1956–, s.v. *maidenhede* (n.), 2c.

16 Julia O'Faolain and Lauro Martines (trans.) *Not in God's Image*, London, Harper & Row, 1973 (from the *Collectio Salernitana* recipes ascribed to Trotula). See now Esther Lastique and Helen Rodnite Lemay, 'A medieval physician's guide to virginity', in Joyce E. Salisbury (ed.) *Sex in the Middle Ages: A Book of Essays*, New York and London, Garland, 1991, pp. 56–79. For Middle English 'Trotula' and related texts, see Monica H. Green, 'Obstetrical and gynecological texts in Middle English', *Studies in the Age of Chaucer*, 1992, vol. 14, pp. 53–88, and, for a hymen recipe, Alexandra Barratt (ed.) *Women's Writing in Middle English*, London, Longman, 1992, p. 37. (Since the hymen is composed of inner folds of flesh, few women are born with an imperforate one. Its cultural construction as imperforate is driven by the demand for blood as evidence of technical intactness. I have pursued these issues further in a paper and workshops, 'What medicine makes of women, or, A short history of the hymen', for the Association of Women in Medicine, London, March 1992. The most lucid modern medical description I have found is in Peter L. Williams *et al.* (eds) *Gray's Anatomy*, 37th edn, Edinburgh, London, Melbourne, New York, Churchill Livingstone, 1989, p. 1446. I am grateful to my colleague, Miss W. Joan Robinson of the University of Liverpool and Alderhaye Hospital, for helpful information.)

17 David Knowles (ed.), Henry Bettenson (trans.), *Augustine: City of God*, Harmondsworth, Penguin, 1972, p. 28; T. Forbes, 'A jury of matrons', *Medical History*, 1988, vol. 32, pp. 22–33; Stephen Spector (ed.) *The N-Town Play*, Early English Text Society, SS 11 and 12, 2 vols, Oxford, Oxford University Press, 1991, vol. 1, pp. 159–61.

18 Jane Tibbetts Schulenberg, 'Strict active enclosure and its effects on the female monastic experience, 500–1100', in *Distant Echoes: Medieval Religious Women* 1, ed. John A. Nichols and Lillian T. Shank, Cistercian Studies Series, vol. 71, Kalamazoo, Michigan, Cistercian Publications, 1984, pp. 51–86.

19 Raymonde Foreville and Gillian Keir (eds and trans.) *The Book of St. Gilbert*, Oxford, Clarendon Press, 1987, ch. 9, pp. 34–5.

20 Georges Duby, *The Knight, the Lady and the Priest: The Making of Modern Marriage in Medieval France*, trans. Barbara Bray with an introduction by Natalie Zemon Davis, London, Allen Lane, 1983; James A. Brundage, *Law, Sex and Christian Society in Medieval Europe*, Chicago, University of Chicago Press, 1987, chs 5–8; Ann W. Astell, *The Song of Songs in the Middle Ages*, Ithaca and London, Cornell University Press, 1990.

21 Roberta Krueger, 'Love, honor and the exchange of women in *Yvain*: some remarks on the female reader', *Romance Notes*, 1985, vol. 25, pp. 302–17.

22 Brundage, 'Reflections on medieval Christianity and modern sexual norms', op. cit., pp. 585–6.

23 All the texts are translated in *Anchoritic Spirituality: Ancrene Wisse and Associated Works*, trans. Anne Savage and Nicholas Watson, New York and Mahwah, New Jersey, Paulist Press, 1991; a selection of texts and facing translations is available in Bella Millett and Jocelyn Wogan-

Browne (eds and trans.) *Medieval English Prose for Women: The Katherine Group and Ancrene Wisse*, Oxford, Oxford University Press, 1990, rev. edn 1992. For editions and secondary material see Roger Dahood, 'Ancrene Wisse, the Katherine Group and the Wooing Group', in *Middle English Prose: A Critical Guide to Major Authors and Genres*, ed. A. S. G. Edwards, New Brunswick, New Jersey, Rutgers University Press, 1984. An updated bibliography edited by Bella Millett is forthcoming in Boydell & Brewer's Annotated Bibliographies series (gen. ed. T. L. Burton). On the question of original audiences see the important new findings in Bella Millett, 'The origins of *Ancrene Wisse*: new answers, new questions', *Medium Ævum*, 1992, vol. 61, pp. 206–28.

24 Bella Millett, 'The audience of the saints' lives of the Katherine Group', *Reading Medieval Studies*, 1990, vol. 16, pp. 127–56; Millett and Wogan-Browne, 1992, op. cit., pp. xi–xiii.

25 Millett and Wogan-Browne, 1992, op. cit., p. 24, ll. 33–4; p. 4, ll. 28–9). Future citations will be referenced by page and line number in the text.

26 No specific source is known for this passage, though it has a generic resemblance to commentary in the *molestiae nuptiarum* tradition (see Millett, 1982, op. cit., p. xxxvii). The social class inscribed in the domestic arrangements here is not incompatible with gentle households: see Dominique Barthélemy and Philippe Contamine, 'The use of private space', in *A History of Private Life*, vol. 2, *Revelations of the Medieval World*, ed. P. Ariès and G. Duby, trans. A. Goldhammer, Cambridge, Massachussetts and London, England, Harvard University Press, 1985, pp. 416–23 and p. 425; on English sources see Joseph and Frances Gies, *Life in a Medieval Castle*, London, Abelard-Schuman, 1974, ch. 3, 'The castle as a house'.

27 On the exegesis of the tower, see Millett and Wogan-Browne, 1992, op. cit., p. xviii.

28 Ann K. Warren, *Anchorites and their Patrons in Medieval England*, Berkeley and Los Angeles, University of California Press, 1985; F. M. Powicke, 'Loretta, Countess of Salisbury', in *Historical Essays in Honour of James Tait*, ed. J. Goronwy Edwards *et al.*, Manchester, printed for the subscribers, 1933, pp. 247–71.

29 Sally Thompson, *Women Religious: The Founding of English Nunneries After the Norman Conquest*, Oxford, Clarendon Press, 1991.

30 Warren, op. cit., table 1, p. 20; Powicke, op. cit.

31 See Tania Modleski, *Loving with a Vengeance*, Hamden, Connecticut, Archon, 1982, ch. 4, 'The search for tomorrow in today's soap operas', and Anne Cranny-Francis and Patricia Palmer-Gillard, 'Soap opera as gender-training', in Terry Threadgold and Anne Cranny-Francis (eds) *Feminine, Masculine, and Representation*, Sydney, London, Boston and Wellington, Allen & Unwin, 1990, pp. 171–89.

32 For saints' lives in English see d'Evelyn, 'Saints' legends', 1970, in Hartung, op. cit., vol. 2, pp. 556–635. For Anglo-Norman lives, see Wogan-Browne, ' "Clerc u lai, muïne u dame" ', op. cit., p. 75, n. 4. Married, urban, female saints are not encountered in vernacular lives in Britain until the end of the thirteenth century: the virgin martyr and the penitent harlot are the major twelfth- and early thirteenth-century types.

33 On the compilation of the Katherine Group see S. R. T. O. d'Ardenne

(ed.) *þe Liflade ant te Passiun of Seinte Iuliene*, Liège, Faculté de Philosophie et Lettres de l'Université de Liège, 1936, and as Early English Text Society, OS 248, repr. London, 1961, pp. xl–xlvii. E. J. Dobson, *The Origins of Ancrene Wisse*, Oxford, Clarendon Press, 1976, pp. 138–9, suggests that the legends were composed for three sisters of the same names. For a recent study of transmission and recopying in the group, see Bella Millett, 'The textual transmission of *Seinte Iuliene*', *Medium Ævum*, 1990, vol. 59, pp. 41–54.

34 See Janice Radway, *Reading the Romance: Women, Patriarchy, and Popular Literature*, Chapel Hill, North Carolina, University of North Carolina Press, 1984, London, Verso, 1987, esp. ch. 3. I have applied Radway's work more extensively to virgin martyr *passio* narratives in a paper, 'The case of the hagiographic heroine', delivered at the International Courtly Literature Society Congress, Amherst, July 1992. See now Brigitte Cazelles, *The Lady as Saint: A Collection of French Hagiographic Romances of the Thirteenth Century*, Philadelphia, University of Pennsylvania Press, 1991.

35 Thus St Katherine is an orphan from childhood whose education is begun by her father (S. R. T. O. d'Ardenne and E. J. Dobson (eds) *Seinte Katerine*, Early English Text Society, SS 7, Oxford, Oxford University Press, 1981, p. 6, l. 27, p. 8, ll. 40–2 (henceforth cited in text by page and line number of edited text: translations mine)): only St Juliana's father is mentioned (d'Ardenne, op. cit., p. 3, ll. 13–14 (MS B), henceforth cited in the text by page and line number references to MS B, except for lacunae, where the reference is to MS R); St Margaret is sent for fostering by her father, and, following the death of her mother, becomes committed to her Christ bridegroom in the rural setting provided by her wet-nurse and fostermother (Millett and Wogan-Browne, 1992, op. cit., p. 46, ll. 1–13, henceforth cited in the text by page and line number).

36 See Elizabeth Grosz, 'Inscriptions and body-maps: representations and the corporeal', in Threadgold and Cranny-Francis, op. cit., pp. 62–74; Margaret R. Miles, *Carnal Knowing: Female Nakedness and Religious Meaning in the Christian West*, Boston, Beacon Press, 1989, part 2.

37 Medieval clerics were capable both of recommending internalisation of violence by rape victims (see Jane Tibbetts-Schulenberg, 'The heroics of virginity: brides of Christ and sacrificial mutilation', in *Women in the Middle Ages and the Renaissance*, ed. Mary Beth Rose (Syracuse: Syracuse University Press, 1986), pp. 29–72) *and* of working closely and cooperatively with female colleagues (the *Ancrene Wisse* writer may complain about his pastoral burden (Millett and Wogan-Browne, 1992, op. cit., 148/9–13), but writes a long, innovative, thoughtful guide for the anchoresses nonetheless). I am grateful to Diane Wolfthal for exchanging ideas on rape with me, and for an early copy of her study of differing traditions of representing rape, ' "A hue and cry": medieval rape imagery and its transformation', *Art Bulletin*, 1993, vol. 75, pp. 39–64. For readings by medieval women, see the works cited in notes 53 and 58 below. For an account of saints' lives and rape, see Kathryn Gravdal, *Ravishing Maidens: Writing Rape in Medieval French Literature and Law*, Philadelphia, University of Pennsylvania Press, 1991. For an argument that

Ancrene Wisse and the Katherine Group illustrate neo-Aristotelian misogyny and construct women only as the corporeal, see Elizabeth Robertson, *Early English Devotional Prose and the Female Audience*, Knoxville, University of Tennessee Press, 1990, esp. chs 3 and 4.

38 For the persecutions of the martyrs, see Eusebius, *The History of the Church from Christ to Constantine*, trans. G. A. Williamson, Harmondsworth, Penguin, 1965 and H. A. Musurillo, *The Acts of the Christian Martyrs*, Oxford, Clarendon Press, 1972; Hippolyte Delehaye, *Les Passions des martyres et les genres littéraires*, Brussels, Bureaux de la Société des Bollandistes, 1921, ch. 1, 'Les passions historiques', ch. 3, 'Les passions épiques', §3 Les supplices, pp. 273–304. For medieval juridical use of torture see Edward Peters, *Torture*, Oxford, Blackwell Publications, 1985, pp. 44–9, and p. 65; on heresy, R. I. Moore, *The Origins of European Dissent*, London, Blackwell Publications, 1977, repr. Oxford, 1985, pp. 250–8 and *passim*; on the 'drama of the ordeal' for literary and historical accused queens, see Robert Bartlett, *Trial by Fire and Water: The Medieval Judicial Ordeal*, Oxford, Clarendon Press, 1986, esp. pp. 17–19; on medieval punitive incarceration, see H. R. T. Summerson, 'The early development of the *peine forte et dure*', in *Law, Litigants, and the Legal Profession*, ed. E. W. Ives and A. H. Manchester, Royal Historical Society Studies in History, 36, London, Royal Historical Society, 1983, pp. 116–25. See also Klaus P. Jankofsky, 'Public executions in England in the late Middle Ages: the indignity and dignity of death', *Omega: Journal of Death and Dying*, 1979, vol. 10, pp. 43–57.

39 For a valuable discussion of twelfth- and thirteenth-century thought on the semiotics and typology of miracles, see Robert Bartlett, *Gerald of Wales, 1146–1223*, Oxford, Clarendon Press, 1982, ch. 4, 'Miracles and marvels'.

40 On the inter-relationships of SJ's and SM's wheels, see d'Ardenne and Dobson, op. cit., pp. xxxix–xl. For texts of Katherine Group sources, see ibid., pp. 132–203; Frances M. Mack, ed. *Seinte Marherete, þe Meiden ant Martyr*, Early English Text Society, OS 193, London, Oxford University Press, 1934, repr. with corr., 1958, pp. 127–42. SJ's source is more closely represented by the text in Bodleian Library, Oxford, MS Bodley 285 than any other known version (see d'Ardenne, *Iuliene*, op. cit., pp. xxii–xxiv, and, for the text, ibid., pp. 2–70 and Jocelyn Price, 'The *Liflade of Seinte Iuliene* and hagiographic convention', *Medievalia et Humanistica*, 1986, NS vol. 14, pp. 37–58, esp. 37–9.

41 Virginity is frequently imaged as gold refined by fire (see, e.g., C. H. Talbot (ed.) '*De institutione inclusarum*' in *Aelredi Rievallensis Opera Omnia*, vol. 1, CCSM I, ed. A. Hoste and C. H. Talbot, Turnholt, Brepols, 1971, pp. 636–82, p. 650, 'Virginitas aurum est, cella fornax, conflator diabolus, ignis tentatio' (Virginity is gold, the cell a furnace, the devil the [bellows-] blower, the fire temptation'); Juliana herself cites the three youths in the fiery furnace (*Daniel* 3.13–25, SJ 29/284–87 and cf. 33/356–35/359. Eleusius's attempt to burn Juliana whole in a fire (not just to mark her with tapers) is thematically apposite (SJ 59/647–61/668).

42 Olibrius threatens to 'forswolhen' ('swallow, devour') Margaret with his

sword (SM 50/25), an unusual use of the verb which aligns him with the dragon who swallows ('forswelh') the saint (SM 60/20).

43 On this theme in SM see further Jocelyn Price, 'The virgin and the dragon: the demonology of Seinte Margarete', *Leeds Studies in English*, 1985, vol. 16, pp. 337–57, esp. pp. 346–53.

44 Among post-Conquest male virgin martyrs, George, for example, among other tortures has his feet pierced (l. 459), his head nailed (ll. 653–4), his foot encased in a hot iron boot (ll. 1171–5), has all the fat burned out of his body (ll. 1132–3) and is sawn in two (ll. 673–4) during his contest with the emperor Dacien (see John E. Matzke (ed.) *Les œuvres de Simund de Freine*, Paris, Société des Anciens Textes Français, 1909, pp. 61–117). In the Katherine Group, each saint's 'leofliche lich' ('beautiful body') lathers in blood: when George is tormented with flesh-hooks, his 'holy *limes* [my italics]' run with blood (Anna Mills and Charlotte d'Evelyn (eds) *The South English Legendary*, Early English Text Society, OS 235, 1956, vol. 1, p. 157, ll. 34–5), and when Lawrence is stripped and beaten, the blood runs down his '*limes longe & grete* [my italics]', ibid., vol. 2, p. 361, ll. 95–6.

45 On body boundaries as social boundaries, the classic work is Mary Douglas, *Purity and Danger: An Analysis of Concepts of Pollution and Taboo*, London, Routledge & Kegan Paul, 1966, repr. with corr., 1969.

46 Peggy McCracken, 'The body politic and the queen's adulterous body in French romance', now printed in *Feminist Approaches to the Body in Medieval Literature*, ed. Linda Lomperis and Sarah Stanbury, Philadelphia, University of Pennsylvania Press, 1993, pp. 38–64. I am grateful to Professor McCracken for generously sending me an early copy of this article.

47 The anchoress is warned against conduct that would make her worthy of being a 'Jew's mate' (Millett and Wogan-Browne, 1992, op. cit., 124/32) and in *AW*, Part Two (J. R. R. Tolkien (ed.) *Ancrene Wisse: MS Corpus Christi College, Cambridge* 402, Early English Text Society, OS 249, London, Oxford University Press, 1962, f. 31a/26): SK refers to Christ, 'þe Giws demden ant heaðene ahongeden' ('whom Jews condemned and heathens hanged', SK 18/119), SM to the Lord 'þe þe Gius fordemden ant drohen to deaðe, and heðene hongeden ant heuen on rode' ('whom the Jews condemned and put to death, [who was] hanged by the heathen [and raised up] on a cross', SM 48/16), SJ to the 'giwes read' ('Jews' advice') (SJ 57/608).

48 This cannot be fully demonstrated here, but it is worth noting that the virgin is simultaneously feminised by being the object of desire and violence, and also masculinised as a *virago* of courage, rationality and heroic endurance. I am not arguing that the exclusionary moves of these texts are acceptable or pleasant, but that we should see their sexual politics within the broader frame of their cultural politics as a whole (I have explored this further in a forthcoming paper, 'Men, women and flesh-hooks: hagiography and the politics of horror').

49 Carol Clover, *Men, Women and Chainsaws: Gender in the Modern Horror Film*, Princeton, New Jersey, Princeton University Press, 1992, pp. 177–8, and see pp. 207–9 (on projective and introjective looking). Medieval theories of perception allow for the gaze to be affected by

what it falls on: see David C. Lindberg, *Theories of Vision from Al-Kindi to Kepler*, Chicago, Chicago University Press, 1976.

50 Clover, op. cit., p. 35–41.

51 On this convention see Millett, 1982, op. cit., p. xliv.

52 See e.g., SJ 13/123–33, 47/521–49/540, SM 56/4–13, SK 44/308–50/351, 52/360–58/413 etc.: the lives' speeches, as also their prayers, deserve fuller analysis than is possible here.

53 See William MacBain (ed.) *The Life of St Catherine by Clemence of Barking*, Anglo-Norman Text Society 18, Oxford, Blackwells, 1964, for a woman's late twelfth-century 'rereading' of the Catherine legend in which nuptial and fecund spiritual love for Christ is used in a critique of courtly love (see W. MacBain, 'Anglo-Norman women hagiographers', in *Anglo-Norman Anniversary Essays*, ed. Ian Short, London, Anglo-Norman Text Society, 1993, pp. 235–50, esp. pp. 243–7). Catherine Innes Parker discusses maternity and fertility in the Katherine Group texts in 'Virgin, bride and lover: a study of the relationship between sexuality and spirituality in anchoritic literature', unpublished Ph.D. thesis, Memorial University, Newfoundland, 1992.

54 J. Wogan-Browne, 'The apple's message: some post-conquest accounts of hagiographic transmission', in A. J. Minnis (ed.) *Late-medieval Religious Texts and their Transmission: Essays in Honour of A. I. Doyle*, York Manuscripts Conferences Proceedings Series, vol. 3, Cambridge, D. S. Brewer, 1993, pp. 39–53, esp. pp. 50–1.

55 Teresa de Lauretis, *Alice Doesn't: Feminism, Semiotics, Cinema* (Bloomington, Indiana University Press, 1984), pp. 37–69, see p. 69.

56 The phrase is Jan Cohn's in her *Romance and the Erotics of Property: Mass-market Fiction for Women*, Durham, North Carolina, Duke University Press, 1988, p. 8: see further ch. 2 'The romance hero', pp. 141–62.

57 For the Loathly Lady figure as a display of antitheses, see, e.g., Chaucer, *Wife of Bath's Tale*, III [D], ll. 1 Chaucer, 1219–226; J. R. R. Tolkien and E. V. Gordon (eds), *Sir Gawain and the Green Knight*, 2nd edn, ed. Norman Davis, Oxford, Clarendon Press, 1967, pp. 26–7, ll. 941–69; on Loathly Lady romances see John Witherington (ed.) *The Wedding of Sir Gawain and Dame Ragnell*, Lancaster, Lancaster University, Department of English, 1991, pp. 13–16.

58 Christina of Markyate, for instance, when forcibly betrothed by her parents, told her bridegroom the story of St Cecilia, the virgin martyr who converted her own bridegroom to Christian chastity on their wedding night (C. H. Talbot (ed. and trans.), *Christina of Markyate: The Life of a Twelfth-Century Recluse*, Oxford, Clarendon Press, 1959, repr. 1987, p. 50; see also J. Wogan-Browne, 'Saints' lives and the female reader', *Forum for Modern Language Studies*, 1991, vol. 27, pp. 314–32).

59 Heloise is a complicated semi-exception: see Linda S. Kauffman, *Discourses of Desire: Gender, Genre and Epistolary Fictions*, Ithaca, New York, Cornell University Press, 1986, ch. 2. On the discourses used here by Chaucer see further P. Delhaye, 'Le Dossier anti-matrimonial de l'*Adversus Jovinianum* et son influence sur quelques écrits latins du XIIe siècle', *Medieval Studies*, 1951, vol. 13, pp. 65–86.

60 See, e.g., among images for the pursuit of Criseyde, bk II, 372–3 (consuming the statues in the temple), 1371 and 1276 (impressing and

smiting), 1380–6 (hacking an oak tree), 1534–5 (driving deer to the bow).

61 For a recent discussion of these issues, see Elaine Tuttle Hansen, *Chaucer and the Fictions of Gender*, Berkeley, Los Angeles and Oxford, University of California Press, 1992, pp. 1–10.

62 Pace Kolve ('Chaucer's Second Nun's Tale and the iconography of St. Cecilia', in Donald M. Rose (ed.) *New Perspectives in Chaucer Criticism*, Norman, Oklahoma, Pilgrim Books, 1981, 137–58 and plates), whatever the usual iconographic visualising of the bath, there is no narrative visualisation here.

63 For an important full-length study, see Sherry L. Reames, 'The Cecilia legend as Chaucer inherited it and retold it: the disappearance of an Augustinian ideal', *Speculum*, 1980, vol. 55, pp. 38–57.

64 Chaucer collocates 'maydenhede' and 'maugre hir heed' when dealing with rape (cf. *Wife of Bath's Tale* [D] ll. 886–8, *Parson's Tale* [I] ll. 973–4, *Legend of Good Women* VII (Philomela), l. 2325–6.

65 A similar argument can be made for the display of maidenhood in *Legend of Good Women* II, though this involves an iconographic rather than a lexical pun. Pyramus, unmanned by his encounter with Thisbe's hymen-like torn and bloodied wimple, decides that Thisbe should never have been allowed out by herself at night (ll. 832, 838–9). The walling about of sexuality by gender roles and by the control of the 'jelos fadres' (l. 900) over its disposition can only be transgressed at the cost of dying, paganly, outside the walls of a city constructed by a queen (707–8), but ruled by patriarchal kin-groups.

66 *Geoffrey Chaucer*, Harvester Feminist Readings, Hemel Hempstead, Harvester Wheatsheaf, 1991, pp. 144–6.

67 SM 48/21–4 for the motif's inversion; cf. *Second Nun's Tale*, [G] ll. 424–7.

68 Sheila Delany argues that Chaucer displaces his sources' social themes and 'forces forward Virginius' determination to kill the girl' ('The haunted work: politics and the paralysis of poetic imagination in *The Physician's Tale*', in her *Medieval Literary Politics: Shapes of Ideology*, Manchester, Manchester University Press, 1990, p. 135); in the generic context of the virgin martyr *passio*, however, Chaucer's stripping-down of the sources has point, and the social themes encoded in the public moment of maidenhead's display and disposal are not in fact ignored by Chaucer. See now Linda Lomperis, 'Unruly bodies and ruling practices: Chaucer's *Physician's Tale* as socially symbolic act', in Lomperis and Stanbury, op. cit., pp. 21–37.

69 See Clover, op. cit., pp. 147–1. The Katherine Group are in one way not 'low-budget' productions (the plain, almost entirely unornamented manuscripts of the group, for example, testify to the voluntary poverty of upper-class women), but they are in a comparable position in relation to the canons of 'high' culture (both in the thirteenth century and their twentieth-century reception).

70 Carolyn Dinshaw, *Chaucer's Sexual Poetics*, Madison, Wisconsin, University of Wisconsin Press, 1989. For discussion of the representation of Cecilia's voice in this tale, see Gail Berkeley Sherman, 'Saints, nuns and speech in the *Canterbury Tales*', in Renate Blumenfeld-Kosinski and

Timea Szell (eds) *Images of Sainthood in Medieval Europe*, Ithaca and London, Cornell University Press, 1992, pp. 136–60.

71 Virgin martyrs have continued to be made in the twentieth century: Maria Goretti, who died in 1902 at the age of twelve from stab wounds received while resisting sexual attack, was canonised in 1950 (D. H. Farmer, *The Oxford Dictionary of Saints*, Oxford, Oxford University Press, 1978, repr. 1982, s.v. *Goretti*; Giovanni Alberti, *Maria Goretti: Storia di un piccolo fiore di campo*, Rome, Citta Nuovà, 1980, repr. 1990). I am grateful to John McKinnell of the University of Durham for kindly providing me with a copy of this work.

9 Reincarnations of Griselda: contexts for the *Clerk's Tale?*

Lesley Johnson

Marlene: 'You really are exceptional Griselda.'

(Caryl Churchill, *Top Girls*)[1]

Biological lives and literary lives are not coterminous. Griselda's physical body may well be dead and buried, as we are reminded in one of the closing gestures of Chaucer's *Clerk's Tale* ('Grisilde is deed, and eek her pacience/And bothe atones buryed in Ytaille', 1177–8), but her literary life is not laid to rest by the version offered by the Clerk in the *Canterbury Tales*, any more than it had been by earlier versions produced by Boccaccio, Petrarch and Philippe de Mézières amongst others.[2] That the story of Griselda had some currency off the page, as a talking point in the late fourteenth century, and as a subject about which wives might be expected to have an opinion, seems to be the implication of the Ménagier de Paris' comments on why he has included Griselda's story in the training manual he prepared for his young wife sometime in the 1390s.[3] The Ménagier finally justifies the place of Griselda's history in his compilation on the grounds that it is important for his wife to be able to engage in discussions about it with other people:

> et desire bien que puis que autres l'ont veue, que aussi vous la veez et sachez de tout parler comme des autres.
>
> (*Le Ménagier de Paris*, I, vi, p. 73)

now that others have seen [the story], it is my wish that you also see it and be able to talk as fully about these things as others.

The continuing value of Griselda's story as a talking point, amongst the upper-bourgeois folk at least, would seem to be attested by the central scene of Maria Edgeworth's novella, *The Modern Griselda* (1805), in which a reading of Chaucer's version of Griselda's history (via a modern translation) is dramatised.[4] And, of course, Griselda's story continues to be talked about today.

The most vociferous modern readers of Griselda's history nowadays are the readers of Chaucer's version of her story, and they are, to some extent, the heirs of the Clerk – the members of the modern scholarly community. As Charlotte Morse's recent survey has shown, there is no shortage of modern readings of the *Clerk's Tale* available now in print.[5] The range of responses in circulation is enormous and varies, obviously, according to the context of the reading, the critical position of the reader, and the kind of model of medieval culture and society with which they are working (a point which is sometimes explicitly discussed, sometimes not). My justification for adding to this scholarly cacophony here is that there is still a place for a relatively brief outline of the kinds of questions which might be asked about the *Clerk's Tale*, and some suggestion of lines of inquiry which might be followed up, in the interests of encouraging feminist interventions in this critical debate. But why should modern feminist readers be interested in this figure of Griselda?

In my view, versions of Griselda's history have offered, and continue to offer, important sites for the promotion of regulatory models of feminine and masculine conduct, and so they deserve some critical attention for that reason alone. But these 'case histories' do not serve regulatory functions in any simple way. Griselda may be cited as an icon of passive, patient and subordinated femininity (frequently represented as the 'ideal' wife), who can be invoked as a counter-model to that of the 'wifely shrew', but the implications of her story, when embodied in narrative form, may offer some challenges to definitions of ideal 'feminine' conduct which abstract 'women' from their place in the social sphere, as I intend to show.[6] My way into the subject will be via a brief review of the variety of the ways in which Griselda's story has been read and reproduced in order to suggest something of the historical mobility of this apparent stereotype of womanhood; then I will move on to consider some of the more specific resonances of the version of Griselda's history credited to Chaucer's Clerk of Oxford.

I

There is no doubt that far from being the last chapter in Griselda's life story, Chaucer's Clerk's version, along with other fourteenth-century versions, continued (and continues) to stimulate further translations, reworkings and revisions of Griselda's history, in England, in narrative and dramatic form. Around 1550, for example, a dramatised version of the story in Latin was devised for the boys of the grammar school at Hitchin by Ralph Radclif; John Phillip's play in the vernacular, *The Commodye of Pacient and Meeke Grissill* ('Whearin is declared, the good example, of her pacience towardes her Husband: and lykewise, the due obedience of children, toward their parentes'), dates from the 1560s, as does William Forrest's English poem, the *History of Grisild the Second*, in which Griselda's story is used as a frame for recounting that of the 'martyrdom' of Katherine of Aragon; Griselda's story was dramatised again by Thomas Dekker, Henry Chettle and William Haughton in *Patient Grissil* (c. 1599), and a prose version of *The Ancient, True and Admirable History of Patient Grisel* was printed in 1619 (and advertises its contents with the subtitle 'How Maides, By Her Example, In Their Good Behaviour, May Marrie Rich Husbands'); in 1739 an amplified translation of Chaucer's *Clerk's Tale* by George Ogle was published, and it is Ogle's version which is read out and discussed at the soirée, organised by Griselda's namesake, which takes place in Maria Edgeworth's novella *The Modern Griselda*, which I have already mentioned. William Carew Hazlitt mentions the productions of puppet versions of Griselda's story in the 1860s.[7] Although Griselda may be dead and buried in Italy, one of the implications of her invitation to the dinner party to celebrate Marlene's promotion in Caryl Churchill's play *Top Girls* (finished in 1980) is that she is a female figure from the past whose story, and exemplary value, continues to have a bearing on the cultural formations of the present and on the models of femininity in circulation now.

Griselda's long and active literary life may suggest that her story offers a model of femininity which transcends time and cultural specificity. Griselda may appear to function as an icon of the unchanging 'good woman' – as 'constant as a wal', to borrow Chaucer's Clerk's description (1047). And yet what is striking when any comparisons are made between particular versions of Griselda's story is the sheer variety of feminine roles which she may fulfil in her different textual incarnations and their changing emphases and permutations. The make-up of a 'good woman' is subject to both historical change and multiple definition at any one time. Although Griselda frequently fulfils the role of obedient wife, she is also variously represented as a dutiful daughter; as an exemplary political and religious subject – as Everyperson, then, not just Everywoman; as a model ruler over the self; as obedient but oppressed wife and martyr to a cruel, impious husband; as a handmaid and chief chambermaid; as organiser of chambermaids; as a nurturing mother who colludes with/passionately protests against the abduction of her children; as a dignified co-ruler who operates outside the household sphere; as psychological tormentor of her husband (the 'Modern' Griselda).[8] There are, in fact, many Griseldas, and the singleness of her figure is something of an illusion. The process of tracking down these varied manifestations of Griselda helps illustrate, in practice, a point that Denise Riley makes in more abstract terms:

> To put it schematically: [the category of] 'women' is historically, discursively constructed, and always relatively to other categories which themselves change; 'women' is a volatile collectivity in which female persons can be very differently positioned so that the apparent continuity of the subject of 'women' isn't to be relied on; 'women' is both synchronically and diachronically erratic as a collectivity.[9]

Examining the variety of Griselda's textual reincarnations also reveals (as Denise Riley's remarks would suggest) the instability of, and contradictions within, this stereotyped construction, and the wider matrix of role-models to which it relates, at any one time (including those of the good man, husband, ruler), and in any single version of her story. This is a point which Catherine Belsey makes in her discussion of some of the Renaissance reworkings of Griselda's story, which, Belsey notes, are themselves indicative of successive attempts by dramatists and writers to resolve some of the difficulties and contradictions in the role-models it contains, particularly those of wife/husband relations. In Belsey's view 'marriage as the story [of Griselda] defines it is entirely absolutist, but the moral superiority of the wife calls into question the justice of this absolutism. . . . In offering a model of absolutist marriage the story challenges the very foundations of marital absolutism.'[10] The promotion of Griselda's exemplary status may require, and yet threaten, that of her husband, the agent of her testing. But the paradigm of the wife/husband relationship may be used to represent relationships between subordinates and superiors in social and spiritual relationships outside the domestic sphere, and this, too, is a factor which may both increase the resonance of Griselda's story and enlarge the range of contradictions and tensions it may encompass, as it does in the *Clerk's Tale*: this is an issue to which I will return.[11]

What is also striking when narrative versions of Griselda's history (or more properly Griselda's histories) are compared is how frequently her story is placed in a discursive context of some kind which (with varying degrees of self-consciousness) draws attention to the way in which its significance may be a matter of debate, a variable to be determined according to the identity of its audience as well as by its writer/producer. Quite complex accounts of the circumstances in which Griselda's story is retold and received are sometimes made part of the fictional framework of the narrative. In its first extant literary form, for example, as the final story in Boccaccio's *Decameron*, the story of Griselda and Walter is reported to have stimulated discussion amongst the ladies present in this story-telling excursion.[12] When Petrarch translates Boccaccio's vernacular narrative into Latin, he necessarily shifts its cultural context, and concomitantly finds rather different resonances in the story. Petrarch's audience, implied and actual, is composed of educated men. In the letter addressed to Boccaccio which accompanies his version of Griselda's history, Petrarch specifically alerts his audience – men of letters – to the exemplary value of the narrative if they read Griselda not so much as an exemplary woman, but as an Everyperson, whose patient conduct offers a behavioural model for all Christians. Yet Petrarch, too, recognises some possible variations in the reactions of an educated male audience to Griselda's history: in a subsequent letter addressed to Boccaccio he reports on two very different responses from his male friends.[13]

When Petrarch's version is given currency in the vernacular again, by French writers, a female audience is anticipated by its narrators, who then have to negotiate between the lessons it apparently contains and their non-gender-specific (Griselda as Everyperson) and gender-specific (Griselda as exemplary woman and wife) applications.[14] When Petrarch's version of the Griselda story is translated into English and embedded in the context of the *Canterbury Tales*, this version of Griselda's story 'addresses a more complex audience than any other translator had imagined'.[15] Accordingly, the possible, and anticipated, range of readings of the figure of Griselda (and Walter) become more disparate too, as is clear from the variety of gestures made towards closing up the narrative and its resonances at the end of the *Tale*.

On these occasions, then, and they are not the only ones, retellings of Griselda's story by Boccaccio, Petrarch and Chaucer are accompanied by some references to the possible composition of its audience and some recognition of how their identity/identities might affect their interpretation of the story's significance. Such references draw attention to the way in which readings of Griselda's story are the product of interactions between its producer, or reproducer, and its audience: clearly, Griselda's story does not speak for itself, and how it is made to speak depends on the circumstances of its production and reception, which can, and do, change. This point, in turn, would suggest that any attempt by modern readers to recover, or claim to have recovered, the single 'medieval' reading of any of these narratives is something of a misconceived critical project.

II

Chaucer's Clerk explicitly introduces his contribution to the *Canterbury Tales* as an act of translation which brings a story written by Petrarch, and set very specifically in Italy, to an audience in England. Modern critics have inevitably responded to this very distinctive feature of the *Tale* and given much attention to detailed comparisons of the Clerk's version with its Latin source, Petrarch's reworking of Boccaccio's tale (revised in 1374). The fidelity of Chaucer's version of Petrarch's narrative is clear enough, but it is clear, too, that some use has been made of a French translation of Petrarch's work, the anonymous *Livre Griseldis*.[16] The distinctive features of Chaucer's version, leaving aside its context in the *Tales*, are to be found in the small-scale details which 'have little to do with narrative and everything to do with interpretation'.[17] Generally, it is agreed, the small-scale changes heighten the affective pitch of the narrative (the narrator, for example, responds much more strongly to Walter's 'assays' and temptings); sharpen the narrative focus on key moments of confrontation; and enhance the thematic organisation of the story (particularly the way in which clothing is used to mark out significant stages of Griselda's career).[18] However, if modern scholarly consensus extends this far, it is much more divided on how best to recover the meaning of these distinctive features of the *Clerk's Tale*: how, that is, to chart their effect on the interpretation of the narrative as a whole and on the understanding we have of Chaucer's response, and his audience's possible response, to the Italian cultural scene in the late fourteenth century and the ethical and aesthetic issues addressed by Petrarch in his reworking of Griselda's story.[19]

In an early exercise in comparative criticism, J. W. Hales read the *Clerk's Tale* against Petrarch's version in an attempt to offer Chaucerian readers of 1875 some guidelines for how they may best recover a 'medieval reading' of Chaucer's version.[20] Hales argued that Chaucer's version aimed at an 'obeisant and faithful reproduction' of Petrarch's narrative which is itself distinguished by the way in which Petrarch 'entered more profoundly into the proper motive of the tale than did Boccaccio', who 'grows somewhat impatient and angry with the figure of Gualtieri' (pp. 173–4). It would be inappropriate and anachronistic, in Hales' view, if modern readers were to respond to Walter's role in the *Clerk's Tale* with anger and impatience. Rather, Hales argues, 'if we would read [the story of Griselda] in the spirit of the day when it became current, we should not vex ourselves into any righteous indignation against the most immediate author of her most touching distress' (p. 174). The key to reading the *Clerk's Tale*, we are told, is simply to concentrate on the one 'theme' of the *Tale*, the patience of Griselda, and to disregard all else:

> In relation to [Griselda] the Marquis has no moral being; he is a mere means of showing forth her supreme excellence; a mere mechanical expedient. He is no more morally than a thorn in the saint's footpath, or a wheel, or a cross.... Indeed, nothing in the tale is of any ethical moment but the carriage of the heroine herself. The eyes and the heart of the old century when she first appeared were fastened devoutly on that single form and let all else go by.
>
> (pp. 174–5)

Hales's argument here is that although Walter and Griselda are situated within the historical world of the narrative, they really should be read as if they existed on different planes: one is a mere narrative prop; the other an example of great virtue. Griselda's history is read as if it were a saint's life. Such reading guidelines as these clearly require modern readers to hold a great deal of the *Clerk's Tale* in suspension and to ignore any signs of possible divergent audience response built into the story's framework, in order that they may be able to extract a single meaning from the *Tale*, on behalf of the imagined response of a unified medieval audience (a single social body) to it.[21]

The guidelines offered in Mr Hales's 'Note on Chaucer's *Clerk's Tale*' deserve some attention here because certain continuities can be traced between the kinds of reading strategies he advocates so clearly and more recent guidelines offered to modern readers for recovering a 'medieval' reading of the *Tale* which also require the construction of a unified medieval response and recommend the suspension of engagement with any other aspects of the narrative which might challenge that view.[22] This is very evidently the case with those critics who represent the medieval period as a Golden Age of hyperstatic orthodoxy, but it may be implicit in more complex critical discussions, some of which may be included in the gamut of feminist readings, as is the case with Jill Mann's recent study of the *Clerk's Tale*, for example.[23]

In *Geoffrey Chaucer*, Jill Mann makes a stimulating case for the 'right' reading of the *Clerk's Tale* as one which interprets the narrative in transcendental terms, but which also recognises Chaucer's innovation in making the figure of Griselda a figure for God himself, in contrast to the identification cued by Petrarch's version of the narrative.[24] At the end of Petrarch's version of Griselda's story, the narrator directs his audience's attention to the model Griselda's experience offers for the conduct of the human subject's relationship with God, and this is the reading re-presented in an abbreviated form in the *Clerk's Tale* as 'what this auctour seith' (1140–62). However, in Jill Mann's view, what happens in the *Clerk's Tale* is that the narrative is recounted in a way which suggests a radical reinterpretation of the traditional homologies between the husband/wife God/human subject paradigms. It is Griselda, Mann argues, whose role is aligned with that of the divine; Walter, in contrast, fulfils the role of the testing, disbelieving human subject, and it is this 'realisation of the divine in a woman's form that is Chaucer's most original development of the meaning of this traditional story' (p. 158).

Some of the specific details of the Clerk's version of the narrative can be used to support Jill Mann's reading of Griselda's numinous role: the narrator's account of Griselda's poor birthplace, for example, gives it a Bethlehem-stable aura (197–210); the resonances of the setting and the scene in which Griselda first meets her lord, Walter, evoke those of the annunciation (274ff.); Griselda's speeches themselves are heavily marked by the inflections of affective devotion and prayer, and her words, on one occasion, echo those of Job (871–2), a figure who could be interpreted typologically as a type of Christ.[25] Walter's experience, in Mann's reading, represents that of 'man [presumably used to mean every person here?] making endless trial of the patience of God, endlessly testing to see how far it will go' (p. 160). In her view, 'how much man asks of God – and receives from him' (p. 160) is indicated in Griselda's response to Walter's warning that she is to be separated from her daughter:

> For wiste I that my deeth wolde do yow ese,
> Right gladly wolde I dyen, yow to plese.

Deth may noght make no comparisoun
Unto youre love.

(664–7)[26]

One general point that emerges from this way of reading the *Clerk's Tale* is that in medieval texts the use of husband/wife relationships to express spiritual relationships may have the effect of unsettling conventional social norms and analogical chains which might link relationships between male/female; husband/wife; soul/body; God/human subject; God/Church (the first of the pair denoting the superior position in each). The effort to express a difference between earthly and spiritual power may produce an empowerment of the feminine and the female in medieval texts which address the subject of Christian spirituality, as some feminist critics have argued.[27] But even so, certain questions about this reading strategy and its adequacy still remain.

If some modern readers choose to read the *Clerk's Tale* as a mystical text (which is what the burden of Mann's comparisons with material drawn from Julian of Norwich's work may imply), there is still no reason why this should be done in an uncritical way. Even if Griselda does embody a divinely empowering ideal of patience to which both sexes should aspire, as Jill Mann argues, that point still does not adequately counter the response that a 'suspicious feminist' might make to this way of reading the *Clerk's Tale*. The suspicious feminist reader might ask, according to Mann's hypothesis, whether 'the assurance that women excel in patient suffering [is] merely a means of confining them in their traditionally subordinate role by praising them for their meek acceptance of it' (p. 161). If we take out the 'merely' here (for why should the putative response of a feminist be constructed in unfairly reductive terms?), a valuable question still remains about the masochistic qualities of the kind of spirituality on offer here and why it might be especially appropriate to realise the figure of a suffering God in female form.[28]

But there is also no reason to limit any reconstruction of the possible resonances of the *Clerk's Tale* to its translation into a transcendental framework of meaning. Petrarch may have recommended this strategy, but then Petrarch, as the Clerk tells his audience at the beginning of his tale, is dead (*Prologue*, 26–38). Other distinctive features of the *Clerk's Tale* include the heightening of the physical, historical and political specificity of the story, and their presence brings into question the adequacy of reading this story exclusively in transcendental terms. For example, what is difficult to accommodate in any reading of the *Clerk's Tale* as a mystical treatise (or a saint's life) is any recognition of how Griselda effectively draws attention to Walter's use of her body in quite specific and material ways in this version of the narrative. Just before Griselda is displaced from Walter's household (to be replaced, it seems, by another, and superior, wife), she reminds him of what she cannot take back to her childhood home:

> My lord, ye woot that in my fadres place
> Ye dide me streepe out of my povre weede,
> And richely me cladden, of youre grace.
> To yow broghte I noght eles, out of drede,
> But feith, and nakednesse, and maydenhede;
> And heere agayn your clothyng I restoore,
> And eek your weddyng ryng, for evermore.
>   . . .
> But yet I hope it be nat youre entente
> That I smoklees out of youre paleys wente
>   . . .
> Wherfore, in gerdon of my maydenhede,
> Which that I broghte, and noght ageyn I bere,
> As voucheth sauf to yeve me, to my meede,
> But swich a smok as I was wont to were . . .

$$(862-86)$$

Griselda is still operating under Walter's 'no complaints' clause (354) – a condition of her marriage which she fulfils in quite an extraordinary way. The narrator has drawn attention to the apparent absolute conformity of Griselda's will to that of Walter's and the apparent absence of any signs of dissent on her part. Yet at this point Griselda's status as a cipher of Walter, as an unchanging being, with no apparent autonomy, with an inner life to which we have no access, is challenged by this sustained speech which draws attention to her marriage as a lived, historical experience which has left its mark on her.[29] Although, up to this point, Griselda seems to have remained silent on the subject of her 'absent' children (606–90), here she talks about her role as a child-bearer for Walter in graphic, physically explicit terms. Her need to negotiate over the value of her 'dowaire' (848), her dowry – that which she brought to him on their wedding day and that which he allows her to take away – moreover, stimulates her reflections on the contrast between past and present experiences in ways unparalleled in the previous versions of the story:[30]

O goode God! How gentil and how kynde
Ye semed by youre speche and youre visage
That day that maked was oure mariage!

But sooth is seyd – algate I fynde it trewe,
For in effect it preeved is on me –
Love is noght oold as whan that it is newe.

(852–7)

In this scene, then, we are given quite explicit reminders of Grisel-da's historical specificity, of her physical womanhood, of the experiential marks of her marriage. And we are reminded of these again in the way in which Griselda is received back by her father: her old coat, which he brings to cover her body, no longer fits (911–17). Her dismissal from court allows another set of expectations about how superiors may treat subordinates to be expressed: Griselda's treatment may cause her father distress, but it comes as no surprise ('this olde poure man/Was evere in suspect of hir mariage', 904–5).[31]

Clearly there are other frames of reference, other areas of social and political interest encoded in the *Clerk's Tale* in addition to its enhanced Christian 'overlay' which need to be accommodated in attempts to recover the contextual resonances of this narrative. And there remains much more to say, indeed much more than has been said, about how concerns with the ethics of governance, and with social ordering and ranking in domestic and wider public contexts, feature in the narrative. In Chaucer's version of Griselda's history some opportunities are developed which allow for critical reflection on the operations of governance, the definition and constitution of social ranking in this society of 'Saluces'. These aspects of the narrative deserve a little more attention here because they throw some interesting light on the co-articulation of class and gender positions in this text.[32]

From the beginning of the narrative, as many critics have noted, relationships of analogy and contiguity are set up between domestic and extra-domestic models of patriarchal governance, in high and low social settings. The opening description of 'Saluces' and its ruler affirms Walter's value as a respected ruler who is served well by his subjects (66–7). Though separated in space and in condition, the palace and Janicula's place are linked by the paradigms of good governance they represent and contain. The obedience and devotion which the people demonstrate in relations with their ruler is mirrored, as Michaela Grudin has pointed out, in Griselda's relationship with her father.[33] Griselda has a place in Saluzzo as one of Walter's subjects, one of Walter's poorest subjects, and she is also part of a paradigm of virtuous domestic governance which then becomes translated into Walter's household when her father assents to her translation into a higher and richer estate. Links between Walter's subjects inside and outside the household are suggested by the extension of the 'no complaints' clause to both (169–70, 354).

Within the household Griselda is absolutely subject to Walter's will, and it is within this arena that the workings of a model of mis-governance, of absolutist rule, are made clear. As Walter discovers that there are no restraints on his power to act upon Griselda, he seems to fulfil perhaps a more familiar role model for some members of Chaucer's immediate reading audience – as one of the tyrants of Lombardy.[34] Walter becomes a potential perpetrator of major acts of transgression: the possibilities of infanticide, usurpation of Papal power (in his use of forged Papal documents to facilitate his mock-divorce) and incest all loom in this hitherto idealised political unit.

But the *Clerk's Tale* is not a political tract any more than a mystical treatise, and it is important not to oversimplify the models of power relations it represents, or to try to make firmer distinctions, or conflations, between public and private paradigms of governance than the narrative allows. If Griselda may be seen to stand in lieu of Walter's subjects within the paradigm of household governance, as I have suggested, Walter's household nevertheless continues to function in a wider public context, and her position within this public/private household is somewhat paradoxical: Griselda is both the most subject of Walter's subjects and a ruler of Saluzzo. Her exemplary conduct as a regent is clear from the account of how her governance in Walter's absence promotes the 'commune profit' (428–41).[35] Moreover, the equivocal role that the people of Saluzzo play in her history also works against any simple alignment of her position with theirs. Although Walter's 'assays' on his wife prompt some criticism from his people (who, more specifically, grow sus-picious of Walter as a child murderer), Walter's subjects commend his action and 'governaunce' (984–94) when they see the attractions of Griselda's replacement. These events (and others) suggest that any simple analogy between Griselda as 'wife' and Walter's subjects, as single substitutable 'bodies', cannot be sustained: the position of the wife of a ruler is both like and unlike that of the body of subjects who are ruled.[36]

But there is another important, and related, area of concern in the narrative which requires attention, if we are to register the full complexity of the way in which the calibration of virtue and rank, for men and women, is explored through the marital history of Walter and Griselda. As Mary Carruthers has pointed out, the issues raised in theory in the old woman's speech in the *Wife of Bath's Tale* (1109–18) about the relationship between gentility of birth and gentility of virtue are played out in practice in the *Clerk's Tale*.[37] Walter, it seems from the opening scenes, is an example of a man who is a legitimate member of the highest social élite through his family line, but he also has a superior ethical stature and a fine sense of discrimination (being 'Discreet ynogh his contree for to gye', 75). He is apparently able to recognise the existence of a virtuous élite, whose being is not dependent on their high birth, but on 'Goddes bountee' (155–8), and, as it transpires, his choice of marital partner is to be from this virtuous stock, and not therefore to be determined by reasons of political and material advantage.[38]

But in a paradoxical way, Walter plays the role both of social innovator and arch disbeliever in his own experiment in affording 'a povre fostred creature' the opportunity to become a fair lady. Walter removes any possible objections to his action in the public sphere through his imposition of a 'no public complaints' condition on his marriage. As events turn out, this clause proves to be redundant: the elevation of Griselda to a social rank that reflects inner virtue is a complete success. Griselda fits her public role as 'markysesse' so well that her social origins become obscured: the people can hardly believe that she is Janicula's daughter, but by 'conjecture/ Hem thoughte she was another creature' (405–6) – indeed 'hevene sent' (440). It is then that Walter begins to ventriloquise all the possible objections to his apparently successful act of social engineering, which does implicitly unsettle hierarchies based on social rank and estate alone (474–83; 631–7; 792–805). These alibis of motive may seem redundant in context: the people do not, in fact, offer any objections to the marriage, nor are they allowed to do so anyway. But the objections which Walter voices to Griselda about his people's putative objections to their match do actually serve to reaffirm the élitist basis on which this society is organised, and continues to be organised, despite Griselda's shift in rank. Her translation into 'swich richesse' (385) does not precipitate any further social reorganisation or any attempts to reduplicate her role-model.

Griselda's history appears to be both exemplary and exceptional, exemplary and aberrant, in gender and class terms, in every sense. The circumstances of her career may seem to validate the proposition that 'a woman may rise to the highest position of hegemonic

power, becoming the honored wife of a wealthy lord and co-ruler
of his kingdom through her archetypally acceptable behaviour', as
Elaine Hansen has suggested.[39] Yet some aspects of her history also
undermine the proposition that there is an 'archetypal' model of
acceptable behaviour for women. For Griselda is not just 'a woman'
(any more than Walter is just 'a man'): she has been 'povre fostred',
and that, as she herself emphasises, makes a difference to her ability
to 'suffer'. When Walter asks her opinion of his young and noble
wife-to-be, Griselda replies with a speech which warns Walter
against any attempt to duplicate her experience ('tormentynge') and
draws Walter's attention to the different constitutions of wives who
have been 'fostred' tenderly and poorly:

> O thynge biseke I yow, and warne also,
> That ye ne prikke with no tormentynge
> This tendre fostred mayden, as ye han doon mo;
> For she is fostred in her norissynge
> Moore tendrely, and, to my supposynge,
> She koude nat adversitee endure
> As koude a povre fostred creature.

(1037–43)

The ramifications of Griselda's comments here for the relationship
between modes of 'norissynge' and their relationship to differentials
of rank and qualities of feminine virtue are extremely challenging:
would 'povre' fostering produce better-quality noblewomen? But
such implications are not pursued by the protagonists of the narrative or by its narrator. Griselda, it seems, has gone far enough.

The subsequent emphasis on Griselda's singularity, if not
aberrancy, as a woman is used to circumscribe any other unsettling
implications of the private and public career of this 'povre fostred
creature'. Walter responds by re-presenting Griselda as his wife,
securing her in her position as Marquess, and positioning her as
an exemplary figure within a category (Woman) which apparently
transcends any rank-specific distinctions ('I have thy feith and thy
benygnytee/As wel as evere womman was, assayed,/In greet estaat
and povreliche arrayed' 1053–5). There is no suggestion that there
are any more 'aristocrats of virtue' around in Saluzzo. Nor are any
female (or indeed male) aristocrats of virtue, rather than birth,
brought in to strengthen the aristocratic stock in the next generation.
Walter's daughter (for she is described in these terms) is married
'richely ... Unto a lord, oon of the worthieste/Of al Ytaille'
(1130–2); Walter's son, who succeeds him, 'fortunat was eek in

mariage/Al putte he nat his wyf in greet assay' (1137–8). This latter comment is followed by a remark by the narrator about the declining strength of the world – which could be taken to apply to the son's failure to duplicate his father's example. Yet this does not get round the awkward principle raised earlier by Griselda: the point is that unless the woman has been 'povre fostred', she will not be able to withstand such an 'assay'.

III

Just how literally should we take Griselda's story? Does her story illustrate the lot of a 'povre fostred creature', or does it offer a pattern for ideal wifely behaviour, or a female embodiment of the operations of divine patience and/or a model for the ideal religious and/or political subject? These possibilities are raised in the body of her narrative, as the Clerk retells it, but they are not all pursued in the readings offered by the narrator at its conclusion (1142–1212). In one way further debate about the meaning of Griselda's story is encouraged by the range of readings offered by the Clerk in these concluding lines; but in another the terms of the debate are circumscribed by the kinds of reading scripts on offer here. There is, for example, no further commentary offered on the ramifications of the translation of a 'povre fostred creature' into 'richesse'. The co-articulation of gender and status issues which I have been tracing in the story are closed off by a more exclusive consideration of how Griselda's *womanliness* should or should not figure in a reading of what she represents.

The closing frames of the *Clerk's Tale* offer shifting evaluations of Griselda's currency as an exemplary figure whose significance is either beyond her sex (as a model spiritual subject for men and women) or for her sex (as an exceptional and singular wife). The shifting evaluations are marked by changes in the clerkly voice of the narrator, and his ostensible audience of address, as he first calls upon his audience as a body to 'Herkeneth what this auctour seith' (1141); later attracts the attention of 'lordynges, herkneth er I go' (1163); and finally produces a song dedicated to the only secular woman on the pilgrimage – the Wife of Bath – and all her 'secte' through which the narrator marks an end to 'ernestful matere' (1175).[40]

If, in the 'auctour's' gloss on the narrative, Griselda offers an intolerable ('importable') role-model for wives, she is, nevertheless, a pattern of constant behaviour in adversity, a role-model for everyone who faces the trials of spiritual life. But then, as the narrator moves beyond the 'auctour's' gloss on the narrative, the issue of Griselda's representational quality is addressed in a different set of terms as a new causal link is made between her singular quality and her identity as a woman. Griselda, it is claimed, literally no longer has any currency as a model woman: 'It were ful hard to fynd now-a-dayes/In al a toun Grisildis thre or two' (1164–5). Griselda's singularity, her scarcity value, becomes a criticism of the quality of women now in circulation ('The gold of hem hath now so badde alayes/With bras' 1167–8). But this pejorative interpretation of Griselda's singularity, her non-portability, is followed by a more celebratory response to the present and future demise of women like Griselda in life and in texts:

> O noble wyves, ful of heigh prudence,
> Lat noon humylitee your tonge naille
> Ne lat no clerk have cause or diligence,
> To write of yow a storie of swich mervaille
> As of Grisildis pacient and kynde,
> Lest Chichevache yow swelwe in hire entraille!
>
> (1183–8)[41]

What wives may think of such sentiments remains, of course, off the record. Those voices which are heard at the conclusion of the *Tale*, those of the Host and the Merchant, suggest that the figure of Griselda still has a positive value for them as that of model wife: they seem not to have heard the 'auctour's' views on Griselda's 'inportable' quality as a role-model in this respect.[42] It seems, then, that although the Clerk's version of Griselda's story may offer some challenges to the ways in which her history is interpreted, it still contributes to the continuing life of a particular formation of femininity (that is Griselda as an icon of the ideal wife).

The literary history of Griselda's story, as it is passed on and between fourteenth-century writers, and produced and received in the context of the *Canterbury Tales*, is, in Carolyn Dinshaw's view, one in which 'once again woman is associated with a text to be read and interpreted by men (and to be read, as well, by women who are being trained by men to be wives)'.[43] In fact, Dinshaw suggests, Griselda's story itself is about the translation of a female body into a text to be read by a man, by Walter. Such a description usefully alerts modern readers to the Pygmalion-type dynamic at work in the production, and continuing reproduction, of Griselda's story, within and beyond the context of the *Canterbury Tales*. But such a description, suggestive as it is, perhaps credits male writers, clerks and makers with too much mastery over their literary subject and homogenises the variety of issues raised by each retelling some of which I have been unpacking in this essay. Male writers, after all, do not have a total monopoly over the productive and receptive contexts of Griselda's histories.[44]

It is true that responses from wives to the Clerk's version of Griselda's story are only ventriloquised at the end of the *Tale*. Though Harry Bailey may wish his wife had heard this 'legende', this 'gentil' tale, she does not form part of its receptive context: she remains 'at hoom' (1212d). But at least we are given a glimpse of the currency of Griselda's history as a subject about which certain bourgeois wives, at least, might be expected to have an opinion in the comments of the Ménagier de Paris. Moreover, as I have been arguing with particular reference to the *Clerk's Tale*, the text of Griselda is not one that is easily or unequivocally 'mastered': it remains the subject of debate and reinterpretation. The sheer variety of textual reincarnations of Griselda suggests that her story has some kind of surplus discursive value which resists total mastery and control: in tracking down the various textual reincarnations of Griselda I think it is important to recognise the radical, and disturbing, potential of the career of this peasant-born noblewoman, even as we register the strategies used to direct its audience to a preferred reading of Griselda's history which might contain and suppress any unsettling ramifications of the narrative.

Griselda's most recent literary reappearance, in the dinner-party scene of Caryl Churchill's play *Top Girls*, suggests that her story still remains part of the historical-cultural baggage of femininity which has yet to be laid to rest. Here again, though, the importance of the context in which Griselda's story is reproduced and received as a determinant of her representative quality is underlined. Here, in this all-female gathering, another distinctive version of Griselda's history is produced. The distinction is marked by Griselda's final hesitant contribution to the dinner-party talk: 'I do think – I do wonder – it would have been nicer if Walter hadn't had to' (Act 1, p. 27).

NOTES

1 Caryl Churchill, *Top Girls*, Methuen Student Edition, London, Methuen, 1991, Act I, p. 25. All further references to this text will be quoted from this edition. All quotations from Chaucer's works are from Larry D.

Benson *et al.* (eds) *The Riverside Chaucer*, 2nd edn, Oxford, Oxford University Press, 1988, and are cited by line number.

2 Boccaccio's version of the Griselda story (c. 1353) forms the tenth story, told on the tenth day, in the *Decameron*: see G. H. McWilliam (trans.) *Boccaccio: The Decameron*, Harmondsworth, Penguin, 1972, pp. 813–24. Petrarch's Latin reworking of Boccaccio's story (c. 1373) is contained in a letter addressed to Boccaccio, in the *Epistolae Seniles*, XVII, 3 (*Letters of Old Age*), reprinted by J. Burke Severs, *The Literary Relationships of Chaucer's Clerkes Tale*, Yale Studies in English, 96, New Haven, Conn., Yale University Press, 1942, pp. 170–2. The text is accessible in translation in Robert P. Miller (ed.) *Chaucer: Sources and Backgrounds*, New York, Oxford University Press, 1977, pp. 136–52. Philippe de Mézières's reworking of Petrarch's Latin version, in French (c. 1384–9), is found at the end of his *Livre de la vertu du sacrement de mariage et du reconfort des dames mariées*: the text is reproduced in Eli Golenistcheff-Koutouzoff, *L'Histoire de Griseldis en France au XIVe et au XVe siècle*, Paris, Droz, 1933, pp. 157–82. For further discussions of fourteenth-century versions of the story of Griselda see Anne Middleton, 'The Clerk and his Tale: some literary contexts', *Studies in the Age of Chaucer*, 1980, vol. 2, pp. 121–50 and Charlotte Morse, 'The exemplary Griselda', *Studies in the Age of Chaucer*, 1985, vol. 7, pp. 51–87. For further discussions of the Griselda story and its European-wide diffusion, see Raffaele Morabito (ed.) *La storia di Griselda in Europa. Atti del Covegno 'Modi dell'intertestualità: la storia di Griselda in Europa', L'Aquila, 12–14 maggio 1988*, L'Aquila, Japadre Editore, 1990. This volume came to my attention after I had completed this chapter.

3 The Ménagier reworked Philippe de Mézières's translation of the Griselda story in the section of his manual addressing the topic of wifely obedience. For a discussion of the distinctive features of the Ménagier's version, see Georgine Brereton and Janet Ferrier (eds) *Le Ménagier de Paris*, Oxford, Clarendon Press, 1981, pp. 332–5. All further references to this edition will be quoted by page number in my text; translations are my own. For a translation of selections from the Ménagier's handbook (including the section on Griselda) see Eileen Power, *The Goodman of Paris*, London, Routledge, 1928.

4 Maria Edgeworth, *The Modern Griselda: A Tale*, London, J. Johnson, 1805.

5 Charlotte Morse, 'Critical approaches to the *Clerk's Tale*', in C. David Benson and Elizabeth Robertson (eds) *Chaucer's Religious Tales*, Woodbridge, D. S. Brewer, 1990, pp. 72–83. This is an extremely useful survey, to which I am indebted.

6 For an example of how the figure of Griselda forms part of an iconographic repertoire of femininity, see Petruchio's comments in Shakespeare's *Taming of the Shrew*, 'For patience she will prove a second Grissel/And Roman Lucrece for her chastity' (II, i, 283–4). Lisa Jardine discusses Griselda as 'the ultimate crystallisation of all demands for wifely obedience and virtue' whose 'print is to be found on Shakespeare's long-suffering female characters', in *Still Harping on Daughters: Women and Drama in the Age of Shakespeare*, Brighton, Harvester Press, 1983, pp. 182–5. But already by 1380 it seems that the figure of

Griselda had some possible currency as a member of the 'Nine Female Worthies' (female equivalents to the Nine Male Worthies): Philippe de Mézières makes this connection in the introduction to his translation of Petrarch's narrative (op. cit.). Philippe de Mézières expresses a wish that Richard II may find a wife like Griselda in his *Epistre au Roi Richard*, edited and translated by G. W. Coopland, Liverpool, Liverpool University Press, 1975, p. 42.

7 For further bibliographical details of the reworkings from 1400 to 1615, not all of which I have listed here, see Helen Cooper, *Oxford Guides to Chaucer: The Canterbury Tales*, Oxford, Clarendon Press, 1989, pp. 420–7; Cyrus Hoy, *Introduction, Notes, and Commentaries to the Texts* in *The Dramatic Works of Thomas Dekker*, Fredson Bowers (ed.), Cambridge, Cambridge University Press, 1980, i, pp. 129–43; Judith Bronfman, 'Griselda, Renaissance Woman' in Anne M. Haselkorn and Betty Travitsky (eds) *The Renaissance Englishwoman in Print*, Amherst, University of Massachusetts Press, 1990, pp. 211–23. Radclif's play is lost, but there is an extant reference to it, as Hoy points out (p. 132). George Ogle's translation is most conveniently accessible in Betsy Bowden (ed.) *Eighteenth Century Modernisations from the Canterbury Tales*, Woodbridge, D. S. Brewer, 1991, pp. 80–106. W. Carey Hazlitt mentions the puppet plays of his time but does not give any further details in his edition of Thomas Warton's *History of English Poetry*, 2 vols, London, Reeves and Turner, 1871, ii, p. 350. For full details of the reworkings of the Griselda story in verse, prose and dramatic form in France, dating from the fourteenth to the sixteenth centuries, see Golenistcheff-Koutouzoff, op. cit.

8 For example, Griselda's role as obedient wife is a central feature of the narratives, but her degree of obedience varies and is sometimes explicitly represented as being in tension with her role as nurturing mother (to startling effect in Dekker *et al.*'s play *Patient Grissil*, where Griselda, with breasts bared, makes an anguished plea for her child). George Ogle elaborates on the tension between Griselda's role as wife and mother in his translation (noting after Griselda's son has been taken away that she 'Fell as a mother, yet she rose as a wife', 1422). In contrast, in Forrest's poem, which departs in many respects from the outlines of the traditional story, Griselda is represented as an exemplary mother who closely supervises the education of her daughter. The direction and value of Griselda's subjectivity to the demands of higher authority are a variable too: Forrest's poem depicts the 'second' Griselda as an ideal religious subject whose Catholic piety contrasts sharply with the impiety of her husband, a barely disguised figure for Henry VIII. The depiction of Griselda and Walter's relationship in George Ogle's translation offers the narrator an opportunity to voice some observations on the slavery he perceives to be an inherent feature of the feudal system (e.g. 1547–50; 1591–3). Obviously a detailed discussion of each of these texts in its socio-cultural context is required, if an adequate account is to be given of these permutations, their differences, and the tensions they set up in individual versions of Griselda's history.

9 'Does sex have a history?' *New Formations*, vol. 1, 1987, pp. 35–45, p. 35.

10 *The Subject of Tragedy*, London and New York, Methuen, 1983,

pp. 167–8. Catherine Belsey discusses the contradictory and unstable qualities of the stereotyped figure of wifely and womanly virtue with which Griselda might be identified on pp. 164–5. Germaine Greer makes some interesting and provocative points about the popularity of the Griselda story in the Renaissance period (it is perhaps 'an indication of the rethinking about marriage that is insensibly and unofficially going on') in *The Female Eunuch*, London, Paladin, 1977, p. 203. Modern commentators on the Renaissance versions of the story seem in general to underestimate the challenging aspects of the earlier versions.

11 Natalie Davis offers some helpful general comments on the varied uses of sexual symbolism in pre-industrial Europe: 'Sexual symbolism, of course, is always available to make statements about social experience and to reflect (or conceal) contradictions within it. At the end of the Middle Ages and in early modern Europe, the relation of the wife . . . to her husband was especially useful for expressing the relation of all subordinates to their superiors, and this for two reasons. First, economic relations were still often perceived in the medieval way as a matter of service. Second, the nature of political rule and the newer problem of sovereignty were very much at issue. In the little world of the family, with its conspicuous tension between intimacy and power, the larger matters of political and social order could find ready symbolization', *Society and Culture in Early Modern France*, London, Duckworth, 1975, p. 127. I would add that this 'ready symbolization' may also result in complex symbolisation as it does in the *Clerk's Tale*, where the interaction between different orders of hierarchical relations complicates the application of the wife/husband paradigm to other kinds of social and political relations. When, for example, Walter's subjects request him to take a wife and to bow 'youre nekke under that blisful yok/Of soverayntee, noght of servyse,/Which that men clepe spousaille or wedlok' (113–15), we see how complex the matter can be: Walter's subordinates ask the Marquis to fulfil their will, but they express their request in terms which suggest that his future marriage would represent an extension of his domain of sovereignty.

12 See the *Decameron*, p. 184. As Anne Middleton observes, 'The beginnings of the literary life of the Griselda story coincide with the beginning of its interpretative history, in a series of explanatory gestures at first surrounding it, and later embedded in it, contexts for reading from which it is never again free', op. cit., p. 124.

13 As Anne Middleton remarks, Petrarch's rewriting, in its language and style, addresses itself primarily to an audience of men, 'those who possess the language of the ancients and of high written eloquence', op. cit., p. 129. Charlotte Morse comments on the female/male shifts in the imagined audience of Boccaccio's and Petrarch's version of the Griselda story in 'The exemplary Griselda', op. cit., pp. 73–4. For general points about the relationship between the use of Latin/vernacular languages and male and female audiences see Susan Schibanoff's chapter in this volume, pp. 221–45. J. Burke Severs outlines the accretative epistolary context of Petrarch's reworking of the Griselda story, op. cit., pp. 7–13; for Petrarch's advice to his readers to extract a Christian lesson from the story see *Sen.*, XVII, 3, vi, 69–91 (in Severs's edition), which is

translated in Miller, op. cit., p. 138: 'My object in thus rewriting your tale was not to induce the women of our time to imitate the patience of this wife, which seems to me to be almost beyond imitation, but to lead my readers to emulate the example of feminine constancy, and to submit themselves to God with the same courage as this woman did to her husband.' Unusually for a female figure, Griselda is allowed to represent 'human', not just 'feminine' virtues here, although only for the benefit of an anticipated male audience. For the two divergent responses to Griselda's story from male peers of Petrarch, see *Sen.*, XVII, 4.

14 Charlotte Morse discusses the varied stances of the French translators on the significance of the story and its application to their anticipated audiences in 'The exemplary Griselda', op. cit., pp. 74–9. Philippe de Mézières's version is interesting since he draws both a general spiritual lesson and a specific lesson in wifely obedience from the story of Griselda and then advises, in cases where the application of both might be in conflict, that wives should please their immortal spouse first, their mortal spouses second. Charlotte Morse draws attention to Philippe's remark, then dismisses its significance with the observation that 'the fourteenth century closed its eyes to such conflict, which might justify wifely disobedience to the mortal husband', 'The exemplary Griselda', p. 79. But Philippe's remark surely suggests otherwise and illustrates potential tensions in the literal and figural applications of the wife/husband paradigm.

15 Morse, 'The exemplary Griselda', op. cit., p. 84.

16 See Severs, op. cit., pp. 135–76.

17 Cooper, 'The Clerk's tale', p. 189. For discussion of the glosses on the text of the *Clerk's Tale* in the manuscripts of the *Canterbury Tales* and one possible reading of their significance, see Thomas J. Farrell, 'The style of the *Clerk's Tale* and the function of its glosses', *Studies in Philology*, 1989, vol. 86, pp. 286–307.

18 For a detailed discussion of the enhanced use of the motif of clothing in the *Clerk's Tale* (stimulated in part by details drawn from the anonymous French version of Griselda's story), see Kristine Gilmartin, 'Array in the *Clerk's Tale*', *Chaucer Review*, 1979, vol. 13, pp. 234–46.

19 In addition to the discussions by Anne Middleton and Charlotte Morse ('The exemplary Griselda') cited above, which offer divergent interpretations of Chaucer's 'reading' of Griselda's story, via Petrarch's version, see also David Wallace, ' "Whan she translated was": a Chaucerian critique of the Petrarchan academy', in Lee Patterson (ed.) *Literary Practice and Social Change in Britain, 1380–1530*, Berkeley, University of California Press, 1990, pp. 156–215 for a detailed and stimulating view of the critical distance separating Petrarch and Chaucer, and their respective literary endeavours.

20 J. W. Hales, 'Note on Chaucer's *Clerk's Tale*', *Originals and Analogues of Some of Chaucer's Canterbury Tales*, Chaucer Society Publications, 2nd Ser., no 10, London, Trubner, 1875, pp. 173–6. All further references to this piece will be cited by page number in my text. See Morse, 'Critical approaches to the *Clerk's Tale*', op. cit., pp. 73–4 for further

comments on the links between Hales' reading and more recent critical trends.

21 It is interesting to note that although Hales' reading of the figure of Griselda in Petrarch and Chaucer conjures up the image of the medieval audience as a single social body ('the eyes and heart of the old century' etc.), his later speculations about why it was necessary to invent a Griselda figure would implicitly contradict that notion. Hales suggests that the very construction of a figure like Griselda is evidence of a chivalric rebellion against a prevailing, clerically inspired, tradition of literature which defamed women. Griselda is the 'figure of a reaction [against this abusive literary tradition]. . . . The hearts of men refused to accept the dishonouring pictures so often drawn of their fellow mortals' (p. 176). Just how these imagined 'chivalrous rebels, who rise in loyal insurrection', are to be reconciled with the identities of the fourteenth-century writers of Griselda's story whom we know is not made clear. Hales is evidently reading the story of Griselda, and its literary contexts, through the prism of varied, and to some extent clashing, images of medieval culture (as one of unified, unquestioning Christian piety, as one in which the code of gentlemanly conduct was first developed).

22 The tendency to write out, or downgrade, evidence of the variety of ways in which the Griselda story was read and interpreted in the four-teenth century is noticeable even in those studies which concentrate on this topic. For example, in Charlotte Morse's essay, 'The exemplary Griselda', op. cit., in which she argues against the dominant tradition of Griselda-reading proposed by Anne Middleton, op. cit., the response of the Ménagier is judged to be 'crass' seemingly because it unsettles the reading which Morse wishes to identify as the dominant, and hence 'right', medieval one (see especially pp. 75–6).

23 Jill Mann, *Geoffrey Chaucer*, Feminist Readings Series, Hemel Hempstead, Harvester Wheatsheaf, 1991. For discussion of the *Clerk's Tale*, see pp. 146–64. All further references to this study will be quoted by page number in my text.

24 See Charlotte Morse, 'Critical approaches to the *Clerk's Tale*', op. cit., pp. 75–6 for an overview of previous allegorising readings.

25 Charlotte Morse describes this process by which Griselda's numinous associations are enhanced as one in which Chaucer weaves 'a text over the subtext of Christianity' and allows 'threads of Christian allusion to show through in the verbal texture of his Griselda', 'The exemplary Griselda', p. 80.

26 For further discussion of Griselda's use of the term 'youre love' (667) rather than 'our love' (as is the usage in Chaucer's sources), see Lars Engle, 'Chaucer, Bakhtin, and Griselda' *Exemplaria*, 1989, vol. 1, pp. 429–59, especially pp. 451–3 and n. 41. Engle traces a wider pattern in Griselda's use of the personal pronoun 'youre', here and elsewhere, to suggest an element of compulsion in her response. Barbara Nolan also comments on Griselda's use of the phrase 'youre love' in her study of how the language of affective devotion and prayer is used in this tale: 'Chaucer's tales of transcendence: rhyme royal and Christian prayer in the *Canterbury Tales*', in Benson and Robertson, op. cit., pp. 21–38,

especially p. 30. Nolan notes, but does not elaborate on, the 'misplaced' faith of Griselda in Walter as an ultimate authority.

27 Elizabeth Robertson sets out a more general case for the way in which 'feminist theory that takes into account the complexities of the relationship between women and religion can help us recognise that what appear in these tales to be extremes of female suffering and violence against women are actually representations of power and strength' in 'Aspects of female piety in the *Prioress's Tale*' in Benson and Robertson, op. cit., pp. 145–60 (p. 145). Jocelyn Wogan-Browne tackles the issue of 'female empowerment' in a subtle and cautious way in her essay in this volume, pp. 165–94.

28 Jill Mann gestures towards this in her discussion of the relationship between the virtue of patience and the experience of childbirth (p. 161), but does not address the kinds of issues raised, for example, by Sara Maitland in her discussion of historical ways of representing the relationship to the divine in the 'sexist and heterosexist' cultures of the past in 'Passionate prayer: masochistic images in women's experience', in Linda Hurcombe (ed.) *Sex and God*, London, Routledge & Kegan Paul, 1987, pp. 125–40.

29 For further comments on the resonances of this speech, and the implied criticism of Walter's behaviour that it contains, see Engle, op. cit., pp. 446–54; Carolyn Dinshaw, *Chaucer's Sexual Poetics*, Madison, Wisconsin and London, University of Wisconsin Press, 1989, pp. 144–55. Judith Ferster offers a helpful analysis of the different modes of representation of the 'self' used in this tale which have a bearing on this passage in *Chaucer on Interpretation*, Cambridge, Cambridge University Press, 1985, pp. 95–121.

30 Walter allows Griselda to take back that which she brought him on their wedding day. Griselda recognises that she brought him nothing except certain qualities of 'person' ('feith, and nakednesse, and maydenhede', 866); her 'maydenhede' is non-returnable and so, in exchange for this, she asks him for a smock in which to return to her father's house. Christiane Klapisch-Zuber discusses the systems of nuptial exchanges in operation in fourteenth-century Italy and offers some particular observations on the exchange system in use in Griselda's history, as told by Boccaccio and Petrarch, in 'The Griselda complex: dowry and marriage gifts in the Quattrocento', in Linda Cochrane (trans.) *Women, Family, and Ritual in Renaissance Italy*, Chicago and London, University of Chicago Press, 1985, pp. 213–46. Klapisch-Zuber suggests that Walter's action in retaining Griselda's rich clothes – hers only as long as the marriage lasts – would have been a recognisable and familiar nuptial practice for Boccaccio's contemporaries (see pp. 228–9). Even so, we should not overlook the extremely unfamiliar nature of the nuptial exchange between Griselda and Walter when considered against the background of the systems operating in Florence and England, in which the bride was normally responsible for bringing to the marriage a larger material endowment than that supplied, for her own use, by the husband. See Klapisch-Zuber for a general discussion of the expected norms and D. Herlihy, 'The medieval marriage market', *Medieval and Renaissance Studies*, 1976, vol. 6, pp. 1–27. Griselda negotiates an exchange for her

virginity in Petrarch's and Boccaccio's versions of her story, but there is no precedent for her using this occasion to muse on the disparity between Walter's apparent promise as a husband and his practice, as she does in the Clerk's version, in which she also gives more emphasis to her 'dowaire' of virginity. Kristine Gilmartin offers a very useful commentary on the disparate readings which Griselda and Walter offer of the significance of clothes in the *Clerk's Tale*, and Griselda's redefinition of her 'dowaire' (from 845–51 to 862–8), op. cit., n. 18.

31 The sceptical response of Walter's subjects (in particular those of Griselda's family) to the ethics of his behaviour as a ruler is substantially developed in later versions of the narrative, particularly in Dekker and co.'s play text of *Patient Grissel*, in which Griselda's brother (another innovation) voices a thoroughly sceptical response to Walter's actions throughout, until he is won over finally by Walter's 'benificent' treatment of Griselda and her family after her testing.

32 I take Cora Kaplan's point here, in 'Pandora's box: subjectivity, class and sexuality in socialist feminist criticism', in *Sea Changes*, London, Verso, 1986, pp. 147–76, that '[m]asculinity and femininity do not appear in cultural discourse, any more than they do in mental life, as pure binary forms at play. They are always, already, ordered and broken up through other social and cultural terms, other categories of difference.... Class and race meanings are not metaphors for the sexual, or vice versa. It is better, though not exact, to see them as reciprocally constituting each other through a kind of narrative invocation, a set of associative terms in a chain of meaning. To understand how gender and class – to take two categories only – are articulated together transforms our analysis of each of them', p. 148.

33 Michaela Paasche Grudin, 'Chaucer's *Clerk's Tale* as political paradox', *Studies in the Age of Chaucer*, 1989, vol. 11, pp. 63–92, especially pp. 80–3. Grudin discusses the *Clerk's Tale* in the light of fourteenth-century controversies over models of political unity and models of rulership, and usefully draws attention to the enhanced political dimension of Griselda's story in Petrarch's version. David Wallace, op. cit., also elaborates on the broader political significance of Griselda's story, and the voice given to the 'commons' in the Clerk's version in ' "Whan she translated was": a Chaucerian critique of the Petrarchan academy'.

34 For a discussion of the distinctive references to Lombardy in the *Clerk's Tale*, the topical associations of the region with the rule of tyrants, and the equivocal representation of Walter, see Phillipa Hardman, 'Chaucer's tyrants of Lombardy', *Review of English Studies*, 1980, vol. 31, pp. 172–7. For a more general discussion of contemporary views on governance and their application to events in Italy in Chaucer's time, see Margaret Schlauch, 'Chaucer's doctrine of kings and tyrants', *Speculum*, 1945, vol. 20, pp. 133–56 and David Burnley, *Chaucer's Language and the Philosopher's Tradition*, D. S. Brewer, Cambridge, 1979, pp. 11–43.

35 'Once she is married to Walter, Griselda becomes not only a perfect wife but, more importantly, a perfect ruler.... What is much more briefly treated in his sources is ... expanded by Chaucer to include two stanzas on Griselda's ability to "redress" the "commune profit" (428–41).... In her ability to "bryngen hem aton", Griselda demon-

strates the qualities of judgement, justice, and love of human welfare emphasised by Dante in his discussion of the ideal monarch', Grudin, op. cit., p. 86.

36 In my view, Carol Falvo Heffernan too easily conflates, and thus oversimplifies, these various levels of analogous action in her discussion of the politics of the *Clerk's Tale*: ' "Tyranny" and "commune profit" in the *Clerk's Tale*', *Chaucer Review*, 1983, vol. 17, pp. 332–40.

37 Mary J. Carruthers, 'The lady, the swineherd, and Chaucer's Clerk', *Chaucer Review*, 1982–3, vol. 17, pp. 221–34.

38 The self-consciousness of Walter's decision not to marry within his own social rank and the fact that Griselda is never revealed to have had noble parents crucially distinguish Griselda's career from those of the female protagonists of certain romances/lais whose social advancement is finally legitimised by revelations of 'hidden' noble origins. Michelle Freeman discusses some parallels and differences between Marie de France's *Lai le Fresne* and the story of Griselda in 'The power of sisterhood: Marie de France's *Le Fresne*', in Mary Erler and Maryanne Kowaleski (eds) *Women and Power in the Middle Ages*, Athens and London, University of Georgia Press, 1988, pp. 250–64 (though Freeman perhaps underestimates the radical significance of Griselda's career in relation to her social origins).

39 Elaine Tuttle Hansen, 'The power of silence: the case of the Clerk's Griselda', in Erler and Kowaleski, op. cit., pp. 230–49, p. 231.

40 If nothing else, our attention is drawn at the end of the *Clerk's Tale* to the way in which clerks may speak in more than one voice: other cultural traditions of 'clerk-speak' (subversive of orthodoxies/advocates for more active models of femininity) are drawn on in this concluding section. John Ganim discusses the changing modulation of the Clerk's voice in this section in 'Carnival voices and the envoy to the *Clerk's Tale*', in *Chaucer Review*, 1987, vol. 22, pp. 112–27. There is some confusion about where the Clerk's voice actually ends in this section. The verse form shifts dramatically with the song and, as Thomas Farrell points out, the song itself is preceded in '[t]wenty-four of the fifty-three relatively complete manuscripts which have the end of the *Clerk's Tale* ... [by] the heading "Lenuoy de Chaucer", spelled or translated in one form or another', 'The "envoy de Chaucer" and the *Clerk's Tale*', *Chaucer Review*, 1990, vol. 24, pp. 329–36, p. 330. Farrell notes the presence of other headings or marginal markers (such as 'cantus', 'songe' etc.) and the attribution of the song to the Clerk. The significance of these varied attributions and headings is open to considerable debate.

41 'Chichevache' is a horned animal who eats patient wives: 'Bycorne', not mentioned here, is a counterpart who feeds on patient husbands. Eleanor Hammond discusses earlier references to 'Chichevache' in her introduction to Lydgate's 'Bycorne and Chichevache': Lydgate's poem reworks some of the material of this song and makes references to Griselda as fodder for 'Chichevache'. See Eleanor Hammond (ed.) *English Verse between Chaucer and Surrey*, New York, Octagon, 1965, pp. 113–18.

42 The editors of the *Riverside Chaucer* note that 'the Host's stanza [at the end of the *Clerk's Tale*] is generally held to have been written early and cancelled when Chaucer wrote new lines for the Merchant's *Prologue*

containing an echo of 1212. It is found in Ellesmere, Hengwrt, and 20 other MSS', p. 884.

43 Dinshaw, op. cit., p. 135.

44 Christine de Pisan recounts Griselda's story on two occasions in her *Livre de la Cité des Dames* (c. 1405); on the first occasion Griselda is presented as an exemplary daughter; on the second, the focus is on her later marital history and exemplary value as a very strong woman. The *Livre de la Cité des Dames* is still most easily accessible in a modern English translation: see Earl Jeffrey Richards (trans.) *The Book of the City of Ladies by Christine de Pizan*, London, Pan, 1983, II.11.2; II.50.1–4. Richards discusses Christine's sources on pp. 265–6; for a more general discussion of Christine de Pisan's strategies for rewriting the texts of selected women from Boccaccio's corpus (using Philippe de Mézières' version here), see Patricia P. Phillippy, 'Establishing authority: Boccaccio's *De Claris Mulieribus* and Christine de Pisan's *Le Livre de la Cité des Dames*', *Romanic Review*, 1986, vol. 77, pp. 167–93, especially pp. 187–8.

10 'Taking the gold out of Egypt': the art of reading as a woman

Susan Schibanoff

The only phenomenon which, in all parts of the world, seems to be linked with the appearance of writing . . . is the establishment of hierarchical societies, consisting of masters and slaves and where one part of the population is made to work for the other part. . . . And when we consider the first uses to which writing was put, it would seem clear that it was connected first and foremost with power . . . exercised by some men over other men [*sic*] and over worldly possessions.

(Claude Lévi-Strauss)

In 1473, Anthony Woodville, Earl Rivers, came across a French version of the *Liber Philosophorum Moralium Antiquorum* and decided to translate it into English for the edification of his royal charge, the Prince of Wales. When he completed his anglicised version, entitled *The Dictes and Sayengs of the Philosophres*, Rivers asked another translator, the early printer and publisher William Caxton, for a professional opinion of his work. No doubt Caxton was pleased to review the Earl's *Dictes*. He was familiar with its French original and was aware that thus far it had not been made available to English-speaking readers, and Rivers – brother-in-law of Richard III – was potentially an important patron and client of Caxton's new press at Westminster. Not surprisingly, Caxton found Rivers's efforts a 'meritory dede', his work 'right wel and connyngly made and translated into ryght good and fayr englissh'.[1] Despite his obvious reluctance to criticise Rivers's work, Caxton did identify one flaw in the translation.

This flaw was in the form of an omission: Rivers had failed to translate a passage of several pages from his French manuscript which Caxton described as 'certayn and diuerce conclusions tow-chyng women' (p. 20). These 'conclusions' were, in fact, a conventional set of anti-feminist proverbs and *exempla* attributed to the classical philosopher Socrates.[2] Actually, Rivers had acknowledged the omitted passage in a brief statement: 'the said Socrates had many seyings ayenst women whiche is not translated'.[3] But Caxton chose to overlook this notice in order to try his hand first at a bit of witticism and then at a well-worn convention. Humorously, Caxton wondered whether the Earl's French manuscript lacked the passage in question or whether the 'wynde had blowe ouer the leef/at the tyme of translacion of his booke' (p. 24). Or, perhaps, Caxton next employed a traditional theme, a female reader had directly or indirectly influenced Rivers's version of the *Liber Philosophorum*: either 'some fayr lady' had objected to the anti-feminist passage and prevailed on Rivers to strike it, or Rivers's own amorous designs on some 'noble lady' had led to the same outcome.

Caxton was too androcentric and conventional to toy with the possibility that Rivers himself found misogyny reprehensible or tedious.[4] Instead, he followed the well-established *topos* of manuscript literature that women readers alone are offended by anti-feminist texts. When men were the fictional audience of anti-feminist material, the author assumed that misogyny neither troubled nor offended them. Instead, the author presented anti-feminist material as a useful encouragement to men to avoid the entrapments of marriage, or as a sympathetic consolation to assuage their grief that resulted from unrequited love.[5] But when women were the fictional audience, the author conceived of misogyny as offending them and in need of apology. Thus, for example, in his address to the audience of the thirteenth-century *Roman de la Rose* (part 2,15135–302), Jean de Meun apologised to his female readers for anything he said against women, just as Chaucer begged forgiveness from his female readers for his depiction of the false Criseyde in *Troilus and Criseyde* (5.1772ff.).

Authorial apologies do not, however, relieve the problems that the anti-feminist text causes the female reader. Instead, they intensify them, for the *topos* commonly includes a justification of the offensive text. In apologising for his malicious words against womankind, Jean de Meun excused himself by noting that he did not invent these words, but nevertheless defended them by explaining that ancient and reputable writers, wise men who never lied, created them. Caxton did likewise. He could not believe that so true a man and noble a philosopher as 'Socrates' 'shold wryte other wyse than trouthe', even if contemporary English women were far more virtuous than the Greek women of 'Socrates'' time. As regrettable as his task might have been, good scholarship demanded that Caxton restore the philosopher's opinions about women to Rivers's text. And Chaucer pleaded with his female readers not to blame him for inventing Criseyde's guilt; 'other bokes' before him record it, and he must follow his written sources. Implicit in this self-excuse by source is the threat that the written texts of anti-feminism are 'fixed': they are autonomous entities that may be neither altered nor discontinued. The female reader is to understand, then, that when writers must choose between pleasing her and venerating the written traditions of anti-feminism created by wise men of the past and noble ancient philosophers, patriarchy has first claim on their loyalty.

Faced with this choice, Caxton honoured patriarchal tradition by restoring the anti-feminist passages from 'Socrates' which Rivers had deleted. Following the restored passage, Caxton again engaged in uncharacteristic badinage with his audience. He advised anyone who was offended by the reinstated anti-feminist material to delete it physically: 'wyth a penne race [scratch] it out or ellys rente [tear] the leef oute of the booke' (p. 30). (To minimise damage to the text, Caxton facetiously located the passage in a conveniently detachable appendix at the end of the book.) In the context of both the written manuscript and the printed book, Caxton's suggested solution to the problem of a hostile text is, of course, ironic. As Rivers or the 'fayr lady' had attempted, a reader could resist offensive material by literally deleting it – but only in his or her own copy or memory, not in the 'work' itself. Caxton and others before him perceived the work as a multiple entity that, thanks to the numerous copies made possible by the technology of writing and printing, possessed a permanence no individual reader could easily undo.[6] One reader could attempt to alter a text; but another, such as Caxton, could restore it to its original form and content by consulting the written exemplar, in this case, a French manuscript, and then producing hundreds of printed copies which would further insure the fixity of the text.[7]

Authorial apologies to the female reader for anti-feminist texts are, clearly enough, something other than heart-felt laments. They are attempts both to intimidate her and, borrowing Judith Fetterley's term, to immasculate her.[8] They warn her that the written traditions of anti-feminism have contemporary guardians and custodians who will not allow these texts to disappear. If the text is 'fixed'[9] in this fashion, then the only solution to the otherwise irremediable problem of the hostile text is for the female reader to change herself:

she must read not as a woman, but as a man, for male readers, according to the *topos*, are neither offended nor troubled by literary misogyny.

In the first chapter of her *Book of the City of Women* (c. 1405), Christine de Pisan depicts the immasculation of a woman reader, the narrator 'Christine'.[10] The work opens with the narrator sitting by herself in her library, hard at work on her literary studies. She decides to relax by reading some light poetry and begins to search among her many volumes for 'some small book' of verse. Instead, into 'Christine's' hands comes a 'strange' book, not one, she assures us, that she has acquired by choice, but one that has been given to her. She opens the volume to find that it contains Matheolus's *Lamentations*, a well-known thirteenth-century anti-feminist diatribe that 'Christine' has heard of but has never been anxious to read. This time, however, she determines to amuse herself by browsing through Matheolus's tirade. Soon, her mother calls her to supper, and 'Christine' puts the book down. When 'Christine' returns to her library the next morning, Matheolus is waiting for her. Again, she starts to read the work and continues for a little while. But despite her resolution to 'enjoy' Matheolus – to read the work with detachment and irony – 'Christine' finds herself increasingly annoyed by its mendacity, immorality and lack of integrity on the subject of women. She browses a bit more, reads the end, and then puts the book down in order to turn her attention to 'more elevated and useful study'.

Physically distancing the text from herself, however, does not halt the negative effects this work has on 'Christine'. The mere sight of the volume sends her memory reeling back over all the other books she has read which present a similarly vicious opinion of women. 'Christine' recalls that she 'could hardly find a book on morals where, even before I had read it in its entirety, I did not find several chapters or certain sections attacking women, no matter who the author was'. Matheolus's text, in other words, is 'fixed' – in 'Christine's' mentality and memory and in the written traditions of Western literature and philosophy. And so 'transfixed in this line of thinking' is this female reader that she feels as if she has fallen into a stupor. 'Christine' is utterly unable to close the floodgates of her reading memories of anti-feminist writers: 'Like a gushing fountain, a series of authorities, whom I recalled one after another, came to mind, along with their opinions on this topic.'

'Christine' is, in Adrienne Rich's phrase, 'drenched' with male assumptions and prejudices about women.[11] Her survival – her self-identity and self-confidence – is at stake, and, at least temporarily, 'Christine' succumbs to the ultimate immasculation, the most extreme form of self-hatred and self-doubt: she agrees with her written authorities that God made an 'abominable work' in creating woman, curses her fate of having been born female, and wishes that she had been born male. The first chapter of Christine de Pisan's *City of Women* ends with its reader-narrator sunk in despair, unable to resolve the problem her hostile and fixed texts have caused her other than through the self-eradicating fantasy of wishing she were a man. She has failed to resist the palpable design the written traditions of patriarchal authority have on her.

Yet, as we know, 'Christine' does survive. By the end of the *Book of the City of Women* she has reclaimed both her self-identity and her self-confidence and has constructed one of the earliest histories of women and critiques of patriarchal society.[12] What I wish to examine more closely here is how Christine does survive, how she 'emasculates' herself as a reader. But first it is useful to look at the case of another fictional female reader contemporary with 'Christine'. She is exposed to the same anti-feminist readings 'Christine' is, but she neither succumbs to them nor loses her sense of self and confidence. Instinctively she knows how to resist an offensive text, and the way in which she automatically reads is the way that 'Christine' must and does teach herself to read in order to survive. It is also the way every female reader since 'Christine' has had to learn to read in order to avoid immasculation. The female reader I refer to here is Chaucer's Wife of Bath.

Most of us will recall that the Wife is a book-burner, and that the text she makes her fifth husband pitch into the flames is his beloved 'book of wicked wives', a manuscript anthology of classic anti-feminist treatises.[13] Night after night Jankyn delights in reading this work to Alysoun, until her anger erupts into a physical assault on the text – she tears three pages from it – and finally to its destruction. As violent as this response is, it is not Alysoun's most radical challenge to the written traditions of patriarchy. Caxton reminds us that written texts are replaceable, hence autonomous, and Chaucer does, too. Soon after the Wife of Bath destroys the book of wicked wives, another Canterbury pilgrim, the Merchant, restores the text that offended her so: to his character Justinus, 'the just one', the Merchant assigns an attack on matrimony which makes use of the same anti-feminist *exempla* Alysoun had consigned to the flames. The technology of writing has made books of wicked wives indestructible, permanently available to merchants and others who, in turn, perpetuate them. In short space, patriarchal tradition thus reasserts and re-establishes itself in the microcosm of experience the *Canterbury Tales* represents. On this score, we hear no further protest from the Wife of Bath. None is possible.

More radical than the Wife's attempt to censor and destroy offensive texts is her appropriation of them, which she demonstrates in her scriptural quotations at the opening of her Prologue. When she quotes scriptural passages, she instinctively and automatically adjusts or interprets them to serve her own needs. To support her argument for female supremacy in marriage, for instance, the Wife repeats Paul's command that husbands love their wives (1 Corinthians 7:3), but she selectively forgets the remainder of Paul's command that wives obey their husbands. And to justify her own multiple marriages, she cites the examples of Abraham and Jacob, both Old Testament patriarchs who were married more than once. More importantly, the Wife chooses to interpret these examples as literal mandates for her own marital conduct rather than, for instance, to read them allegorically as Jerome had, as examples of conduct sanctioned under the Old Law but not under the New.[14] In these and other uses of Scripture, the Wife implicitly calls attention to the existence of two 'texts': the fixed one, which consists of words on manuscript and printed pages, and the variable one, which consists of the meaning or significances readers assign to these words. In claiming her right to produce her own variable text, the Wife is at her most radical, for she demonstrates that Jerome's text, no matter how sanctified by tradition and authority, is in fact exactly that, *Jerome's* text, not the Wife of Bath's. And in selectively forgetting Paul's command about wifely obedience, the Wife is no more and no less biased and self-serving than Paul was in issuing the command. The Wife survives – welcome ever the sixth husband! – not because she burns books, but because she rereads old texts in new ways. And on this score, none of Alysoun's Canterbury companions, clerical or secular, wishes to confront her directly; her rereadings go unchallenged. Only the Pardoner manages the oblique criticism of dubbing her a 'noble prechour'.

What accounts for the Wife's ability to survive in this fashion? It does not proceed, I suggest, from a conscious analysis of the situation of the female reader in a patriarchal society. Nor does it proceed, as one modern critic suggests, from the Wife's 'perverse' inclination to misquote, misunderstand and misinterpret holy writ.[15] Rather, the Wife's survival skills as a reader are, at least in part, a function of the *way* in which she reads. As we often fail to distinguish, Alysoun is an aural reader, not a visual reader – an ear-reader, not an eye-reader.[16] In modern terms, she must be classified pejoratively as 'illiterate'; her texts are read to her by her priests, her husbands and others. Her choice of texts is largely controlled by the men who read to her, and, as her Prologue witnesses, she is probably as well versed in anti-feminist traditions as is 'Christine', her contemporary.

Although aural readers such as the Wife of Bath live in a world of written records – a manuscript culture – in at least one important respect they behave as if they exist in a totally oral culture, one altogether devoid of written records. Oral cultures preserve their literary and other 'texts' through continual recitation and repetition, but neither ancient nor modern oral cultures display anything near a *verbatim* recollection of their verbal works.[17] Instead, as these works are repeated over the years, they change form and content, and the alterations proceed according to the demands of relevance and utility. Oral cultures, in other words, constantly 'reread' their 'texts'; each retelling of a narrative is slightly different from the previous one, and there is a built-in, unconscious procedure of updating oral traditions over the years. Anthropologists term this phenomenon 'structural amnesia', and numerous modern examples exist in which that 'part of the past with no immediately discernible relevance to the present ha[s] simply fallen away' in oral tradition.[18] The implication is that orally composed, aurally perceived, narratives reflect a society's present cultural values; what fails to harmonise with these values is forgotten or altered. In Walter Ong's words, 'Oral societies live very much in a present which keeps itself in equilibrium or homeostasis by sloughing off memories which no longer have present relevance.'[19] Authority and tradition are readily and naturally altered, sometimes deleted altogether, to serve the needs of present experience.

As an aural reader, the Wife of Bath utilises 'methodology' and procedures that resemble those of oral tradition. She has no concept of the 'fixed' text of written tradition; unconsciously, she alters or destroys those authorities that conflict with her values or experiences. Her much-noted self-confidence, vitality and eagerness for yet more marital adventure are not due merely, as she would hold, to her astrological inheritance; they are also due to her ability to keep the world around her in equilibrium with her concept of self. To be sure, she achieves a precarious homeostasis that demands constant vigilance, but unlike her literate counterpart 'Christine', the Wife never succumbs and subscribes to anti-feminist views of women. She resists immasculation because she instinctively rereads authority and tradition, a survival skill that does not come easily to the literate reader burdened by the immobile written records of the past.

Written cultures do, of course, update or modernise the texts they receive from the past, but the process by which they do so is both more cumbersome and more restricted than that of oral society. A case in point here is the method by which early Christian writers of the fourth and fifth centuries attempted to harmonise the Old Testament with their own values. In many instances, the Old Testament appeared immoral or contrary to new Christian doctrines and ethics. What to do, for instance, with a scriptural passage such as the Wife quotes, in which an Old Testament patriarch practises bigamy? To the literate reader, the written text itself was fixed; it was the word of God transcribed, and both its literal and its historical form had to be preserved. Nor could one simply 'forget' troublesome passages. Instead, the past could be brought into equilibrium with the present only by creating an interpretation or meaning for the fixed text which complemented contemporary values. As Augustine phrased it, hermeneutics or exegesis allowed Christians to take the gold out of pagan cultures and convert it to their own use:

> Just as the Egyptians had not only idols and grave burdens which the people of Israel detested and avoided, so also they had vases and ornaments of gold and silver which the Israelites took with them secretly when they fled, as if to put them to a better use. They did not do this on their own authority but at God's commandment, while the Egyptians unwittingly supplied them with things which they themselves did not use well. . . . When the Christian separates himself in spirit from their miserable society, he should take this treasure with him for the just use of teaching the gospel. And their clothing . . . should be seized and held to be converted to Christian uses.[20]

With written texts such as the Old Testament, the method of converting the past and putting it to better use often took the form of allegorical interpretation. Thus, the patristic exegete explained, many passages in the Old Testament were to be understood by Christians as containing an *allegoria*, literally, a 'something other', beneath their literal surface. In some cases, the *allegoria* or inner significance was the direct opposite of what the literal surface suggested. While the Old Testament patriarch is, on the surface, an immoral bigamist, allegorically he may be understood as Christ, his wives as faithful Christian souls, and the intimacies between husband and wives as the loving relationship between divine and human in the Christian religion. The rationale patristic exegetes offered for such ironic interpretation *per antiphrasim*, 'by opposites', was complex. They maintained that immoral surfaces or literal meanings acted as a protective shroud over inner and true meanings. The unworthy, the scornful or the ignorant, as was appropriate in the opinion of the church fathers, would be distracted by the glitter of the literal surface and thus denied access to the inner kernel of Christian truth, while the worthy and the faithful would know how to penetrate surfaces to reach essences.[21]

Although patristic exegesis is the literate equivalent of homeostasis and structural amnesia in oral culture, a method of preserving and harmonising the traditions of the past with those of the present, it suffered from the same problem it attempted to remedy: by recording its interpretations of scriptural texts in writing, it gave to its reading a fixed character that became no less authoritative and ineradicable than sacred writing itself. What began as a method of revitalising earlier texts became inert and unchangeable.[22] In Christine de Pisan's era, almost a thousand years after Augustine wrote *De Doctrina*, Augustine's 'modernisations' of scriptural texts were still being cited, despite the fact that both Christian culture and Western society had obviously undergone enormous changes. For an aural reader, such as Alysoun of Bath, this petrification of an earlier point of view and set of values causes little problem; she freely adapts the opinions and readings of church fathers to reflect her own times and experiences. But for literate readers, such as Christine de Pisan, these earlier endeavours to update the past become in themselves part of the burden of the past which oppresses her fictional reader, 'Christine', as well as herself. What she must learn and practise is what the Wife unconsciously knows: in order to survive, to read as a woman, she must, in fact, reread, enter old texts from new critical directions.

As reflected in the fictional experiences of the narrator of the *City of Women*, Christine de Pisan herself learned this survival skill slowly and somewhat painfully. Her progress from immasculated reader to woman reader can be traced over a series of her works, including *Epistle of the Goddess Othea to Hector* (c. 1399–1400); *Epistle to the God of Love* (1399); her letters, which form a part of the debate over the *Romance of the Rose* called the *Querelle de la Rose* (c. 1400–2); and, finally, the *City of Women* (c. 1405). In the *Othea*, Christine schooled herself in the art of reading as a man or, more accurately, a patristic exegete. The work consists of one hundred chapters, each divided into three sections: 'texte', 'glose' and 'allegorie'. The 'texte' is a short narrative, usually no longer than a quatrain, from classical mythology, the story of Troy, or another source. Following the 'texte', the 'glose' explains or elaborates the passage, frequently employing illustrative or edifying quotations from the ancient moralists and philosophers (Aristotle, Socrates, Hermes, Diogenes, Pythagoras and others). Each chapter concludes with an 'allegorie', an interpretation or rereading of the text according to patristic – and patriarchal – tradition. The 'allegorie', or what I have earlier termed the 'variable text', is studded with appropriate quotations from the church fathers and other clerical authorities – Jerome, Gregory, Origen, Bernard, Augustine, Ambrose and others – and Scripture.

Christine's chapter on Briseyde (the English 'Criseyde') demonstrates her ability to read the text as a patristic exegete would. The 'glose' provides a brief summary of the love affair between Troilus and Criseyde, of Calchas's removal of his daughter to the Greek camp, and of Criseyde's affair with the Greek warrior Diomede. It closes with an indictment of Criseyde for having so 'light a corage' and warnings to good men to avoid 'such a lady as Criseyde was'.[23] In Hermes' words, she represents 'evil fellowship'. The 'allegorie' then interprets the text, the significance of which is made unequivocably clear: 'Criseyde . . . is vainglory, with which the good soul should not acquaint himself, but flee it with all his power, for it is quick and overtakes too suddenly.' Augustine is called on to witness the dangers of vainglory, the hardest of sins to overcome, and the rereading ends with Paul's admonishment in Corinthians to take one's glory in God.

Christine's allegorisation of the story of Troilus and Criseyde is anything but original, for this text had often been reread to yield an *exemplum* against the female vices of duplicity, pride and fickleness which seduce and ruin good men such as Troilus.[24] It is still reread in this fashion by modern patristic exegetical critics.[25] In fact, Christine's allegorisation is so conventional it appears that she is unaware that any other interpretation is possible; the 'allegorie' or variable text is fixed for her, and she shows no inclination here, or elsewhere in the *Othea*, to assign her own significances to the texts she reads. Perhaps because of its very traditional and patriarchal rereadings, the *Othea* was extraordinarily successful; more contemporary manuscripts (forty-three) of this work can be verified than of any of Christine's other numerous writings. Within a hundred years, it had been translated into English at least three times, and early publishers, such as Caxton, frequently printed and reprinted the *Othea*.

At almost the same time, however, that Christine was perfecting the art of patriarchal reading in the *Othea*, she was beginning to detect and criticise the anti-feminist bias of two important literary works of her day, Ovid's *Art of Love* and Jean de Meun's *Romance of the Rose*. In her *Epistle to the God of Love*, she briefly attacked both works for their vicious and illogical slanders against women. By modern standards, her critique of Ovid and Jean might appear tame and attenuated, and in itself her analysis did not confront the central question of who is privileged to determine the variable meaning of a text, each individual reader or the dominant set of readers in a culture. Despite its mildness, Christine's *Epistle to Love* provoked an immediate, strong and hostile response. By 1402, Thomas Hoccleve had turned out a smutty anglicised parody of it,[26] and three erudite French men – Pierre and Gontier Col and Jean de Montreuil – rose to Jean de Meun's defense and engaged Christine in a lengthy debate known as the *Querelle de la Rose*. Although Christine's opponents wished to reform her errant, that is, feminine, reading of the *Romance of the Rose*, in fact they enlightened her and motivated her to read as a woman.

The central portion of the debate took the form of a series of letters written by and circulated among Jean de Meun's defenders, the Cols and de Montreuil, and his opponents, Christine and her semi-ally, Jean Gerson. At the heart of the debate was the question of how different readers respond to the *Romance*. Jean's defenders maintained that all readers should interpret the work as they did, as an ironic discouragement of vice and a promotion of virtue. When, they argued, Jean narrates an assault on the castle – rape – it is not because he wishes to condone immorality; rather, his purpose is of the highest morality, for he describes the assault 'in order to teach more effectively how gatekeepers should guard the castle'. When Jean invents speeches of vicious anti-feminism for his character the Jealous Husband, it is not because the author wishes to promote misogyny, but because he wishes to 'demonstrate and correct the enormous irrationality and disordered passion of jealous men'.[27] In the opinion of Jean's admirers, the *Romance*'s literal scurrility and anti-feminism must be interpreted allegorically as 'something other' in their purpose and intent, and readers must interpret its surface *fabula* or narrative *per antiphrasim* ('by opposites') in order to detect its true meaning.[28]

Christine did not concern herself with the question of how the *Romance* ought to be read, but with how, in her opinion, the work *would* be read by different readers. Basically, she argued that readers would interpret the *Romance* according to their own lights. The virtuous, she conceded to her opponents, might well find in the *Romance* a powerful and persuasive praise of virtue (p. 63). But, by the same token, the vicious would easily find in the work an endorsement of vice. To Pierre Col's defence of the Jealous Husband's misogyny, Christine responded that a reader who was actually a jealous husband would recognise only the poem's misogyny and read it literally as a justification rather than a condemnation of his vice:

> Not long ago, I heard one of your familiar companions and colleagues, a man of authority, say that he knew a married man who believed in the *Roman de la Rose* as in the gospel. This was an extremely jealous man, who, whenever in the grip of passion, would go and find the book and read it to his wife; then he would become violent and strike her and say such horrible things as, 'These are the kinds of tricks you pull on me. This good, wise man Master Jean de Meun knew well what women are capable of.' And at every word appropriate, he gives her a couple of kicks and slaps. Thus it seems clear to me that whatever other people think of this book, this poor woman pays too high a price for it.
>
> (p. 136)

If, Christine continued logically and pragmatically, only the erudite or the pure were able to pierce through the *Romance*'s scurrilous surface to its inner moral message, then its message or meaning was wasted on those who most needed to hear it, the foolish and the vicious. Again and again Christine argued the point that an ironic discrepancy between a poem's immoral *fabula* or narrative surface and its moral *sententia* or inner meaning ran the risk of inculcating the superficial values, for readers read – and create texts – in their own images. On this score, Jean Gerson agreed with Christine; he wished that the *Romance* inculcated virtue in the way that Scripture did:

> That is, to reprove evil in such a way that every man might perceive that condemnation of evil and that approbation of good, and (what is most important) that all those things could have been done without excessive frivolity. But no. . . . Everything [in

the *Romance*] seems as true as the Gospel, particularly to those
foolish and vicious lovers to whom [Jean] speaks.

(p. 181)

Christine phrased it more succinctly: 'There is no point in reminding
human nature, which is naturally inclined to evil, that it limps on
one foot, in the hope that it will then walk straighter' (p. 55).

Inadvertently, Jean's defenders proved Christine's point. Although
they continued to justify the morality of the *Romance* on the basis
of an ideal reading – *their* reading – increasing frustration with
Christine's attack led them to admit that other readers were, in fact,
understanding the work differently, or, in their terms, misreading it.
Among these misreaders, of course, was Christine de Pisan. Jean de
Montreuil complained that Christine and other detractors of the
Romance lacked the intelligence and sophistication necessary to
perceive the moral purpose of Jean's work: 'They do not understand
how that teacher has fulfilled the function of a satirist and is therefore permitted many things prohibited to other writers' (p. 154).
In Christine's case, he charged more specifically, the misreading
proceeded from the regrettable fact that she was reading (just) like
a woman; to him, she sounded like 'Leontium the Greek whore, as
Cicero says, who dared to criticize the great philosopher Theophrastus' (p. 153). Similarly, Gontier Col identified female pride as the
source of Christine's misreading of the *Romance*. He exhorted and
begged her to correct the 'manifest error, folly, or excessive willful-
ness which has risen in [her], a woman impassioned in this matter,
out of presumption or arrogance' (p. 60). Pierre Col also charged
that Christine read – that is, misread – like a woman, and prescribed
a hundred readings of the *Romance* to rid Christine of this unfortunate point of view:

> Oh excessively foolish pride! Oh opinion uttered too quickly and
> thoughtlessly by the mouth of a woman! A woman who condemns
> a man of high understanding and dedicated study, a man who, by
> great labor and deliberation, has made the very noble book of
> the *Rose*, which surpasses all others that ever were written in
> French. When you have read this book a hundred times, provided
> you have understood the greater part of it, you will discover
> that you could never have put your time and intellect to better
> use.

(p. 103)

Christine's male ally, Jean Gerson, was also accused of reading like a woman, even though he possessed sufficient 'manly' intellect to arrive at a proper understanding of the *Romance*'s worth:

> And granted that the book was more attentively read by one of these detractors [i.e., Gerson] and, that brooding over the processes and nuances of the work, it was given to him to understand, still he was led to speak and feel differently because of his religious vocation and vows, or perhaps he is simply the kind of man who is rendered useless for the propagation of the species, which is, after all, the purpose of this book.
>
> (p. 154)

In the course of the debate, Christine replied often to the accusation that she read the *Romance* like a woman – that envy, pride or foolishness led her to misunderstand the work. Her responses range from ironic comment on the double standard to outright denial and, finally, to a redefinition of the charge: she was not reading *like* a woman, she was reading *as* a woman. To Jean de Montreuil she argued that if she were reading like a woman, then Jean de Meun deserved even more censure for writing like a man: 'And may it not be imputed to me as folly, arrogance, or presumption, that I, a woman, should dare to reproach and call into question so subtle an author, and to diminish the stature of his work, when he alone, a man, has dared to undertake to defame and blame without exception an entire sex' (p. 56). To de Montreuil, she denied that her reading proceeded from 'feminine bias' (p. 53); to Pierre Col, that pride, envy or indignation produced her reading (pp. 142–3); and to Gontier Col, that folly and presumption motivated her attack on the *Romance* (pp. 62–3).

Christine's denials of the charge that she read like a woman were futile, judging from the number of times such pejorative comments recur in the debate. But in the course of defending herself, Christine gradually began to develop a positive view of the way in which she was reading. In a letter to Gontier Col, she redefined his insult about her sex into a compliment:

> And if you despise my reasons so much because of the inadequacy of my faculties, which you criticize by your words, 'a woman impassioned', etc., rest assured that I do not feel any sting in such criticism, thanks to the comfort I find in the knowledge that there are, and have been vast numbers of excellent, praise-worthy women, schooled in all the virtues – whom *I* would

rather resemble than to be enriched with all the goods of fortune.

(p. 63)

To Jean de Montreuil, she defended her reading of the *Romance* as an anti-feminist work not on the basis that she had arrived at a universal interpretation of the work, but on the basis that as a woman she possessed a more authoritative understanding of women than did Jean de Meun: 'And it is precisely because I am a woman that I can speak better in this matter than one who has not had the experience, since he speaks only by conjecture and chance' (p. 53). As Christine phrased this new understanding in her final entry in the debate, 'Nothing gives one so much authority as one's own experience' (p. 143). In part, Christine's experience as the only female participant in the *Querelle de la Rose* taught her to read authoritatively, to read, that is, as a woman.

Christine also learned from the debate the art of deconstructing a text, of recognising and examining the means by which readers construct the variable meanings of a text. It appears she never convinced her opponents that readers inevitably recreate the texts they read in their own images, even though she herself was charged with reading in precisely that way. Nor did she convince them specifically that the *Romance* was morally ineffective because it was especially vulnerable to being recreated in diverse, often opposite, ways. Jean de Meun's defenders held fast to their conviction that there was only one correct reading of the *Romance*, that the variable text was in fact fixed, and that the goal of each reader should be to arrive at this same reading. As Christine left the debate, in 1402, she remarked with evident weariness and frustration on the futility of arguing the issue further:

> You know that it happens with the reading of this book as with the books of the alchemists. Some people read them and understand them in one way; others read them and understand them in a totally opposite way. And each thinks he understands very well indeed. . . . So it is with you and me and many others. You understand the book in one way, and I, quite the opposite. You quote; I reply. And when we have worked and worked, it is all worth nothing.

(p. 125)

I do not know why we are debating these questions so fully, for I do not believe we will be able to change each other's opinions.

You say that [Jean de Meun] is good; I say that he is evil. Now show me which of the two is right.

(p. 140)

As her *Book of the City of Women* witnesses, however, the debate was worth much to Christine de Pisan, for it had transformed her from being the immasculated reader who composed the *Othea* into the woman reader, one who claimed her right to reread texts according to her own experiences and knowledge. She would not again subscribe to a patristic 'allegorie' or interpretation of a 'texte'; instead, she created her own readings of standard texts which, in many cases, were startling in their divergence from other readings. As I have suggested, the *City of Women* may be read as a quasi-autobiographical work, and the extreme immasculation of the fictional reader, 'Christine', reflects in part its author's early experiences. The narrator's subsequent transformation into a woman reader also, I think, reflects Christine de Pisan's experience in the *Querelle de la Rose*. The turning point in 'Christine's' reader identity occurs shortly after she experiences the depths of self-hatred and self-doubt. The allegorical personification, Reason, appears to her, determined to rescue her from the blind ignorance that so clouds her intellect that she 'shun[s] what [she] know[s] for a certainty and believe[s] what [she does] not know or see or recognize except by virtue of many strange opinions' (p. 6). 'Christine's' wish that she were male strikes Reason as utter folly: 'You resemble the fool in the prank who was dressed in women's clothes while he slept; because those who were making fun of him repeatedly told him he was a woman, he believed their false testimony more readily than the certainty of his own identity. Fair daughter, have you lost all sense?' (p. 6).

Reason then proceeds to show 'Christine' how to read as a woman, specifically, how to reread both Matheolus's *Lamentations* and Jean's *Romance* in a way that does not immasculate her, and she does so in a completely irrational fashion:

As far as the poets of whom you speak are concerned, do you not know that they spoke on many subjects in a fictional way and that often they mean the contrary of what they say? One can interpret them according to the grammatical figure of *antiphrasis*, which means, as you know, that if you call something bad, in fact, it is good and vice versa. Thus I advise you to profit from their works and to interpret them in the manner in which they are intended in those passages where they attack women.

(p. 7)

In a patently outrageous conclusion, Reason demonstrates that both the *Lamentations* and the *Romance* actually praise women. Despite the facetious tone in Reason's instructions on the art of reading as a woman, there is a serious dimension to her observations. She has taken the methodology used by both patristic exegetes and the defenders of the *Romance* – interpretation 'by opposites' – and turned it to women's advantage. In doing so, she points squarely at the issue of how readers create texts in their own images and claims the same privilege for female readers that male readers have always enjoyed, even though the latter have often claimed that their readings are the 'correct' and universal ones sanctioned by God and Reason.

'Christine's' instruction in the art of reading as a woman serves her well, and much of the remainder of the *City of Women* contains her rereadings of women's history as presented by male writers. She does not continue in the outrageous and comic mode of her instructor, Reason, although many of her rereadings are unusual for their boldness and originality. Two examples from the *City* must suffice here to indicate the extent to which 'Christine' – and her creator, Christine de Pisan – learned to enter old critical texts from new directions, to take the gold from Egypt and convert it to better use. The first is the story of Circe, a figure Christine de Pisan had earlier treated in her *Othea* and 'Christine' discusses in the *City of Women*. To the *Othea* author, Circe may be read either as a woman full of wantonness and idleness who led Ulysses' knights astray (p. 118), or as the female deceiver and enchantress whom the good knight should avoid (p. 51). Christine's reading of Circe as the 'wicked woman' who leads men astray is traditional enough; Boccaccio, for instance, had interpreted her meaning in precisely the same way in *Concerning Famous Women* (c. 1355–9).[29] In the *City of Women*, however, 'Christine' completely rereads the significance of Circe; she is no longer the wicked woman par excellence, but a historical example of a woman of great learning who proves that women were not naturally inept in the much-respected ancient art of divination. Circe excelled so in this art 'that there was nothing which she might want to do that she could not accomplish by virtue of the strength of her spells' (p. 70). As an example of Circe's art, 'Christine' briefly narrates the Ulysses episode, as Christine earlier had in the *Othea*. But again, she rereads the meaning of Circe's transformation of Ulysses' men into swine. In the *Othea*, Circe's spell is capricious and unmotivated, the action of a fickle and malicious woman. But in the *City of Women*, 'Christine's' Circe behaves as a woman might when she is suddenly confronted by ten strange men: 'Ulysses . . . sent his knights to her in order to find out whether it would please her for them to land. But this lady, *thinking they were her enemies*, gave the ten knights a drink of her concoction, which immediately changed them into swine. *Ulysses quickly went to her, and the men were subsequently changed back to their proper form*' (p. 70; italics mine).

The second example is brief, but striking: Leontium. To Boccaccio, she was a scholar who, 'moved either by envy or womanly temerity', dared 'write against and criticize Theophrastus, a famous philosopher of that period'. Although Leontium was 'brilliant', Boccaccio admits, she ruined her reputation because she 'threw away womanly shame and was a courtesan, or rather a harlot': 'We must certainly bewail the fact that so brilliant a mind, given by heaven as a sacred gift, could be subjected to such filthy practices.'[30] And to Jean de Montreuil (as well as Cicero), Leontium was nothing more than 'the Greek whore . . . who dared to criticize the great philosopher Theophrastus'; Leontium also reminded him of his opponent in the *Querelle de la Rose*, Christine de Pisan. In her *City*, Christine de Pisan, however, detected an entirely different woman: 'I could tell you a great deal about women of great learning. Leontium was a Greek woman and also such a great philosopher that she dared, *for impartial and serious reasons*, to correct and attack the philosopher Theophrastus, who was quite famous *in her time*' (p. 68; italics mine). As Christine had earlier turned the insult, reading like a woman, into a beneficial methodology, reading as a woman, so here she transformed a woman reviled by male readers into a woman both admired and understood. Her gold from Egypt – women's experience as presented by men – was converted to better use.

Unlike the earlier *Othea*, Christine's *City of Women* was allowed to fall into obscurity. To date, no critical edition of the original French text has been published, and the first modern English translation of it did not appear until 1982. Modern readers have frequently labelled it an 'imitation' of Boccaccio's *Concerning Famous Women*, which it decidedly is not.[31] Not only does it contain straightforward analyses and critiques of patriarchal culture that are altogether absent in Boccaccio's work, but, as I hope the two examples above may indicate, it also entirely rereads Boccaccio and other male authorities who had, until Christine's time, controlled the production of the written records of women's history. Her achievement is, I think, stunning, but still undervalued. Almost single-handedly, Christine came to the realisation that in order to read as a woman, she would have to reread almost the entire corpus of men's writings about women; the *City of Women* rereads the written narratives of more than one hundred and twenty women, ranging from the ancient poet, Sappho, to the modern queen, Isabella of Bavaria. From her experiences in the *Querelle*, Christine must also have realised that she would again be accused of reading like a woman in the *City*; perhaps for that reason, the *City* is a work about women for women readers. She addressed the work specifically to women and presented the dedication copy to the queen. No *Querelle de la Cité* ensued. Instead, Christine went on to write a continuation of the *City, The Book of Three Virtues*.

Christine de Pisan's transformation from immasculated reader to woman reader occurred at a critical point in the history of Western women: as Christine herself witnesses, more and more women, secular as well as religious, were gaining the formerly male prerogative of literacy.[32] In many cases, women were doing so with the aid rather than the opposition of those who controlled their access to learning. Although Christine's mother opposed her academic pursuits, her father encouraged them and made them possible.[33] Even such conservative moralists as Geoffrey La Tour Landry – who argued, for instance, that bad husbands deserve good wives in order to remedy their faults – advised other parents to teach their daughters how to read.[34] And the so-called Renaissance increased women's access to literacy and learning. As always, when considering such apparent progress, we must reread, by, in this case, asking the question '*Cui bono?*' If Christine's experiences tell us anything, it is that we must be cautious in assuming that women were necessarily the primary beneficiaries of their own literacy. As my two paradigms, 'Christine' and the Wife of Bath, suggest, female literacy brought women into a more submissive relationship to men's texts.[35] (There was, of course, little else to read.) Even women's courtesy books – on the art of being a good woman – were largely male-authored and contain male views of ideal female behaviour: modesty, obedience, chastity, humility.[36] Renaissance educational writers frequently remarked that women should be taught to read in order not to be learned, but to be good. Literacy was and remains an effective and efficient means of indoctrination, of immasculation. When we ask why, between Christine and the Wife of Bath's time and the sixteenth and seventeenth centuries, women's status declined and roles narrowed, increased female literacy may, in fact, provide part of the answer.[37]

At the same time, however, literacy provided some women the opportunity to take the gold from Egypt, to reread and thus reclaim their own history from anti-feminist texts. That relatively few women developed the feminist exegetical methodology of a Christine de Pisan until recently is perhaps less significant than the fact that a few did so in the face of opposition and hostility. What is still crucial for us to examine now is how and why some female readers resist immasculation and others succumb to it, for our literary texts and traditions remain largely male-made. In Christine's case, literacy and learning were crucial factors in her development of a feminist exegesis. But, as I have noted earlier, Christine also credits personal experience for her new-found authority. And one dimension of that experience was evidently in the oral rather than the literate mode. 'Christine' recounts that she frequently talked with other women, 'princesses, great ladies, women of the middle and lower classes, who . . . graciously told me of their most private and intimate thoughts' (p. 4).[38] Presumably, Christine de Pisan did likewise and found it just as hard to reconcile what she heard from them with the written opinions of male authorities on women's base and immoral character. If one of the mainsprings which motivated Christine's rereadings was the conflict between what she heard from women and what she read by men, then perhaps it is well for us to remember that modern feminist oral traditions – such popular forms of feminism as the consciousness-raising sessions, the discussion group, the workshop – have a vital role to play in the otherwise intellectual and literate act of rereading, reading as women. We must, I believe, continue to honour the methods and mentalities of both the garrulous Alysoun of Bath and the scholarly Christine de Pisan if we are to succeed in repossessing all of our gold.

NOTES

1 W. J. B. Crotch (ed.) *The Prologues and Epilogues of William Caxton*, Early English Text Society, OS 176, London, Oxford University Press, 1928, reprinted 1956, p. 16. N. F. Blake speculates that Rivers had already granted financial assistance to Caxton in *Caxton and his World*, London, Andre Deutsch, 1969, p. 86.

2 E.g., 'And [Socrates] saw a long mayde that lerned to wryte / of whom he sayde that me[n] multiplied euyl vpon euyll', Caxton, op. cit., p. 26.

3 Curt F. Bühler (ed.) *The Dicts and Sayings of the Philosophers*, Early

English Text Society, OS 211, London, Oxford University Press, 1941, p. 345, note on 100.24–102.29.

4 Rivers's family library did include a copy of Christine de Pisan's *The Book of the City of Women*; from this manuscript, Harley 4431, evidently the first translation was made for English readers.

5 Thus, Ruffinus in Walter Map's *De Nugis Curialium* (c. 1181–93), Walter in the third book of Andreas Cappellanus's *De Arte Honeste Amadi* (c. 1185), and January in Chaucer's *Merchant's Tale* (1380s) listen to anti-feminist material in order to dissuade themselves from matrimony or devotion to women, while the anonymous dreamer in Boccaccio's *Corbaccio* (c. 1355) is consoled for his unsuccessful love affair by the same means. Another version of the topos that employs men as the fictional audience of misogyny does so by encoding anti-feminist statements in Latin. See, for example, Chauntecleer's 'mulier est hominis confusio' in Chaucer's *Nun's Priest's Tale*; and the destroying burden 'cuius contrarium verum est', in poems that otherwise praise women. In his *Philobiblon* (1345), Richard de Bury comments that 'biped beasts' (i.e., women) would even be more opposed to the clergy if they 'could see our innermost hearts . . . had listened to our secret counsels . . . had read the book of Theophrastus or Valerius, or only heard the twenty-fifth chapter in Ecclesiasticus with understanding ears', E. C. Thomas (ed.), New York, Barnes & Noble, 1970, pp. 43–5. The 'book of Valerius', or *De Nugis Curialium*, op. cit.; Theophrastus's *Liber Aureolus de Nuptiis*; and *Philobiblon* are, of course, all in Latin. In 'Latin language study as a Renaissance puberty rite', *Studies in Philology*, 1959, vol. 56, pp. 103–24; *The Presence of the Word: Some Prolegomena for Cultural and Religious History*, New Haven, Yale University Press, 1967, pp. 249–52, and *Orality and Literacy: The Technologizing of the Word*, New York, Methuen, 1982, pp. 112–15, Walter J. Ong discusses Latin as a sex-linked language written and spoken only by males. Josephine Donovan, 'The silence is broken', in Sally McConnell-Ginet, Ruth Borker and Nelly Furman (eds), *Women and Language in Literature and Society*, New York, Praeger, 1980, pp. 205–18, examines the effects of the masculinising of Latin on early women writers.

6 Ong, *Orality*, op. cit., p. 82, argues that 'writing is in a way the most drastic of the three technologies. It initiates what print and computers only continue, the reduction of dynamic sound to quiescent space, the separation of the word from the living present, where alone spoken words can exist.' M. T. Clanchy, *From Memory to Written Record: England, 1066–1307*, Cambridge, Mass., Harvard University Press, 1979, pp. 88–115, characterises writing as a 'special skill in the Middle Ages which was not automatically coupled with the ability to read', and discusses the tools of this technology. While I do not wish to sweep aside the often cogent distinctions between chirographic (or script) and print cultures made by such recent writers as Elizabeth L. Eisenstein, *The Printing Press as an Agent of Change*, 2 vols, Cambridge, Cambridge University Press, 1979, I do take the point of view here that script and print cultures are similar in that they use their respective technologies to achieve a uniformity and permanence among texts which would be impossible in an oral culture. The ancient maxim 'vox audita perit, littera

scripta manet' ('the heard voice perishes, the written word endures') was used by scribe and early printer alike to justify the production of written and printed books, e.g., de Bury, op. cit., pp. 19–21, and Caxton, op. cit. For a complementary view of similarities between script and print cultures, see Donald P. Howard, *The Idea of the Canterbury Tales*, Berkeley and Los Angeles, University of California Press, 1976, pp. 60–7.

7 The number of copies Caxton printed is not known, but H. S. Bennett, *English Books and Readers, 1475 to 1557*, Cambridge, Cambridge University Press, 2nd edn, 1969, pp. 224–5, speculates that 'between four and five hundred copies would be a fair average for a book published' between 1480 and 1490 on the Continent.

8 Judith Fetterley, *The Resisting Reader: A Feminist Approach to American Fiction*, Bloomington, Indiana University Press, 1978, p. xx: 'Though one of the most persistent of literary stereotypes is the castrating bitch, the cultural reality is not the emasculation of men by women but the immasculation of women by men.'

9 I use the term 'fixed' as does Franz H. Bauml, 'Varieties and consequences of medieval literacy and illiteracy', *Speculum*, 1980, vol. 55, n. 31, p. 248: 'The fixity of the written word, of course, does not necessarily imply "stability" of a written text in its transmission. It merely means that, in contrast to the spoken word, the written word does not change or disappear without being made to change or disappear – unless the written symbol changes.'

10 Christine de Pisan, *Book of the City of Women*, trans. Earl Jeffrey Richards, New York, Persea Books, 1982, pp. 3–5. Subsequent references are cited parenthetically in the text.

11 Adrienne Rich, 'When we dead awaken: writing as re-vision', *College English*, 1972, vol. 34, p. 18. Also, Fetterley, op. cit., p. xix.

12 Joan Kelly, 'Early feminist theory and the *Querelle des Femmes*, 1400–1789', *Signs*, 1982, vol. 8, p. 20 characterises the *City* as one of the 'first attempts' at women's studies.

13 Included are Map's *Valerius to Ruffinus* (or *De Nugis Curialium*), Theophrastus's *Golden Book of Marriage*; Jerome's *Epistle against Jovinian*, Ovid's *Art of Love*, etc.

14 Graham D. Caie, 'The significance of the early Chaucer manuscript glosses (with special reference to the *Wife of Bath's Prologue*)', *Chaucer Review*, 1976, vol. 10, p. 354, notes that early fifteenth-century glossators of the *Canterbury Tales* cite Jerome's reading from the *Epistola Adversus Jovinianum*.

15 Caie, op. cit., p. 353.

16 An exception is Paula Neuss, 'Images of writing and the book in Chaucer's poetry', *Review of English Studies*, 1981, vol. 32, NS., p. 394, who recognises that Alysoun cannot write or read, but assumes that she wishes to emulate men 'and so the only way that she can take a leaf out of Jankin's book is literally'. For some of the distinctions between hearing and seeing, illiterate and literate, see Clanchy, op. cit., pp. 175–91. Franz H. Bauml, 'Transformations of the heroine: from epic heard to epic read', in Rosemarie Thee Morewedge (ed.) *The Role of Women in the Middle Ages*, Albany: State University of New York Press,

1975, pp. 23–40, compares aural and visual reception of literature about women.

17 Ong, *Orality*, op. cit., pp. 46–9.

18 'Structural amnesia' is a phrase coined by J. A. Barnes in 'The collection of genealogies', *Rhodes-Livingston Journal: Human Problems in British Central Africa*, 1947, vol. 5, pp. 48–56. The quotation is from Ong, *Orality*, op. cit., p. 48. For discussion, examples, and bibliography, see Ong, *Orality*, op. cit., pp. 46–9, and Jack Goody and Ian Watt, 'The consequences of literacy', in Jack Goody (ed.) *Literacy in Traditional Societies*, Cambridge, Cambridge University Press, 1968, pp. 1–27.

19 Ong, *Orality*, op. cit., p. 46.

20 Augustine, *De Doctrina Christiana* II. 40, in D. W. Robertson, Jr (trans.) *On Christian Doctrine*, New York, Liberal Arts Press, 1958, p. 75.

21 Robertson, op. cit., p. 83. Macrobius, *Commentary on the Dream of Scipio* I. ii, in William Harris Stahl (trans.), New York, Columbia University Press, 1952, p. 85, similarly maintains that 'a modest veil of allegory' insures that only 'eminent men of superior intelligence gain a revelation of [Nature's] truths'.

22 Jack Goody and Ian Watt, 'Literate culture: some general considerations', in Robert Disch (ed.) *The Future of Literacy*, Englewood Cliffs, N.J., Prentice-Hall, 1973, pp. 51–2, term this phenomenon *culture lag* and maintain that it was surely 'this lack of social amnesia in alphabetic cultures which led Nietzsche to describe "we moderns" as "wandering encyclopedias", unable to live in the present and obsessed by a "historical sense that injures and finally destroys the living thing, be it man or a people or a system of culture" '.

23 Christine de Pisan, *Epistle of the Goddess to Hector*, trans. Stephen Scrope, in Curt F. Bühler (ed.) *The Epistle of Othea*, Early English Text Society, OS 264, London, Oxford University Press, 1970, p. 102. Subsequent references are cited parenthetically in the text.

24 Gretchen Mieszkowski, *The Reputation of Criseyde: 1155–1500*, Hamden, Conn., Archon Books, 1971, pp. 71–153, documents the widespread reading of Criseyde as a 'type of fickle woman'. For exceptions, see Susan Schibanoff, 'Argus and Argyve: etymology and characterization in Chaucer's *Troilus*', *Speculum*, 1976, vol. 51, pp. 647–58, and Susan Schibanoff, 'Criseyde's "impossible" *Aubes*', *Journal of English and Germanic Philology*, 1977, vol. 76, pp. 326–33. For innovative aspects of Christine's work, see Mary Ann Ignatius, 'Christine de Pizan's *Epistre Othea*: an experiment in literary form', *Medievalia et Humanistica*, 1979, NS vol. 9, pp. 127–42.

25 E.g., D. W. Robertson, Jr, 'Chaucerian tragedy', in Richard J. Schoeck and Jerome Taylor (eds) *Chaucer Criticism: Troilus and Criseyde and the Minor Poems*, Notre Dame, Ind., University of Indiana Press, 1961, pp. 86–121, interprets Chaucer's work as an 'echo' of the Adam and Eve story.

26 F. J. Furnivall (ed.) 'The Letter to Cupid', in *Hoccleve's Works: The Minor Poems*, 1892, vol. I; revised by Jerome Mitchell and A. I. Doyle, London, Oxford University Press, 1970. Diane Bornstein, 'Antifeminism in Thomas Hoccleve's translation of Christine de Pisan's *Epistre au dieu d'amours*', *English Language Notes*, 1981, vol. 19, pp. 7–14, finds the

'Letter to Cupid' subtler in its methods of undermining feminism than I do.

27 Joseph L. Baird and John R. Kane (trans.) *La Querelle de la Rose: Letters and Documents*, North Carolina Studies in the Romance Language and Literatures, Chapel Hill, University of North Carolina Press, 1978, no. 199, p. 104. Subsequent references are cited parenthetically in the text.

28 E.g., Pierre Col argues that one must not take the *Romance* literally, 'but rather according to what was previously said and the intention of the author', in Baird and Kane, op. cit., p. 102.

29 Boccaccio, *De Claris Mulieribus*, trans. Guido A. Guarino, New Brunswick, N. J., Rutgers University Press, 1963, pp. 77–8. Subsequent references are cited parenthetically in the text.

30 ibid., p. 132.

31 E.g., Francis Lee Utley, *The Crooked Rib: An Analytical Index to the Argument about Women in English and Scots Literature to the End of the Year 1568*, New York, Octagon Books, p. 120.

32 Reliable statistics on the literacy rate for men or women in the fourteenth and fifteenth centuries are hard to come by, but M. B. Parkes, 'The literacy of the laity', in David Daiches and Anthony Thorlby (eds) *The Medieval World*, London, Aldus Books, 1973, p. 557, notes that from the twelfth century on there were didactic treatises addressed to women: 'one of them, written in the early 14th century, discusses whether it is proper that a woman should learn to read. Such a discussion would be pointless if by that time reading had not already become something of a habit. This evidence is supported in the literature itself.' See also Joan M. Ferrante, 'The education of women in the Middle Ages: theory, fact, and fantasy', in *Beyond Their Sex: Learned Women of the European Past*, New York, New York University Press, 1980, pp. 9–42.

33 de Pisan, op. cit., pp. 154–5.

34 William Caxton, *The Book of the Knight of the Tower*, in M. Y. Offord (ed.) Early English Text Society, SS 2, London, Oxford University Press, 1971, p. 122. Geoffrey argues that women should learn to read in order to recognise better perils to the soul; there is no use, however, in teaching women to write. (Cf. n. 2 above.)

35 Another aural reader of the early fifteenth century, Margaret Kempe, readily accommodated the written lives of the women saints to her own secular life and aroused both suspicion and hostility by practising celibacy in marriage. See *The Book of Margery Kempe*, (ed.) Sanford Brown Meech and Hope Emily Allen, Early English Text Society, OS 212, London, Oxford University Press, 1940, reprinted 1961.

36 Diane Bornstein, *The Lady in the Tower: Medieval Courtesy Literature for Women*, Hamden, Conn., Archon Books, 1983, p. 120.

37 Both Joan Kelly-Gadol, 'Did women have a Renaissance?', in Renate Bridenthal and Claudia Koonz (eds) *Becoming Visible: Women in European History*, Boston, Houghton Mifflin, 1977, pp. 139–52, and Ruth Keslo, *Doctrine for the Lady of the Renaissance*, Urbana, University of Illinois Press, 1956, have considered this question. Jane Tibbetts Schulenburg, 'Clio's European daughters: myopic modes of perception', in *The*

Prism of Sex: Essays in the Sociology of Knowledge, Madison, University of Wisconsin Press, 1977, p. 37, remarks that both the Wife of Bath and Christine de Pisan 'coincide with a period in which women's experimental realm had become substantially circumscribed; in general, their previous options in political, religious, and economic spheres had sharply contracted'. See also her 'Sexism and the celestial gynaceum: from 500 to 1200', *Journal of Medieval History*, 1978, vol. 4, pp. 117–33.

38 Garrulous and frequently 'illiterate' women are often viewed as threatening androcentric values and institutions; the satirical caricature of these women as 'gossips' is an attempt to silence them.

Further reading

The following is not a neutral reading list. It represents our version of some reference points which may be of use for readers who are interested in feminist analyses of medieval literary texts, but it does not attempt to cover the field. That would be difficult anyway, given that such readers come from a variety of disciplines and make use of multidisciplinary approaches. Each of the chapters in this collection also contains further reference points and contextualising aids (see Chapter 8, for example, for further reading on constructions of virginity and sexuality in the period). We have included material on aspects of medieval culture, although the main focus is on criticism of literary texts. Readers' attention is also directed to two North American journals, the *Medieval Feminist Newsletter* and *Exemplaria*. Both regularly carry specifically feminist articles on medieval texts and culture: the former is especially valuable for its bibliographical resources. Subscriptions to the *Medieval Feminist Newsletter* can be secured by writing to (UK) Lesley Johnson, School of English, The University, Leeds, LS2 9JT, England or (USA) Elizabeth Robertson, Dept of English, University of Colorado, Box 226, Boulder, Colorado 80309. The *Journal of Medieval History* also publishes feminist scholarship. A recent special issue of the journal *Speculum* focuses on gender and medieval studies: *Studying Medieval Women: Sex, Gender, Feminism: Speculum*, 1993, vol. 68. An entire issue of the journal *Signs* was devoted to medieval women: see *Working Together in the Middle Ages: Perspectives on Women's Communities, Signs: A Journal of Women in Culture and Society*, 1989, vol. 14. It is significant that no British journal of medieval studies provides, or has provided, a critical platform for critics who wish to engage with the conjuncture of sex/gender and the Middle Ages.

An obvious starting-point is feminist criticism of Chaucer. The following books are especially recommended:

Elaine Tuttle Hansen, *Chaucer and the Fictions of Gender*, Berkeley, University of California Press, 1992.
Carolyn Dinshaw, *Chaucer's Sexual Poetics*, Madison, Wis. and London, University of Wisconsin Press, 1989 (notable for its development of a detailed thesis about the gendering of literary activities in the Middle Ages in relation to key texts of Chaucer and his critics.

Sheila Delany, *Writing Woman: Women Writers and Women in Literature, Medieval to Modern*, New York, Schocken Books, 1983 (Delany's essay 'Sexual economics' (this volume, pp. 72–87) appeared previously in this volume. Delany declares herself a Marxist rather than a feminist, but the essays on Chaucerian texts are nevertheless thoroughly informed by feminist arguments, and are productive for feminist readers).

Sheila Delany, *Medieval Literary Politics: Shapes of Ideology*, Manchester and New York, Manchester University Press, 1990 (Marxist-feminist readings of Chaucer, Christine de Pisan and aspects of medieval culture).

Jill Mann's *Geoffrey Chaucer*, Hemel Hempstead, Harvester Wheatsheaf, 1991. (This appears in a series called 'Feminist Readings', but is not in fact written from an explicitly feminist or theoretical standpoint. However, it has value insofar as it identifies a number of *topoi* in Chaucer's texts (the betrayed woman, the feminised hero, etc.) which gender-conscious medievalists might want to engage with in making their interventions or organising their critical readings of Chaucer, even though it is defensive and/or cautious about the potential radicalism of such readings.)

CULTURE

Meanings are historical and cultural. There are certain areas of late medieval culture, especially of European culture in the fourteenth century (the central concern of the present volume), which are crucial for feminist readers trying to construct or reconstruct textual meanings for the period. A good starting place might be Shulamith Shahar, *The Fourth Estate: A History of Women in the Middle Ages*, trans. Chaya Galai, London, Methuen, 1983, or Edith Ennen, *The Medieval Woman*, trans. Edward Jephcott, Oxford, Basil Blackwell, 1989, or Margaret Wade Labarge, *A Small Sound of the Trumpet: Women in Medieval Life*, Boston, Beacon Press, 1986, or one of the anthologies listed below. One of the most accessible feminist histories of the period is Bonnie S. Anderson and Judith P. Zinsser, *A History of Their Own: Women in Europe from Prehistory to the Present*, vol. 1, New York, Harper & Row, 1988; repr. Harmondsworth, Penguin, 1990. An invaluable sourcebook for the period 500–1500 is Emily Amt (ed.) *Women's Lives in Medieval Europe: A Sourcebook*, New York and London, Routledge, 1993. See also Diane Bornstein, *The Lady in the Tower: Medieval Courtesy Literature for Women*, Hamden, Conn., Archon Books, 1983.

Medieval anti-feminism in general, and anti-matrimonialism in particular, is a central feature of the late Middle Ages; Chaucer's texts engage repeatedly with these issues. However, this area has to be approached with caution: critics who merely identify anti-feminist elements in medieval writing are not necessarily performing a feminist reading, although they may believe themselves to be doing just that. One of the best resources is the anthology of medieval texts that attack or defend women which has been edited by Alcuin Blamires with the assistance of Karen Pratt and C. W. Marx, *Woman Defamed and Woman Defended: An Anthology of Medieval Texts*, Oxford, Oxford University Press, 1992. Robert P. Miller (ed.) *Chaucer: Sources and Backgrounds*, New York, Oxford University Press, 1977, has useful sections on 'Marriage and the good woman' and 'The antifeminist tradition'. Of related interest is a volume consisting of modern translations of three late thirteenth- and early fourteenth-century French *dits* dealing with the vices and virtues of women: Gloria K. Fiero, Wendy Pfeffer and Mathé Allain (eds) *Three Medieval Views of Women*, New Haven and London, Yale University Press, 1989. More provocative and controversial (for feminists) is an article by R. Howard Bloch, 'Medieval misogyny', *Representations*, 1987, vol. 20, pp. 1–24, which attempts (though not from a feminist standpoint) to problematise the discourses of anti-feminism; this needs to be read in conjunction with the series of feminist responses which appeared in the *Medieval Feminist Newsletter*, 1988, vol. 6, pp. 2–15, and Bloch's reply, in *Medieval Feminist Newsletter*, 1989, vol. 7. On men in medieval feminism, see Allen J. Frantzen, 'When women aren't enough', in *Studying Medieval Women: Sex, Gender, Feminism: Speculum*, 1993, vol. 68, pp. 445–71.

Another important, and related, area of later medieval culture is that of 'courtly love', which intersects in interesting and problematic ways with anti-feminism, most notably in the twelfth-century Latin text *The Art of Courtly Love*, by Andreas Capellanus, available in a modern translation by John J. Parry, New York, Columbia University Press, 1941, repr. 1969, and in the encyclopedic thirteenth-century French allegorical love-vision, *Le Roman de la Rose*, the first part of which was written by Guillaume de Lorris, the second by Jean de Meun, available in a modern translation by Charles Dahlberg, *The Romance of the Rose*, London and Hanover, University Press of New England, 1971, repr. 1983. Feminist readers can initially follow up the critical inquiries (medieval and modern) that have been sparked off by these two primary texts: firstly, by reading a stimulating article by Toril Moi, 'Desire in language: Andreas Capellanus and the controversy of courtly love', in David Aers (ed.) *Medieval Literature: Criticism, History, Ideology*, Brighton, Harvester, 1986, which intervenes in the debate about whether or not the interests of aristocratic women (and medieval women in general) were served by courtly literature, by offering a feminist post-structuralist reading of Andreas Capellanus; and secondly, by considering the large corpus of feminist and proto-feminist literature which is a response to the supposed misogyny of Jean de Meun's portion of *Le Roman de la Rose*, beginning in the early fifteenth century with Christine de Pisan's *Book of the City of Ladies*, available in a modern translation by Earl Jeffrey Richards, London, Pan Books, 1983.

The specific debate over *Le Roman de la Rose* has far-reaching implications for the understanding of late medieval culture; the best starting-place is an influential article by Joan Kelly, 'Early feminist theory and the *querelle des femmes*, 1400–1789', in Joan Kelly, *Women, History and Theory: The Essays of Joan Kelly*, Chicago and London, Chicago University Press, 1984, pp. 65–109, although readers should perhaps be warned that Kelly essentialises the phenomenon she identifies as the 'querelle des femmes', and that it is by no means as self-evidently 'there' as she assumes; see also Susan Schibanoff, 'Comment on Kelly's "Early feminist theory and the *Querelle des Femmes*" ', *Signs*, 1983, vol. 9, pp. 320–6. A sharp discussion of what has been, and is, at stake for modern male – and female – critics in analysing 'courtly love' is Arlyn Diamond, 'Engendering criticism', *Thought*,

1989, vol. 64, pp. 298–309. Also useful is Anne McMillan's translation of *The Legend of Good Women*, Houston, Rice University Press, 1987, the introduction of which has a useful contextualising discussion of material relating to the *querelle*.

Elizabeth Fox-Genovese, 'Culture and consciousness in the intellectual history of European women', *Signs*, 1987, vol. 12, no. 3, pp. 529–47, is an extremely useful review article which covers many aspects of women and historiography, from the Middle Ages to the present, and offers a useful overview of feminist and woman-orientated medieval historical scholarship. It is both generous and cautious about the field of modern historiography and the supposed objects of its inquiry. Readers are also directed to the important work of the historians Judith Bennett, Susan Mosher Stuard and Martha Howell: see, for example, Judith M. Bennett, *Women in the Medieval English Countryside: Gender and Household in Brigstock Before the Plague*, Oxford, Oxford University Press, 1986; Judith M. Bennett, 'Feminism and history', *Gender and History*, 1989, vol. 1, pp. 251–72; Judith M. Bennett, 'Medieval women, modern women: across the great divide', in David Aers (ed.) *Culture and History 1350–1600: Essays on English Communities, Identities and Writing*, Hemel Hempstead, Harvester Wheatsheaf, 1992, pp. 147–75; Susan Mosher Stuard, 'The chase after theory: considering medieval women', *Gender and History*, 1992, vol. 4, pp. 135–46; Martha Howell, *Women, Production and Patriarchy in Late Medieval Cities*, Chicago and London, Chicago University Press, 1986. See also David Herlihy, *Opera Muliebra: Women and Work in Medieval Europe*, New York, 1990.

An essay by Natalie Zemon Davis, 'Women on top', in Natalie Zemon Davis, *Society and Culture in Early Modern France*, London, Duckworth, 1975, pp. 124–51, although not explicitly concerned with medieval texts, offers an importantly radical model of carnival which is potentially very useful for feminist readings of drama and fabliau, as well as of other genres in which comic inversion is an element. Zemon Davis's work challenges the perspectives of 'status quo' anthropologists, opening up to feminist analysis anthropological discussions of cultural practices like carnival.

On the subject of the widespread phenomenon of medieval female mysticism, Sarah Beckwith's 'A very material mysticism: the medieval mysticism of Margery Kempe', in David Aers (ed.) *Medieval Literature: Criticism, History, Ideology*, Brighton, Harvester, 1986, pp. 34–57, provides a sophisticated critical model which effectively changes the reading-agenda both for *The Book of Margery Kempe* and for current feminist claims for female mysticism as a site where the patriarchal Symbolic can be resisted. Beckwith's piece is stimulating because it does not just use current feminist theory to interpret medieval texts, but challenges that theory through specific readings of those texts.

The subject of sexuality and the body in medieval culture has been enormously opened up in the work of the social historian Caroline Walker Bynum: see especially Caroline Walker Bynum, 'Fast, feast, and flesh: the religious significance of food to medieval women', *Representations*, 1985, vol. 11, pp. 1–25, later developed into a book, *Holy Feast and Holy Fast: The Religious Significance of Food to Medieval Women*, Berkeley, University of California Press, 1987 (for a recent controversial critique of the premises and processes of *Holy Feast and Holy Fast*, see Kathleen Biddick, 'Genders, bodies, borders: technologies of the visible', *Speculum*, 1993, vol. 68, pp. 389–418); Caroline Walker Bynum, *Jesus as Mother: Studies in the Spirituality of the High Middle Ages*, Berkeley, University of California Press, 1982; Caroline Walker Bynum, *Fragmentation and Redemption: Essays on Gender and the Human Body in Medieval Religion*, New York, Zone Books, 1992. Karma Lochrie, *Margery Kempe and Translations of the Flesh*, Philadelphia, University of Pennsylvania Press, 1991, has much useful discussion of the medieval body in theory and practice. See also Linda Lomperis and Sarah Stanbury (eds) *Feminist Approaches to the Body in Medieval Literature*, Philadelphia, University of Pennsylvania Press, 1993, and Danielle Jacquart and Claude Thomasset, *Sexuality and Medicine in the Middle Ages*, trans. Matthew Adamson, Princeton, Princeton University Press, 1988. An invaluable discussion of the problematic of medieval sexualities is opened up in a collection of brief articles by E. Ann Matter, Simon Gaunt, Carolyn Dinshaw, Sylvia Huot, Susan Schibanoff and Mary Anne Campbell in *Medieval Feminist Newsletter*, 1992, vol. 13, pp. 1–15. Further references to medieval sexuality and the body are available in the notes to Chapter 8 of this volume.

On the subject of women and literacy, see Joan M. Ferrante, 'The education of women in the Middle Ages in theory, fact, and fantasy', in Patricia H. Labalme (ed.) *Beyond Their Sex: Learned Women of the European Past*, New York and London, New York University Press, 1980, pp. 9–42 and Carol Meale (ed.) *Women and Literature in Britain, c. 1150–1500*, Cambridge, Cambridge University Press, 1992. An influential article by Roberta Krueger, 'Love, honour and the exchange of women in *Yvain*: some remarks on the female reader', *Romance Notes*, 1985, vol. 25, pp. 302–17, deals with the inscription of women as readers in certain medieval texts; despite its focus on Old French texts, this piece sets up an initial premise that has implications for reading a range of late medieval *English* texts. On the relation of class to literacy, see Jennifer C. Ward, *English Noblewomen: The Later Middle Ages*, Harlow, Longman, 1992.

Alexandra Barratt's anthology, *Women's Writing in Middle English*, Harlow, Longman, 1992, opens with an introductory essay which discusses some of the issues related to categorising and classifying medieval texts according to whether or not they are signed with a female signature: the collection itself draws attention to the work of some little-known late medieval female translators. We have discussed the problematic relationship between use of a female voice in a text and assumptions of authorship in 'The *Assembly of Ladies*: a maze of feminist sign-reading?', in Susan Sellers (ed.) *Feminist Criticism: Theory and Practice*, Hemel Hempstead, Harvester Wheatsheaf, 1991, pp. 171–96. For a collection of medieval English religious texts which appear to have been written *for* a particular group of women, see Bella Millett and Jocelyn Wogan-Browne (eds) *Medieval English Prose for Women*, Oxford, Oxford University Press, 1992. See also Elizabeth Robertson, *Early English Devotional Prose and the Female Audience*, Knoxville, University of Tennessee Press, 1990. Katharina Wilson has collected texts attributed to female authors from several countries and from several centuries in her edition *Medieval Women Writers*, Athens, Georgia and Manchester, University of Georgia Press, 1984. Further discussion of 'women's writing' is found in Marcelle Thiebaux, *The Writings of Medieval*

Women, New York, Garland, 1987 and Peter Dronke, *Women Writers of the Middle Ages: A Critical Study of Texts From Perpetua to Marguerite Porete*, Cambridge, Cambridge University Press, 1984.

COLLECTIONS OF CRITICAL ESSAYS

Arlyn Diamond and Lee R. Edwards (eds) *The Authority of Experience: Essays in Feminist Criticism*, Amherst, University of Massachusetts Press, 1977, repr. 1988.

S. Fisher and J. Halley (eds) *Seeking the Woman in Later Medieval and Renaissance Writings*, Knoxville, University of Tennessee Press, 1989.

Derek Baker (ed.) *Medieval Women*, Oxford, Basil Blackwell, 1978.

Mary Erler and Maryanne Kowaleski (eds) *Women and Power in the Middle Ages*, Athens and London, University of Georgia Press, 1988.

Susan Mosher Stuard (ed.) *Women in Medieval History and Historiography*, Philadelphia, University of Pennsylvania Press, 1987 (very useful introduction surveying, roughly, the last decade of feminist historical scholarship; written by a historian).

Julius Kirshner and Suzanne F. Wemple (eds) *Women in the Medieval World*, Oxford, Basil Blackwell, 1985.

Carole Levin and Jeanie Watson (eds) *Ambiguous Realities: Women in the Middle Ages and the Renaissance*, Detroit, Wayne State University Press, 1987.

Mary Beth Rose (ed.) *Women in the Middle Ages and the Renaissance: Literary and Historical Perspectives*, Syracuse, Syracuse University Press, 1986.

John A. Nicholas and Lillian T. Shank (eds) *Distant Echoes: Medieval Religious Women* i, Cistercian Studies Series 71, Kalamazoo, Michigan, 1984.

P. J. P. Goldberg (ed.) *Woman is a Worthy Wight: Women in English Society c. 1200–1500*, Stroud, Alan Sutton, 1992.

Judith M. Bennett *et al.* (eds) *Sisters and Workers in the Middle Ages*, Chicago, Chicago University Press, 1989.

Juliette Dor (ed.) *A Wyf Ther Was: Essays in Honour of Paule Mertens-Fonck*, Liège, University of Liège Press, 1992.

Christiane Klapisch-Zuber (ed.) *Silences of the Middle Ages*, vol. 2 of Georges Duby and Michelle Perrot (gen. eds) *A History of Women*, Cambridge, Mass. and London, England, Bellknap Press of Harvard University Press, 1992.

Barbara Kanner (ed.) *The Women of England from Anglo-Saxon Times to the Present*, Hamden, Conn., Archon Books, 1979.

Index